HN 49 .C6 B87 1993
People first : a guide to
Burkey, Stan

190811

DATE DUE

BRODART   Cat. No. 23-221

About the Author

Stan Burkey started university life at Pennsylvania State University where he studied Forestry for two years before winning a scholarship to Yale University where he took a degree in Engineering. He subsequently did post-graduate studies at Oxford University in Development Economics and at the Massachusetts Institute of Technology (MIT) in Business Administration.

His interest in the Third World began during a three-year teaching stint in Nigeria in the early 1960s. Afterwards he moved for personal reasons to Norway where he first worked at the National Computer Centre and later for the Norwegian Scout Movement. In 1977 he joined Redd Barna as a programme co-ordinator which work took him to countries as diverse as India, Thailand, the Maldives, Guatemala and Kenya. In 1981 he was posted for three years to Sri Lanka as Redd Barna's Country Representative. After a short period as a development consultant, he went to Uganda in 1986 to set up and run self-reliant participatory development programmes there for the development consortium, ACORD. Since 1990 he has been employed by Quaker Service Norway training change agents throughout Uganda.

People First: A Guide to Self-Reliant Participatory Rural Development is Stan Burkey's first book. It is deeply influenced both by pioneer thinkers and animateurs in other parts of the world, as well as by his own considerable experience in training Third World change agents.

Go to the People
Live with them
Love them
Learn from them
Work with them
Start with what they have
Build on what they know
And in the end
When the work is done
The People will rejoice:
'We have done it ourselves!'

STAN BURKEY

PEOPLE FIRST

A Guide to Self-Reliant Participatory
Rural Development

ZED BOOKS LTD

London & New Jersey

People First: A Guide to Self-Reliant Participatory Rural Development was first published by Zed Books Ltd, 57 Caledonian Road, London N1 9BU, UK and 165 First Avenue, Atlantic Highlands, New Jersey 07716, USA, in 1993.

Cover designed by Andrew Corbett.
Cover photograph by Paul Weinberg.
Typeset by EMS Photosetters, Thorpe Bay, Essex.
Printed and bound in the United Kingdom
by Biddles Ltd, Guildford and King's Lynn.

A catalogue record for this book is
available from the British Library.

ISBN 1 85649 081 5 Hb
ISBN 1 85649 082 3 Pb

Contents

Abbreviations   ix
Preface   xi
Introduction   xv

Part I: Analysis   1

1. **Understanding Poverty**   3
   Basic Needs and Poverty   3
   What are the Causes of Poverty?   6
   Analysing Poverty   11

2. **What is Development?**   26
   Theories of Development   27
   Recent Trends in Development Thinking   32
   Development from Below – People First   35

3. **Self-Reliant Participatory Development**   40
   What is a Community?   40
   Social and Cultural Change   45
   What is Self-Reliance?   50
   What do We Mean by Participation?   56
   Participatory Development and the Time Factor   68

Part II: Action   71

4. **Agents of Change**   73
   What Part can Development Agencies Play?   73
   What is a Change Agent?   76
   The Role   78
   Formal Qualifications   83
   The Staying Power of Change Agents   86

5. **The Training and Support of Change Agents**   88
   Participatory Training   88
   Follow-up and Support   104
   Organisation and Leadership   107

6. Getting Started 115
Preparatory Studies 116
Planning and Proposals 121
Programme Monitoring 128

7. Working with People 130
The Dialogical Method 131
What is an Interest Group? 134
How Groups are Formed 135
Group Activities 148
Common Causes of Failure 159
Summing Up 163

8. External Relationships: Inside Looking Out 164
Local Elites and the Power Structure 165
Government Officials 169
Combining with Other Groups 174
Dilemmas of Participatory Development 178

9. Savings, Credit and Inputs: Essential Components 180
Factors of Production 181
External Credit 189
Donations and Matching Grants 193
Introducing New Technologies 195

Part III: Reflection 203

10. Objectives and Principles of Self-Reliant Participatory Development 205
The Objectives 206
Basic Principles 207

11. Two Steps Forward, One Step Back 212
Two Steps Forward 212
One Step Back ... 212
Stepping Out 216

Appendix: Questions for Discussion 219

References 234

Index 239

List of Case Studies

1. Changing Marriage Customs 46
2. The Importance of Common Interest 137
3. Nok Cibo Acaye Group 139
4. Can Ocuka Women's Group 147

5. Jocan Penindo Women's Group   155
6. Can Deg Ming Men's Group   162
7. Getting out in front   168
8. Paroketo Fishermen's Association   177
9. Nga Konyi Mixed Group   185
10. Setting up a Group Loan Fund   187

Abbreviations

CIDA – Canadian International Development Agency, Ottawa.

FAO – United Nations Food and Agriculture Organisation, Rome.

FFHC/AD – Freedom from Hunger Campaign/Action for Development Programme, FAO, Rome. A programme networking with participatory development programmes. Publisher of *Ideas and Action*, a quarterly newsletter.

GRIS – Grass Roots Information Service. A programme implemented by the Society for International Development (SID).

IFAD – International Fund for Agricultural Development, Rome.

IFDA – International Foundation for Development Alternatives, Nyon, Switzerland. Publishes articles and news on matters of alternative development in its quarterly journal *IFDA DOSSIER* (ceased publication 1991).

IIED – International Institute for Environment and Development, London. Networking and publishing (Earthscan).

IPPF – International Planned Parenthood Federation, London.

ILO – United Nations International Labour Organisation, Geneva.

IRED – Innovations et Reseaux pour le Developpement (Development Innovations and Networks), Geneva. A very active network of participatory development initiatives. Seven regional offices. Quarterly journal *IRED Forum*.

OECD – Organisation for Economic Co-operation and Development, Paris.

ORAP – Organisation of Rural Associations for Progress, Bulawayo, Zimbabwe.

PIDA – Participatory Institute for Development Alternatives, Colombo, Sri Lanka. One of the first NGOs to use a 'pure' change agent (action researcher) approach to rural development. One of the early recipients of the Right Livelihood Award (the alternative Nobel Prize as it is called).

PORP – Participatory Organisations of the Rural Poor Programme, ILO, Geneva. A programme for researching self-reliant participatory development and organisations of the rural poor. Publisher of many useful booklets.

SID – Society for International Development, Rome. Publisher of the journal *Development: Seeds of change – village through-global order* and GRIS Notes.

SIX S's – Se Servir de la Saison Sêche en Savane et dans le Sahel, Burkina Faso (translation: 'Making use of the dry season in the savannah and the Sahel'). A network of people's organisations in French-speaking West Africa.

UNICEF – United Nations Children's Fund, New York. Implements social service and infrastructure programmes.

UNRISD – United Nations Research Institute for Social Development, Geneva. Popular Participation Programme aims to clarify, operationalise and render more useful and socially relevant the idea of participation. Publishes occasional papers.

WHO – United Nations World Health Organisation, New York. Carries out research on health matters and implements international health programmes.

Preface

This book is a result of encounters I had a few years ago with two women! They were both Sri Lankans – one a Tamil lady, a 45-year-old widow, struggling together with her 20-year-old son to scratch a living from two acres of dry-zone highland in the north of Sri Lanka; the other an unmarried 35-year-old rural development officer, a Singhalese, living and working among poor village women along the south coast.

I met the Tamil lady while walking through her settlement. I was trying to figure out what could be done to help these people. She had been there five years, having come from the south after communal disturbances. After a year in a tent camp she and her son had been settled by the government on her two-acre plot. For the past three years she had been part of a project run by a large European non-governmental aid agency. She came out of her hut together with her son, and with a pleading voice asked me, 'Please Sir, may I have permission to root out these mulberry bushes? I want to plant chillies?' She, like everyone else, had half an acre of mulberry bushes (and a dilapidated silkworm rearing shed) which was her 'share' of a 600,000 rupee silkworm project from which she had not earned a single cent and was (at least in the office records) Rs. 2,000 in debt. Her annual income was at most Rs. 500.

I said to her, 'Madam, they're your mulberry bushes. You may do with them what you like!' But in my mind I was thinking – My God, we've spent all these years and all that money, and this poor woman doesn't even realise that she owns her own land.

I met the second woman when I stopped unannounced at her village on the way back from a project visit further south. I had heard about her work with the Change Agent Programme and wanted to see for myself. We asked around and found her house, and someone went to fetch her from a nearby village. We sat in the shade and for five hours she told us what the women in the surrounding villages had accomplished on their own during the past three years. From having been completely in the hands of the middlemen, they now had their own Coir Women's Producer Association and were delivering coir rope directly to the exporters in Colombo. We later went to where some of the women were grading, weighing and packing the rope which the members had brought in that day. They told us all about their association after first asking us directly why we wanted to know. Our new friend, the change agent, didn't say a word on behalf of the women; they spoke for themselves.

I later thought to myself – I've never in all my travels met a government employee who was so enthusiastic about her work. She had been specially chosen and trained for this pilot project. She was on secondment, and I asked her whether she would go back to her old position if the project was terminated. She said, 'No, I would resign and stay here. This is the only way the rural people will rise above their oppression.'

The first encounter woke me up; the second pointed me in a new, exciting and personally very rewarding direction. Later I was able to provide 'change agent' training and support for young village workers in Sri Lanka and Uganda and see how many of them became totally dedicated to working with the poor. I have been privileged to spend many afternoons and evenings sitting under a tree or in dimly lit village houses listening to proud groups of poor men and women tell how they have worked together to try to overcome the constraints in their lives.

I am convinced that self-reliant participatory development is the only foundation for true development – human, economic, political and social. It is a slow and difficult process – one totally dependent on men and women themselves, assisted by those who are willing to live and work among them.

This book is intended for those who want to begin learning about self-reliant participatory development, but no book can, by itself, teach such a basically human process. There are no fixed rules, no formulae, no quantitative measurements. There have been lessons learned, lessons based on the hard-earned experiences of poor men and women in Asia, Africa and Latin America. What they and the dedicated 'change agents' working with them have learned is slowly becoming better known through the research and writings of various observers, mainly social scientists and practitioners from the Third World itself. Self-reliant participatory development is a practical, field-level methodology. It is the result of trial and error throughout the Third World. It has developed in the Third World and will, hopefully, eventually develop the Third World. Ultimately, the peoples of the so-called developed world may also rediscover these basic principles of genuinely human endeavour.

In addition to my own experiences, I have tried to bring together the research and writings of many observers working with participatory development. Significantly, much of this has been carried out by Asian and Latin American social scientists. Some excellent work is also being done in Africa, but Africa is so over-burdened with 'traditional' Western development assistance that these efforts are little noticed. Participatory development has only recently begun to emerge in Africa in a few isolated pockets, and little has been written about these efforts. For the past six years I have had the great good fortune of having the opportunity of introducing the methodology in three separate areas of a re-emerging Uganda. The insights gained have added considerably to my understanding.

This book provides an introduction to self-reliant participatory development. It is very definitely not a 'how to' handbook in which you would expect to find clear, specific instructions as to 'what to do next'. Although I have tried, wherever possible, to give guidelines based on cumulative experiences, these should be seen as just that, no more. Actual practice must ultimately be determined by individual change agents, groups or associations. Hopefully, this book will provide a background and a framework for discussing the conceptual basis for, and the practical problems of, implementation of the self-reliant participatory methodology. It is strongly recommended that this material be used as a starting point for small group discussions at workshops and training sessions for field personnel, programme administrators and coordinators. To help in this, I have posed questions for discussion which are found as an annex at the end of the book. Some may be relevant for your situation, others not. But hopefully they can provide a start for your own dialogues.

Although primarily intended for field workers in the Third World and students of development everywhere, it should also be useful to managers and administrators both in the field and in home offices. As change agent trainees said to me in Uganda, 'Please take this training back to the people in our home office, so that they too can begin to understand what we are trying to do, and stop setting targets for our work based on their own priorities, instead of the priorities of the people with whom we are working.'

This book could not have been written without the benefit of the field experiences and writings of numerous practitioners and researchers working in many countries of the world. On a firsthand practical basis, the efforts of the core trainers of the Change Agent Programme in Sri Lanka and the action researchers of the Participatory Institute for Development Alternatives (PIDA), also in Sri Lanka, have been particularly useful. The writings and personal advice of the following have been especially valuable: Ms Kamla Bhasin, Programme Officer, FFHC/AD FAO, India; Dr Md Anisur Rahman, Director, Participatory Organizations of the Rural Poor Programe, ILO, Geneva; Dr Ponna Wignaraja, former Secretary-General, Society for International Development, Rome; Dr Orlando Fals-Borda, Director, Foundation for the Analysis of Colombian Reality, Colombia; Prof S. Tillakaratne, PIDA, Colombo, Sri Lanka; and Dr Ian Askew, Research Officer, Institute of Population Studies, University of Exeter, England.

Special thanks must go to the 65 change agents and their programme coordinators in the ACORD rural development promotion programmes in Uganda, and particularly Rose Ayenga and Rita Laker-Ojok who shared many trials and tribulations with me under often difficult and not entirely safe conditions. These men and women are living in scattered rural settlements, trudging through dust and mud, and patiently sharing their ideas and experiences with several thousand poor rural men and women struggling to improve their own lives. I have been privileged to share hundreds of hours of training, discussion and dialogue with them in trying to learn together the art of self-reliant participatory development.

Ultimately, we are all greatly indebted to the many poor women and men in Africa, Asia and Latin America who have, through their persistent fight against poverty and oppression, shown us the power and potential of genuinely self-reliant participatory efforts.

Sincere thanks are also due to Robert Molteno, without whose support and encouragement this manuscript might not have been published.

Introduction

I once visited an agricultural settlement project where a large, respected international non-governmental organisation had been assisting about 200 of the settler families for over three years. The NGO had already invested about US$ 3,000 per settler family. A full-time staff of 25 were working in the project. They had built two small agro-based factories, invested US$200,000 in silkworm propagation, and had constructed an elaborate system of tubewells (boreholes), diesel pumps and water storage tanks.

Driving into the settlement area, the project administrator indicated where the project began. Along both sides of the road there were two-acre allotments, each with a small, rather dilapidated hut made completely of plaited palm fronds (*cadjans*). Around the huts were rather parched areas of weeds and the remains of previous crops. A few young coconuts were struggling to survive, and most plots had about 100 mulberry bushes. Some had small plots of chillies, and occasionally we passed a bare-chested farmer watering his chillies from an earthenware pot. The two factories were not in operation, and there was no sign of any silkworm propagation. After three years, it didn't look very prosperous.

Suddenly, just before the administration compound, we came to an allotment which looked like an oasis. There was a large wattle-and-daub house with a sheet-iron roof. The house was surrounded by tall, thick banana trees. There was an open-pit well about 10 metres from the house. Dispersed over the allotment were fairly mature mango trees and young coconuts. The two acres were completely planted with chillies, *brinjal* (egg plant), lady's fingers and cowpeas. The farmer was watering his brinjals from his own hand-dug well with a small kerosene-fuelled pump. It was beautiful.

I turned to the project administrator and said, 'That fellow is really doing well. He must be one of your best settlers.' The project administrator gave a little snort of a laugh and replied, 'He's not in the project! He borrowed some money privately and has done all that himself.' Later, I discovered several other families scattered throughout the settlement who had done well in developing their allotments. In each case, they were not being assisted directly by the project.

What had happened? Was this project atypical? The project staff and the NGO leadership had done everything possible to help these people. They had consulted experts; they had made detailed plans and work schedules; they had constructed and built professionally; they had held meetings; they had hired qualified instructors; but the people in the project had not responded. Those who had purposefully stayed out of the project were the ones who had progressed. Yet the project staff all talked about 'self-reliance' and 'people's participation'. The programme director spoke of 'not sewing pillows under the arms of the participants'; meaning they were expected to do things themselves. But the reality was that the project and its staff had planned and organised everything themselves, and the participants had only 'participated' in carrying out the instructions of the staff.

We have now seen over three decades of so-called development programmes and thousands of development projects designed and implemented by hundreds of thousands of local and expatriate, governmental and non-governmental consultants, experts, administrators, trainers, volunteers, etc. Yet everyone who has any familiarity with the Third World knows that poverty is well and thriving, that the numbers of poor are not only increasing but their poverty is deepening. What is wrong?

During the past few years an increasing number of development researchers, practitioners and progressive support agencies have expressed considerable concern over this situation. A typical expression of this concern was provided by a group of 18 international specialists participating in the Inter-Agency Working Group on Community Participation in Family Planning & Mother Child Healthcare sponsored by WHO, IPPF, UNICEF and OECD:

> Until fairly recently, programmes and projects aimed at improving the socio-economic and health conditions of the poor tended to be initiated, designed and implemented from the 'top-down' by agencies and institutions without systematic consultation and involvement of the intended beneficiaries. The basic idea was that the introduction of modern technology and science would automatically lead to a decent standard of living for all and that the availability of modern health services would defeat illness and disability.
>
> However, with experience has come the awareness that top-down approaches to development create an increasing dependence of the people on outside resources and also sharpen social divisions. Moreover, the cost of this approach to welfare and development is so high that no government in any low-income country can reasonably expect to meet the needs of all its people in the near future. It also became clear that the intended beneficiaries of development and health care do not necessarily share the perception programme planners have of their priority needs. As a result services offered to the people were often rejected or underutilised because they did not meet their needs, respect their sensitivities or respond to local realities.
>
> (Askew, 1983)

Huge amounts of money and millions of man-hours of 'expert' efforts have been put into rural development projects. Yet the results for hundreds of millions of poor men, women and children have been discouraging in the extreme. Much effort has also recently been put into analysing why the results have been so meagre. A study carried out for CIDA (Canadian International Development Agency) by a group of consultants, who interviewed approximately 150 rural development theorists and practitioners in Europe, Asia and North America, indicated seven main reasons for disappointing results of traditional rural development programmes (Léger, 1984):

1. Target groups are not homogeneous;
2. Technological options do not always correspond to the motivations of target groups and to the constraints of the environment;
3. Equitable distribution of revenues and benefits may be a myth;
4. Government and NGO strategies for project conception and implementation do not necessarily represent the aspirations and interests of target groups;
5. The human and social factors are too often neglected;
6. Projects are planned in a rigid manner, based on an overly idealised economic, political and institutional environment;
7. The already existing or newly created organisational entities do not foster efficient/effective project management.

Léger, who at that time was the Director of the CIDA International NGO Division, maintained that a successful externally-sponsored rural development programme remained an exception.

My own view is that all too many development professionals unconsciously believe that rural development will be achieved through the efforts of governments and development agencies. They do not reflect on the possibility that sustainable rural development will only be achieved through the efforts of the rural people themselves working for the benefit of themselves, their families and, hopefully, their communities. Governments and agencies can assist this process, but they cannot do it themselves. Unfortunately, after decades of this type of paternalism, all too many rural people have also come to believe – they have been told so many times – that this government or that agency is going to develop them. The result is apathy interspersed with small peaks of expectation as one or another 'new' development programme comes their way. Rather than promoting development, such programmes have ended up developing 'dependency thinking'.

Yet during this same period of increasing doubt as to the effectiveness of 'top-down' approaches to development, there have been numerous small, local initiatives throughout the world which have successfully merged self-help traditions with modernisation and development. In Brazil and other countries of Latin America tens of thousands of 'base communities' have organised for neighbourhood improvements within the context of the Roman Catholic Church. In Asia organisations such as PIDA (Participatory Institute for Development Alternatives) in Sri Lanka, and SARILAKAS ('own strength') in the Philippines are helping groups of poor producers to organise for economic and social development. In Africa ORAP (Organisation of Rural Associations for Progress) is organising village groups in Zimbabwe, while thousands of miles to the north-west an organisation called Six S's (Se Servir de la Saison Sèche en

Savanne et au Sahel) has helped over 1,000 farmers' groups in West Africa to improve their agriculture through autonomous village associations.

These grassroots movements have given impetus to a shift in the approach to development from top-down to bottom-up, from specialised to integrated, from lecturing to dialogue, from modern technology to appropriate technology. Some development agencies, and some few governments, have adopted new policies to guide their activities based on the principle well expressed in the saying: 'Start with what the people have, build on what they know'.

This book is not an attempt to define a new theory of poverty and development. It is not an analysis of the macro-relationships between rich and poor nations or between rural and urban centres in the developing countries. Nor is it an analysis of the various development theories or about national development policies. It is concerned with poverty and its causes at the immediate level of the rural people. It is concerned with development at the level at which the rural people themselves can do something to change their own lives. Obviously, national and international relationships and policies do indeed affect the rural poor and their ability to develop themselves. The problems of changing macro-conditions is left to others; here we are concerned with starting a process that with good fortune will not be smothered by negative external influences.

No process can begin in a vacuum. There must be a background environment whose components either nurture or retard the development of the process. The first step in nurturing the process must be to examine the social, economic and political environment, study the constraints to development, and identify possible actions to remove or lessen these constraints.

It is for this reason that this book is divided into three parts. Part I – Analysis – discusses 'theory': poverty analysis, development concepts and the rationale for self-reliant participatory development. An important element of self-reliant participatory development is the Analysis–Action–Reflection cycle; hence the need to analyse theory before attempting action. Chapter 1 begins with a review of the most commonly held theories of poverty. Some readers may wish to skim this section, but the second part of the chapter illustrates how poverty needs to be analysed at the local level in order to respond to root causes rather than symptoms. Likewise, Chapter 2 begins with a brief review of the more common theories of development and ends with an illustration of how development needs to be seen from the grassroots. The macro-theories tend to disregard the role of ordinary people in development as well as to ignore the important relationships between human, economic, political and social development.

Part II – Action – looks at practice: the methodology of the self-reliant participatory approach to development. Naturally, this section of the book accepts and builds upon the theoretical basis for self-reliant participatory development defined in Part 1. Finally, Part 3 – Reflection – is a summing up of the general objectives and the basic principles of self-reliant participatory development followed by a final cautionary chapter which attempts to analyse the obstacles, risks and traps which practitioners may expect to encounter as well as the limitations of grassroot development in a hostile external environment.

Part I
Analysis

1.   Understanding Poverty

There is no use trying to help these people. These dirty, ignorant people are putting too many children into the world. They won't work; they have no discipline. They misuse every opportunity they get. Every time they get some money in their hands it all goes to drinking and senseless waste. All the help we give them is just an incentive to laziness, and another opportunity to produce even more children.

The statement above was written by an English industrialist working in Norway in the 1880s. Norway was indeed a poor country 100 years ago. The fact that nearly every Norwegian family has relatives in Canada or the United States, who emigrated 'for a better life', attests to the widespread poverty during the last century. And yet Norway today has one of the highest incomes per capita of the industrialised nations. But what do we mean by poverty? And what are its causes? This chapter attempts to show how poverty can be analysed so that its root causes can be identified in a given situation.

Basic Needs and Poverty

Basic needs are those things that an individual must have in order to survive as a human being. Essentially, these are clean (unpolluted) air and water, adequate and balanced food, physical and emotional security, physical and mental rest, and culturally and climatically appropriate clothing and shelter.

However, the survival of the human race depends not on the survival of a single individual, but on the survival of communities. It is thus necessary to expand the list of basic individual needs to include those of a community. These might be defined as sexual regeneration, a system of communication (language), a belief and educational system for cultural continuity, physical and cultural security, a political system defining leadership and decision-making, and systems of health and recreation for maintaining well-being among sufficient numbers to maintain the community.

Poverty can be defined in terms of basic needs. A group of development workers in Uganda defined absolute poverty as the inability of an individual, a community or a nation to satisfactorily meet its basic needs. They defined relative poverty as the condition in which basic needs are met, but where there is an inability to meet perceived needs and desires in addition to basic needs. They also discussed an expression much abused by development agencies: the poorest of the poor. These were considered those unfortunate individuals who, because of serious mental or physical handicaps, were incapable of meeting their basic needs by themselves.

In terms of external assistance, people existing in a situation of absolute poverty need immediate relief in order to survive while those existing in relative poverty can hopefully benefit from development assistance which ideally should help them to become independent of such assistance. Needless to say, many handicapped or disabled people can be assisted to manage on their own. However, the truly 'poorest of the poor' must survive on charity which ultimately must be provided by their own family or community either privately or through governmental programmes. Development assistance should aim at making this possible.

Identifying and measuring poverty

The wealth of nations is often measured in terms of Gross National Product (GNP – the total value of a nation's annual output of goods and services). GNP measurements are usually presented in terms of per capita figures. The World Bank annually publishes comparative lists showing low income, middle income and high income countries. In 1987, Ethiopia had one of the lowest per capita GNPs listed of US$ 120. Norway's GNP per capita was US$ 17,110. Countries like Thailand (US$ 840) and Guatemala (US$ 940) are classified as middle income. Yet both these countries have hundreds of thousands of people who are little better off than an average Ethiopian.

Per capita GNP figures are aggregate numbers, i.e. they are based on averages. But averages can be highly misleading. A fair number of very wealthy families in an otherwise very poor country will pull the average higher than observation might expect. The man with his head on an ice block and his feet in the fire cannot exactly be said to be comfortable.

As a counterweight to the national economic statistics approach to measuring poverty, the Physical Quality of Life Index (PQLI) has been developed. Various ways of putting together the index have been proposed. All of these are based on the selection and measurement of physical factors which indicate the state of people's health and welfare. The standard factors are usually life expectancy, child mortality and adult literacy.

These factors are measured and averaged on a national basis. The averages are given relative weights, and an index is produced. Other factors can also be used in generating the index, such as malnourishment, child morbidity and school attendance. Generally speaking, Physical Quality of Life Indices give a better indication of the standard of living for an average person than the national economic statistics. However, the PQLI does not tell the whole story. Sri Lanka is perhaps the best example of this. With its high literacy rate (about 80%), high life expectancy (69 years) and low child mortality (32 per 1,000), Sri Lanka rates high on nearly all PQLI measurements. Yet it is classified as a low income country (GNP per capita US$ 400) and any casual observer travelling in the country can attest to the widespread poverty.

In recent years, a third way of identifying and measuring poverty has been developed – the Basic Needs Approach. In this method the presence or absence of minimal basic human requirements for life as well as essential services indicate the degree of poverty or, if you wish, the level of the standard of living. The basic requirements for a family are considered to be adequate food, safe drinking water, suitable shelter and clothing as well as basic household equipment. The essential services are considered to be sanitation, public transport, health and educational facilities. There are various measurements and standards used to quantify these needs, e.g. food: calories per day; water: litres per day; shelter: sq. metres per person, etc.

There are numerous problems involved in attempts to identify and quantify poverty. No one set of measurements will give a complete picture. And what about immeasurable factors of welfare such as happiness, security, togetherness? Is an African villager less well-off in these terms than an elderly person sitting alone and isolated in a cold big-city flat in Europe?

For most development workers, estimates of the levels of family income, food and nutrition, infant mortality, shelter, potable water, sanitation, indebtedness, etc. are adequate to identify those areas and groups of people who are most in need of developmental efforts.

Rural poverty unperceived

We have all been exposed numerous times to media presentations of the appalling human suffering arising under conditions such as drought, floods and civil wars, yet many of us, including even experienced development administrators, are not personally aware of the real extent of persistent poverty in rural areas of the Third World. Although the vast majority of the poor live in rural areas, our mental image of poverty in the Third World is usually based on the unavoidable confrontation with the deplorable conditions in the shanty towns of the major cities.

Robert Chambers in his book *Rural Development: Putting the last first* has thoughtfully analysed why rural poverty is often unperceived and how development workers can rectify this serious deficiency. He writes in his introductory chapter:

> Outsiders are people concerned with rural development who are themselves neither rural nor poor. Many are headquarters and field staff of government organisations in the Third World. They also include academic researchers, aid agency personnel, bankers, businessmen, consultants, doctors, engineers, journalists, lawyers, politicians, priests, school teachers, staff of training institutes, workers in voluntary agencies, and other professionals. Outsiders underperceive rural poverty. They are attracted to and trapped in urban 'cores' which generate and communicate their own sort of knowledge while rural 'peripheries' are isolated and neglected.
>
> The direct rural experience of most urban-based outsiders is limited to the

brief and hurried visits, from urban centres, of rural development tourism. These exhibit six biases against contact with and learning from the poorer people. These are **spatial** – urban, tarmac and roadside; **project** – towards places where there are projects; **person** – towards those who are better off, men rather than women, users of services and adopters of practices rather than non-users and non-adopters, and those who are active, present and living; **seasonal** – avoiding the bad times of the wet season; **diplomatic** – not seeking out the poor for fear of giving offence; and **professional** – confined to the concerns of the outsider's specialisation. As a result, the poorer rural people are little seen and even less is the nature of their poverty understood.

If we are seriously concerned with helping the rural poor to improve their lives, then we must minimise rural development tourism and learn to eliminate those biases which are preventing us from finding and working with the genuinely poor and vulnerable in the rural areas of the Third World.

What are the Causes of Poverty?

There are almost as many theories explaining the causes of poverty in the Third World as there are development theorists. For many people the statement by the English businessman quoted at the beginning of this chapter adequately sums up the problem – if he had been talking about Africa instead of Norway! But even the serious students of development problems disagree, often substantially, as to the real causes of poverty. Some of these arguments are coloured by ideological convictions, education and training, class prejudices, etc.

The reasons that have been given for the continued existence of poverty in the Third World can be grouped under five headings:
1. Lack of modernisation tendencies
2. Physical limitations
3. Bureaucratic stifling
4. Dependency of Third World countries
5. Exploitation by local elites

Those who explain poverty in terms of a lack of modernisation tendencies in Third World communities often group their reasons into two main categories: lack of modern technology, and lack of 'modern' outlooks among the people. They are inclined to believe that if these 'growth-inhibiting factors' can be removed and replaced with modern technologies and motivations, then development will take-off for the betterment of all concerned.

Lack of modern technology
It is argued that poverty exists because the poor lack modern techniques of agriculture, fishing, industry, etc. Farmers lack not only modern equipment, improved seeds, fertilisers and pesticides, but also the necessary knowledge to use these techniques. They lack irrigation, roads, cooperatives and other

support facilities. Fishermen lack motorised boats and equipment. Industry needs modern equipment, electricity, management, etc. Those who interpret the causes of poverty in this way tend to believe that introducing modern technologies together with the required training and extension programmes will lift the poor out of their destitute situation.

Although these ideas were widely accepted during the first two development decades, many more recent researchers have vigorously pointed out the weaknesses in these arguments. They maintain that the development of modern cash-crop agriculture has not led to a generalised improvement of the incomes and living standards of the rural population. They point out that export crops have replaced food crops and, although incomes have risen, food consumption has often decreased. Profits have become concentrated in the hands of merchants, middlemen, large landowners and government bureaucrats. The high cost of modern inputs has increased the debt of small producers. Mechanisation has produced a pool of under-employed landless. Violent price fluctuations in the international markets have severely affected small producers as well as national incomes.

It has also been pointed out that no amount of modern technology is going to help peasant farmers unless they also have access to land, reasonable credit and fair market prices.

Lack of a modern outlook

> I have been thinking about this 'resistance-to-change' accusation. And I say it now clearly: it is the landlords and the government who are resistant to change! I mean have they not done everything to fight our demand for a change in the ownership of the land?
>
> *Mang Pedring*, peasant farmer, Philippines
> (quoted by Bhasin, 1980a)

Viewpoints relating to the presumed 'lack of modern outlook' among the poor vary from the derogatory to the genuinely serious, and tend to be based on the broad concept of resistance to change. Poor people are said to resist change because they are ignorant, superstitious, fatalistic, traditional, etc. They have a limited world view and are unable to see the advantages of modernisation. They lack innovativeness and are unable to perceive the advantages of 'investing today for a better tomorrow'. They have limited aspirations and are unable to defer today's gratifications to the future. They are either dependent on or hostile to government and other outside interventions.

Rural economists have shown that poor peasants as well as other poor producers will tend to adopt production strategies that minimise the risk of failure. Because they have nothing to fall back on, they concentrate on producing adequate quantities of food and a little surplus to sell in order to purchase necessary consumer goods. They cannot afford to risk everything on maximising profits. They tend towards mixed farming to spread their risk. They avoid hybrid seeds which require expensive fertilisers and insecticides and which are often more susceptible to bad weather conditions and pests. Poor farmers are not afraid to make money, but they are deathly afraid of losing an entire harvest.

Physical limitations

Another set of explanations for poverty relate to the physical limitations of geography. Many areas of the Third World are subject to long periods of drought; rain, when it comes, tends to come all at once causing flooding and waterlogging; soils are thin and very delicate; cyclones and earthquakes supplement drought and flooding in a frequent cycle of natural disasters.

Often, however, the problem is not the natural disaster, but a nation's inability to respond to it effectively. After the 1974 floods in Bangladesh which devastated standing crops, there was enough rice stockpiled during the subsequent famine to feed the entire nation for four months. But the vast majority of the people were too poor to buy it. The ability to overcome physical limitations often depends on addressing other causes of poverty.

Poverty and population pressures intensify the physical limitations. Deforestation caused by over-grazing or the need for more land and firewood leads to desertification, soil erosion, flooding and micro-climatic changes.

The physical conditions of the poor resulting from their destitute condition create new barriers to development. The symptoms of poverty become the causes of continued poverty. Malnutrition, disease, lack of clean water and proper sanitation weaken the poor and often make it physically difficult for them to break the vicious circle. High rates of childbirth weaken women physically, and lead to greater pressure on the environment.

However, physical limitations can be overcome assuming that political and social conditions, especially population growth, can be changed rapidly enough to reverse environmental deterioration.

Bureaucratic stifling of development

> Welfare programmes are instruments of manipulation and ultimately serve the purpose of dependence and domination. They act as an anaesthetic, distracting the oppressed from the true causes of their problems and from the concrete solutions of these problems.
>
> (Freire, 1972)

A third set of reasons, often proposed by non-governmental organisations, is the stifling of development by bureaucratic heavy-handedness. Third World governments are, in this view, saddled with overgrown bureaucracies attempting to control all aspects of rural peoples' development. Over-centralisation leads to decisions and programmes which are not only unrelated, but also often detrimental, to the real interests of the people. The lack of genuinely representative local government prevents the emergence of local initiatives. Government bureaucrats and politicans are said to be part of an elite who are uninterested in or, even worse, antagonistic to the real needs of the poor. Their formalism makes it impossible for them to communicate with the common man and woman. Programmes and projects initiated from the top-down either never reach the poor or actually make their situation worse. Finally, there is a widespread conception that all bureaucrats and government officials are corrupt, that their actions and decisions are related primarily to their desire for personal gain and prestige.

Where government programmes are temporarily successful in reaching the rural poor, such programmes are often based on the provision of subsidised inputs. And as Paolo Freire has pointed out, they create even greater degrees of dependency and domination. When such programmes inevitably collapse, the people tend to sit back and say, 'When is the government coming back to develop us?'

Dependency of Third World countries

The ideas contained in this section are often espoused by observers with more politically radical tendencies although not exclusively so. These arguments are based on a particular analysis of capitalism and international economic relationships. It is maintained that colonialism was the beginning of a process in which the profits or surplus from the production of exported foodstuffs, minerals and other raw materials were expropriated by the colonial powers, thus draining the colonised countries of their wealth. Before independence the process was maintained through military force, but it has continued since independence in the more subtle form of neo-colonialism in which economic power has replaced military power.

Third World countries are dependent on the developed countries for capital, technology and markets. The rich countries of the West set the interest rates, the terms of trade, the tariffs and import barriers and generally, through their economic power, drain off the surpluses produced in the poor countries. Even worse, in the eyes of these observers, is the fact that the bankers and governments of the West seem able to dictate the policies adopted by Third World governments thus perpetuating their dominant position. The world has been polarised into the rich and powerful 'haves' and the poor and dependent 'have nots'.

Capitalism in the form of all-powerful transnational corporations have monopolised the production and extraction of raw materials, the production of manufactured goods, commerce, marketing, banking and information. It is maintained that they use not only their enormous economic power, but also corruption and unfair or immoral practices, to eliminate competition and preserve their dominance. The submission of the Nestlés Corporation to charges of improper marketing tactics in the promotion of the sale of powdered milk to nursing mothers in the Third World is given as proof of the existence of such tactics. The continued marketing of unsafe pharmaceuticals and agricultural chemicals is credited to the ruthlessness of international capitalism.

Some observers maintain that so-called development assistance is another mode of domination leading to an especially pernicious form of dependency.

Aid is often given on terms which benefit the donor countries' own bankers, industrialists and industrial workers – not to speak of those benefits which accrue to the expatriate 'experts'. It is suggested that many Third World leaders and bureaucrats are dependent on aid programmes to maintain their positions and lifestyles. Aid projects are exported from the high-technology donor economies and placed in very inappropriate situations. Even 'good' development projects perpetuate attitudes of inferiority, and dependence on outsiders for progress.

Exploitation of the poor

> They used to say we were unproductive because we were lazy and drunkards. All lies. Now that we are respected as men, we're going to show everyone that we were never drunkards or lazy. We were exploited!
> *Chilean peasant leader* (quoted by Freire, 1972)

The final set of explanations for continued poverty focuses on the local socio-economic situation of the poor. It is here maintained that the immediate causes of poverty lie in the domination of poor people and their resultant dependence on powerful local elites in the form of landowners, merchants and middlemen, moneylenders, corrupt officials and sometimes even religious leaders.

Exploitation of the poor in this context takes many forms. Unable to accumulate their own savings or obtain reasonable loans from established credit institutions, they must borrow from money-lenders at usurious terms in order to purchase agricultural inputs, food and supplies in lean pre-harvest periods, or to meet the unexpected expenses such as funerals and weddings. In order to secure such loans, they mortgage their land and all too often lose it thus becoming landless labourers, sharecroppers or even indentured/bonded labourers little better off than slaves.

As sharecroppers they must pay excessively high rates of sharecropping rentals (often as much as 50% of their harvests) without the landowners contributing to any of the production input costs. As agricultural labourers they are paid minimal wages and are thereby denied their rightful share of the production surplus.

On every hand they are cheated. Not only do they pay high prices for their purchases of agricultural inputs, food and supplies, but these essential supplies are often short-weighted, diluted, impure and of inferior quality. When selling their products, they are subject to exceedingly low sales prices resulting from their inability to store produce for later sale as well as to monopolistic pricing by the merchants or government marketing boards. And again they are short-weighted; high quality produce is low-graded resulting in lower prices. The merchant is usually the moneylender, and the cycle is complete.

Observers, in their indignation, maintain that the poor are never visited by the government extension agents. They can't get bank credit. They have no say in co-operative decisions. Their children are discriminated against at school, as are the women at health clinics. They can't draw water at the wells controlled by the wealthy and the high-caste. They are always at the tail-end of irrigation systems and never receive their rightful share of the precious water. The list of oppressions is endless.

Many poor people consciously enter into dependency relationships with wealthy merchants or landowners. These patron–client relationships are not as irrational as they might look. If something goes wrong – a poor harvest, illness or death in the family – the patron can be relied upon to provide a loan or wage labour. Obliged by circumstances, the poor peasant is forced to adopt a short-term strategy to solving problems which inevitably leads to greater debt and dependency. Organising to break out of these exploitative relationships carries a high risk of violent repression by the patrons.

Any strategy of development, if it is to be successful, must act upon the factors that create dependency without creating a new and unbearable high-risk situation.

Analysing Poverty

We have looked briefly at some of the explanations given to explain the continued existence of extreme poverty in the Third World. Some observers tend to hold to one set of explanations. Technocrats and practitioners are inclined to put their faith in the lack of modernisation, the physical limitations, and the bureaucratic stifling viewpoints. Academics and leftists tend to emphasise local and international exploitation and dependency relationships as well as blaming the capitalists and the transnational corporations.

Chambers (1983) has pointed out the dangers in the tendency of both practitioners and academics towards partiality: they tend to concentrate on one or a few explanations and actions and ignore others. He then argues eloquently for the need for pluralism – recognising multiple causation, multiple objectives and multiple interventions. He defines pluralism in rural development as standing on three legs, the two cultures – academic and practical – joining together with a third:

> The third culture, of the rural people in a particular place, is the true centre of attention and of learning. As some officials were once told, 'The village is the centre; *you* are peripheral.' The micro-level is again and again out of focus; and when in focus it is seen from a distance, through the urban professional's telescope. To understand rural poverty better, and to judge better what to do, outsiders, of whatever persuasion, have to see things from the other end.

It would therefore be wise to analyse each given situation individually, starting with an examination of the local causes and finishing with an evaluation of how national and international political and socio-economic relationships affect the poor in each particular programme area. In each situation we will undoubtedly find a complex network of interrelated causes – some from each of the categories listed above. This network of inter-related causes for one particular area will differ from that of another area, although within the same country there will normally be a high degree of similarity. This similarity lessens as the comparison moves to other countries and continents.

The first step in assisting poor rural people onto the path of development must therefore be an analysis of the causes of poverty affecting a particular people in their own particular situation. This analysis should preferably be carried out with the active participation of the people themselves. The remainder of this chapter shows how some development workers in Uganda analysed the situation of the people with whom they were working.

Symptoms versus causes

Question: What is the cause of underdevelopment in your country?
Answer: Ignorance, disease and poverty.

This refrain seems to be a permanent fixture in many Third World school curricula; but I have also heard it said by ministers, presidents and development workers. Sometimes it is stated as the goal of development: eliminate ignorance, disease and poverty, which seems to imply that the remedy is simply books, medicines and money.

If you push a bit harder, you can get people to make a list of what they think are the causes of poverty. Interestingly, the list made by a European businessman will not differ very much from that made by a Third World government official. Topping the list will be ignorance, disease and possibly poverty itself. A typical list might look like Table 1.1.

Table 1.1
Causes of Poverty

Malnutrition	Low income	Lack of clean water
Illiteracy	Lack of transport	Low productivity
Poor sanitation	Overpopulation	Poor housing
Laziness/idleness	Drunkenness	Superstition
Backwardness	Hunger	Corruption
Drought/floods	Indebtedness	Exploitation
Deforestation	Lack of tools	Unemployment
Lack of markets	Low prices	Lack of skills
Colonialism	Poor management	Lack of industry
Traditions	Lack of credit	Lack of initiative
Lack of capital	Mistrust	Lack of cooperation

With a little effort this list could go on and on. But are all of these really *causes* of poverty? If so, then the thought of development really becomes daunting! Is poor housing a cause of poverty? Or is poor housing a pretty good indication that the people living in the house are poor? Is idleness a cause of poverty, or are people apparently idle because they have nothing productive to do with their time? A symptom is a sign, an indication of something else. We need to separate the symptoms from the real causes.

Vicious circles of poverty
It's all very well saying that some things are symptoms of poverty while others are the real causes, but is it all that simple? Surely disease and malnourishment cause poor health; and if you are sick, you can't work as well in your fields; and if you don't work well your production is going to be lower than it would have been and your income will also be lower. On the other hand, what are the root causes of debilitating disease and malnourishment? We all get sick at one time or another, but poor people seem to get sick more often and recover more slowly or not at all. Why is that? Part of the answer is that they don't get proper treatment. Why not? If there is a hospital or a doctor around, poor people may not be able to pay for treatment because they have low incomes. Why doesn't the government provide a free medical service or build more clinics and hospitals? The government doesn't have enough money to pay for all these things. Where does the government get its money from? By taxing the surplus of production. But production is low because people are sick!

Yes, we are going around in circles; and that is what is meant by a *vicious circle of poverty*. One problem causes another which in turn causes a third, and we keep finding new linkages until we are right back where we started from and the vicious cycle starts all over again.

At this point it might be instructive to draw a diagram of what we have so far discovered about disease and malnutrition:

Figure 1.1
A Vicious Circle

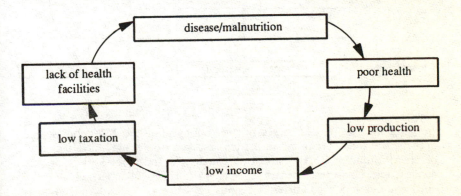

This is a simple drawing of a vicious circle of poverty. The real world, unfortunately, is even more complicated. There are factors other than the lack (or unaffordability) of health facilities causing illness in poor families and communities. Three of these are poor sanitation (the lack of toilets or sewage facilities), lack of clean drinking water and poor housing. Why are these lacking? Once again, low taxation and/or low income.

Does everything boil down to a lack of money (capital)? Not quite. Some people have money, but they don't improve their sanitation or housing (a crude, but adequate, rural pit latrine is a very inexpensive innovation). Why not? Some people lack the knowledge of the close connection between health, sanitation and clean drinking water. Some people don't care; perhaps the man in the family prefers to use the little surplus money they have on a bicycle or a watch, or perhaps drinking – this is what we can call misdirected priorities. Some people don't like the taste of water from a borehole; they prefer river water. Some people will not build or use a latrine because they are afraid that jealous neighbours will bewitch the latrine or the pathway leading to it and they will fall ill and die. Thus superstition and social traditions also play a role in the vicious circle of disease and poverty. Not only are there monetary (economic) factors involved, but also social factors.

The following illustration shows how these factors can also be integrated into the diagram of the vicious circle of disease/malnutrition and poverty:

Figure 1.2
A Vicious Circle of Poverty and Disease

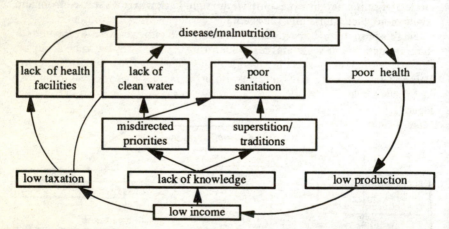

Our diagram is getting a bit messy, but we're not yet finished. Most poor people in the world today are found in the tropics. The tropics may have beautiful beaches for tourists, but they are also a tough place for poor people. Not only do the tropics have those diseases which have been brought under control in the northern developed countries – typhus, dysentery, typhoid, pneumonia, measles, malaria, hookworm, leprosy, tuberculosis – but also quite a number of exotic diseases such as schistosomiasis, trypanosomiasis, filariasis and onchocerciasis, which kill or handicap millions annually. Many of these diseases are transmitted with the help of vectors (mosquitoes, flies, snails, etc.) which are not found in colder climates. Thus there are also physical factors relating to disease and poverty.

Some of the diseases mentioned above can be controlled to some extent through mass social mobilisation to eliminate the vectors. Communities could also dig a cement-lined open well, or protect a spring, or even have a borehole drilled. Why aren't these things done? For one thing, many rural poor do not trust each other or their leaders. They will not pool their meagre funds because they are afraid that someone will misuse them. They lack cooperation, they lack social cohesion and they lack local organisational structures. All of these are social factors which contribute to the continuation of the vicious circle of poverty.

Some governments in the Third World do have enough revenue to considerably improve the health facilities, carry out the water programmes and implement the disease-eradication programmes that their people need. But the funds get diverted to fight civil wars, to finance prestige projects or through blatant corruption. What are the underlying causes of these failures of public accountability? Some of the reasons identified by the Ugandan rural development workers were political instability, lack of representational government, over-centralisation and lack of local government.

So in addition to economic, social and physical factors, we also have a series of political factors which are contributing to the perpetuation of the vicious circle of disease and poverty. I shall not attempt to put all of the factors which we have now identified into the diagram. Perhaps you can give it a try?

There are many other vicious circles of poverty that can be analysed and diagrammed. Below are some more which were developed by the same group of rural development workers in Uganda. They are shown in a simplified form. Perhaps you can elaborate on them with other factors that you can think of.

Figure 1.3
More Vicious Circles

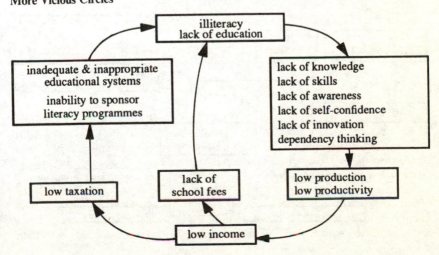

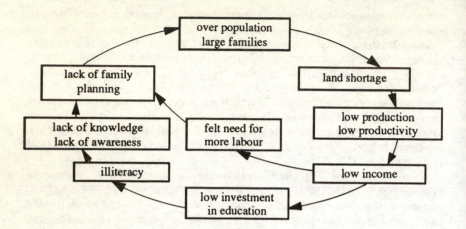

You may have noticed that in all of the vicious circles illustrated above there were several common elements: low income, low production, lack of knowledge, lack of awareness. Two of these are economic constraints to development and two are social constraints. There is a vicious circle of economic constraints, and these are so important to development efforts that they need to be looked at more closely:

Figure 1.4
The Vicious Circle of Economic Constraints

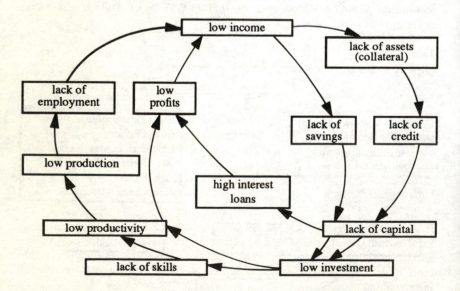

From the diagrams above, it is apparent that the analysis of the symptoms and causes of poverty, even in relatively isolated rural communities, is quite complex. If we are to find ways of breaking out of any of these vicious circles of poverty, we will need to make our analysis more systematic.

Causes of poverty

In the analysis of the vicious circles of poverty we discovered that some of the causes were economic, some were social and others were political or physical. Earlier it was noted that some causes had their roots in local communities, others at national level and even some in the realm of international relationships. This gives us a number of categories on which to sort out the causes of poverty. This categorisation may help us to identify the key constraints to development at each level of intervention – local, national and international.

In making such lists there will obviously be duplication as some constraints, such as corruption, will be found at two or more levels. There will at times also be an element of arbitrary placement of certain constraints. For example, lack of clean water could be considered either physical, social, economic or even political if you think it is the government's obligation to provide clean water for its citizens. As we shall see later, this arbitrariness does not lessen the value of categorisation.

Although the categories will be the same, the contents of such an analysis will vary from region to region and from nation to nation. An analysis in Asia is more likely to include land scarcity and debilitating indebtedness than an analysis done in Africa. An analysis in Latin America and the Philippines is more likely to mention exploitation by large landowners. For the sake of continuity, we shall continue with the analysis done by our friends in one area of Uganda as seen in Tables 1.2 and 1.3.

Table 1.2
Physical causes of poverty

Local	National	International
Poor soils	Land destruction:	Tropical disease
Unreliable rainfall	Deforestation	Vectors
Lack of surface water	Erosion	Land-locked nation
Lack of natural	Overgrazing	
resources	Lack of energy sources	
Unfavourable terrain		

It was realised that the placement of a particular cause under the category local, national or international was a bit arbitrary inasmuch as land destruction and tropical disease vectors were also local problems. It was felt, however, that land destruction was a major national problem and disease vectors an international problem.

It was realised that a cause such as land destruction, which was included in the list of physical causes, could perhaps more rightly be said to be social since it is more often than not caused by humans. It could also be political – if the causes were land tenure systems or other government policies.

The legacies of colonialism

Perhaps you are questioning why neo-colonialism and legacies of colonialism are listed as international and national social constraints, respectively, rather than political or economic constraints. This is an appropriate place to examine this contentious issue. It is worth keeping in mind that this analysis is based on discussions held in Uganda. Uganda has been independent for over 25 years. Most other former colonies have been independent for 10, 25 or even 40 years. Yet it is still not uncommon to hear politicians and intellectuals pronounce that 'colonialism is the root cause of our poverty'.

Table 1.3
Social causes of poverty

Local	*National*	*International*
Lack of knowledge	Ethnic differences	Neo-colonialism
Lack of skills	Social classes	Racial prejudice
Lack of awareness	Corruption	
Lack of cooperation	Mismanagement	
Misdirected priorities:	Legacies of colonialism	
Unnecessary		
consumption	Land destruction	
Drinking/smoking	Deforestation	
Laziness/apathy	Erosion	
Dependency thinking	Overgrazing	
Lack of initiative	Lack of family planning	
Resistance to change	programmes	
Traditional beliefs	Inappropriate school	
Religious beliefs	curriculum	
Mistrust	Poor social services	
Corruption		
Jealousy and fear		
Division of labour		
Large families		

Recognising that Uganda has been independent for 25 years, the analysis turned to looking back at how colonial policies contributed to poverty:

- Over-emphasis on cash crops for export;
- Exploitation of natural resources, especially minerals, for export;
- Land alienation;

- Discouragement of local manufacturing;
- Centralised and monopolistic control of export marketing;
- Centralised and bureaucratic domestic pricing policies;
- Export-oriented communications and transport;
- Centralised government structures;
- Lack of genuine local government;
- Centralised appointment of local administrative officers;
- Imposition of external law and institutionalisation of customary laws and 'foreign' constitution;
- Inappropriate educational systems and curricula;
- Religious conflict;
- Acceptance of European values as better than local cultural values;
- Class conflict and prejudice;
- Regional favouritism;
- Creation of dependency thinking and lack of participation in decision-making;
- Lack of democratic tradition.

What struck these young Ugandan development workers most – they were all children at the time of independence – was that after 25 years of self-government few of the colonial policies had been changed. These policies were still contributing to the continuation of poverty. These legacies of colonialism were still in place because of the mind-set of the country's ruling elites. The problem was therefore as much a social problem as either a political or an economic problem (see Tables 1.4 and 1.5).

Table 1.4
Political causes of poverty

Local	*National*	*International*
Lack of local governmental institutions	Political instability	Neo-colonialism
Sectarianism	Civil war	East-West bloc politics
Nepotism & favouritism	Lack of democratic decision-making	National rivalry
Lack of law and order	Lack of interest in poor people	Refugees
Corruption	Legacies of colonialism	
Lack of local participation	Corruption & nepotism	
Lack of political education	Lack of good administration	
	Breakdown of legal system	

The division between local and national causes was found to be somewhat arbitrary with national conditions dominating and seriously affecting local conditions. Uganda, in particular, has suffered the consequences of an inappropriate and unchanged political system inherited from colonial times.

Table 1.5
Economic causes of poverty

Local	National	International
Lack of capital	Inflation	Neo-colonialism
Lack of savings	Central marketing	Fluctuating
Lack of credit	Lack of crop finance	commodity prices
Lack of skilled labour	Late payments to	Tariffs & quotas
Lack of management	producers	Unfair trade
skills	Low producer prices	practices
Lack of enterpreneurs	for export crops	External debt
Lack of storage	Inefficient parastatal	
facilities	industries	
Lack of tools and	Lack of effective demand	
equipment	Lack of transport and	
Exploitation by traders	communication	

The above examples, though not rigorous, show how perceived causes of poverty can be categorised into more manageable groups. This is an important first step in analysing the causes of poverty in a given area within a given country. The exercise is still daunting: in the examples above there are listed 38 perceived causes of poverty at the local level. Since this book is only concerned with rural development at the micro-level, the further analysis is limited to local causes of poverty, i.e. those immediate causes which can possibly be alleviated by local initiatives. These initiatives may or may not be successful as they can be positively or negatively affected by what is happening at the national and even international levels. This is, however, beyond the scope of this book. Those development administrators and policymakers working at national level will need to analyse the national causes of poverty keeping a close eye on how their decisions may or may not affect the local initiatives being taken to alleviate poverty.

Primary and secondary causes
We have so far seen that some things can be seen as symptoms of poverty because there are more important underlying causes which are producing these symptoms, such as poor housing being caused by low income and misdirected priorities. The examples of vicious circles of poverty have shown the complex series of causes and effects involved in the analysis of any one factor – disease and malnutrition, lack of education/illiteracy, over-population, low income, etc. Separating causes into physical, social, political and economic categories as well as into local, national and international levels has helped to identify those causes which can be addressed by local developmental initiatives.

Local initiatives cannot attempt to alleviate all of the local causes of poverty at once. Trying to alleviate the symptoms without first identifying the real underlying causes will not lead to sustainable results. For example, building a

Table 1.6
Analysis of poverty by Ugandan development workers

Symptom	Secondary cause	Primary cause
1. Disease	Lack of clinics	Lack of knowledge
	Lack of drugs	Lack of awareness
	Malnutrition	Lack of capital
	Lack of clean water	Misdirected priorities
	Lack of sanitation	Dependency thinking
2. Malnutrition	Lack of food	Lack of knowledge
	Wrong type of food	Lack of awareness
	Low income	Lack of skills
	Lack of tools	Lack of capital
	Lack of land	Drought
3. Lack of clean water and sanitation	Ignorance	Lack of knowledge
	Lack of tools	Lack of skills
	Superstition	Lack of awareness
	Misdirected priorities	Lack of capital
		Dependency thinking
		Lack of cooperation
4. Over-population	No family planning	Child mortality
	No child spacing	Lack of land
	Lack of education	Lack of knowledge
	Low income	Lack of awareness
5. Illiteracy/ Lack of education	Lack of schools	Lack of capital
	Lack of teachers	Lack of awareness
	Gender discrimination	Lack of cooperation
	Lack of school fees	Low income
6. Poor housing	Lack of materials	Lack of capital
	Lack of land	Lack of skills
	Poor management	Lack of awareness
	Misdirected priorities	Lack of cooperation
	Low income	
7. Low income	Lack of employment	Lack of skills
	Lack of investment	Lack of capital
	Low production	Lack of cooperation
	Low productivity	Lack of awareness
	Lack of markets	Lack of initiative
8. Low agricultural productivity	Simple tools	Lack of skills
	Labour-intensive	Lack of knowledge
	Lack of fertilisers	Lack of capital
	Lack of pesticides	Lack of cooperation
	Lack of water	Lack of markets
	Poor soils	

health clinic may not significantly reduce the burden of illness if the people being served cannot afford treatment or there is no local governmental body able to manage and fund the continued operation of the clinic.

It therefore becomes imperative to continue the analysis of the causes of poverty in an attempt to isolate those factors which are crucial for sustainable development in a given area. This further analysis involves identifying symptoms, secondary causes and primary causes. A secondary cause is one which, at first glance, appears to be the immediate cause of the symptom. A primary cause is one which, on deeper analysis, turns out to be the real origin of the secondary cause and, more importantly, is an entry point for breaking a vicious circle. Once we have identified the entry points, we can begin to promote local initiatives for breaking the vicious circles.

The examples in Table 1.6 are taken from the analysis carried out by a group of Ugandan development workers. They are some of the more typical symptoms of poverty. These are the symptoms that most development agencies choose to attempt to alleviate. You will also have noted that some of the primary causes are included as secondary causes and even as symptoms, for example malnutrition and low income. This is part of the analysis process. What might seem to be a primary cause may, with closer analysis, be perceived as a secondary cause or even a symptom. In reality, we could have several layers of secondary causes; and the above examples are therefore simplifications. What is important is to gradually peel away the layers in order to identify the root or primary causes.

Table 1.7
Analysis of poverty by Ugandan development workers

Symptom	Secondary cause	Primary cause
1. Soil erosion/ degradation	Poor farming methods	Lack of knowledge
	Overgrazing	Lack of awareness
	Deforestation	Lack of land
	Farming on slopes	Common land
	Misdirected priorities	Lack of capital
2. Low producer prices for crops	Marketing boards	Government policies
	Corruption	Over-centralisation
	Exploitation	Government involvement in economy
	Lack of transportation	Lack of accountability
	Lack of storage	Lack of cooperation

The examples in Table 1.7 show how the analysis can move into physical and political causes of poverty as well as social and economic ones. Both also illustrate the need to continue peeling away the secondary causes to get at the root causes. For example, is the common ownership of land a root cause of overgrazing and deforestation? Or is lack of cooperation a root cause of the problems arising from common ownership?

There are many more examples that could be illustrated, such as lack of transportation, absence of industry, low fish production and lack of energy supplies. It would be counter-productive here to try to generate all of the possible combinations because the analysis must be specific to the locality being analysed. No two sets of symptoms, secondary causes and primary causes will be exactly identical. What is important is the method of analysis – the gradual peeling away of symptoms and secondary layers of causes until the root problems are revealed.

The root causes

Once the analysis of secondary and primary causes is completed, these lists can be analysed for elements which keep turning up in the lists of primary causes. These will be good indicators of the root causes of poverty in the particular situation being analysed.

Although the example given above is an incomplete representation of the analysis done by the Ugandan development workers, it still contains a number of common elements pointing at the root causes of poverty in that particular area of Uganda. Some of these need to be looked at more closely, for example lack of capital.

Lack of capital shows up in seven of the 10 lists shown above. But what is lack of capital? Where does capital come from? Analysis shows that there are four sources: savings, credit, grants and plundering. Plundering (banditry, colonialism, exploitative taxation, etc.) is no longer a viable social policy. Grants are not particularly viable or sustainable, and often come with strings attached. Credit (and taxation) are someone else's savings. So lack of capital is actually lack of saving, both individually and in the community in general. Thus lack of saving is a root cause of poverty where lack of capital is identified as a primary cause.

Some of the terms used above may have underlying causes, but we might still find the term useful in identifying root causes. What are the underlying causes of lack of co-operation? These might be mistrust and disunity, jealousy and fear, sectarianism, exploitation and fear of reprisals and, more often than not in co-operation involving money, the lack of book-keeping skills.

Some of the terms are rather vague. What lies behind misdirected priorities? Possibly drunkenness, tradition, superstition, prestige (e.g. keeping large numbers of unproductive cattle), family pressures, unessential expenditures on items of consumption (e.g. beer, tobacco), many children, expensive weddings and funerals. Much of this is also referred to as short-term perspectives. But who is to say what are misdirected priorities? This is where another vague term, lack of awareness, comes into the picture.

Lack of awareness encompasses a lack of awareness of the costs and consequences of misdirected priorities; a lack of awareness of the possible opportunities for alternative use of money, time and other resources for the benefit of the individual and his/her family; and a lack of awareness of political rights and responsibilities which might also have economic and social consequences. Coercion is not a viable long-term method of changing individual priorities although negative incentives such as taxation and loss of social benefits are a means of making the individual aware of the cost of his/her priority choices. Real change occurs only when the individual is consciously aware of the costs and consequences as well as the alternatives.

There is a great danger, however, that terms such as misdirected priorities and lack of awareness become jargon if one forgets the underlying content of the terms. Development workers should guard against this tendency.

Let us end this chapter on poverty by completing the analysis carried out by the development workers in rural Uganda as seen in Table 1.8. This is the list of root causes of poverty in the area of Uganda in which they worked, together with a short clarification where necessary.

Through analysis the Ugandan rural development workers reduced their long lists of symptoms and causes down to eight root causes of poverty in their working area. In spite of very irregular rainfall and, relative to Uganda, poor soils in their area, they did not list any root physical causes because they felt these could be overcome in time through increased awareness, skills training and increased investment.

Table 1.8
Root social causes of poverty in rural Uganda

1. Misdirected priorities	People spend too much money and time on drink, and drunkenness affects their work and families. Too much money and time is spent on weddings and funerals. Cattle are kept only for prestige purposes.
2. Dependency thinking	People expect government or agencies to develop them, bring inputs, water, etc.
3. Lack of awareness	People are unaware of the social and economic costs and consequences of misdirected priorities, superstitions, mistrust, etc. Unaware of improvement options and opportunities. Unaware of rights and responsibilities.
4. Lack of skills and knowledge	People lack skills and knowledge relating to improved methods of agriculture and fishing, disease and health, book-keeping, investment analysis, etc.
5. Lack of cooperation	People mistrust and fear (superstition) each other. Jealousy is rife. Past experiences with government cooperative societies negative. Lack of bookkeeping and organisational skills, etc.

Root economic causes

6. Lack of capital   Lack of savings; lack of credit facilities; inflation;
                        corruption

Root political causes

7. Political instability   Civil war/banditry, dictatorships, lack of elections,
                            sectarianism, ethnic nationalism (tribalism).

8. Over-centralisation   Lack of democratic local government, government
                            over-involvement in production, marketing, etc.;
                            corruption; non-accountability.

This chapter has hopefully illustrated the type of analysis of the causes of poverty that every group of development workers should be carrying out in their working areas, and preferably in conjunction with the people themselves. It cannot be over-emphasised that such an analysis will produce a particular list of root causes for each particular region analysed.

Once the root causes of poverty are identified then strategies can be developed and priorities set for helping the people to break their vicious circles of poverty and begin their own process of development. Perhaps this type of poverty analysis will also help development agencies to break their own vicious circles of treating symptoms, rather than working to alleviate the root causes of poverty.

2. What Is Development?

Poverty is unfortunately a growth industry!

Anonymous development worker

Most countries in Central and South America have been independent for well over 100 years. It is now over 40 years since India and the other countries of the subcontinent gained their independence, and 25 years since most of the new countries of sub-Saharan Africa joined the United Nations as independent countries. With the end of colonialism, expectations were high that the former colonies would experience a period of rapid economic growth and positive social transformation. The post-war recovery of Europe with assistance from the U.S. Marshall Plan, as well as the Japanese development miracle, had led economists and statesmen to foresee the possibilities for similar progress in the Third World.

Spurred on by the independence movements throughout Asia, Africa and the Caribbean islands, as well as Cold War manoeuvring, development assistance agencies and programmes were established during the 1950s. The decade beginning with 1960 was declared by the UN as the Development Decade; the 1970s became the Second Development Decade. Significantly, the 1980s were not declared the Third Development Decade (although the Women's Decade is over and we are presently nearing the end of the Water Decade). However, despite all of these 'decades', the high expectations for development and the eradication of poverty have not been fulfilled.

During the 1950s economists, political scientists and others began directing their attention towards the practical and theoretical problems of development in the Third World countries, or, as they were then called, the underdeveloped countries. Since then, thousands of scholarly papers, articles and books have been published. Magazines on all aspects of development have been established. Specialised institutes of development studies and research have been founded, and theories of economic and social development have proliferated.

A whole new jargon as well as a jet set has grown up. Discussions on development are peppered with expressions like 'modernisation', 'community development', 'dependency theory', 'structural adjustment', 'ecodevelopment', 'appropriate technology', 'self-reliance', 'participation', 'women in development' (now called 'gender awareness') and 'vulnerable groups'. The educated developmentalist refers knowingly to Rostow's 'take-off', *The Peasant's Charter*, the *Brandt Commission Report*, *The Limits to Growth*, *Another*

Development and *The Cocoyoc Declaration*. The old work-horses capitalism and socialism are saddled alternately, or even simultaneously, with responsibility for both causing and curing underdevelopment.

Theories of Development

The field of development studies is a veritable jungle, inhabited by theories, counter-theories, approaches, paradigms and programmes of all sizes, shapes and colours. This book is not intended as a taxonomy of this fauna, but it aims to help in the recognition and, to some extent, comprehension of the behaviour of some of these exotic species. A brief description of the principal theories is given below. The book by Magnus Blomstrom and Björn Hettne, *Development Theory in Transition*, is excellent for those who wish to increase their understanding of the many components of present-day development theories.

The final section of this chapter looks at development through the perspective of development workers living and working in rural areas of the Third World and, in particular, examines what is meant by human, economic, political and social development as these apply to rural communities.

Modernisation – development through growth

Development theory has until recently been dominated by theories and models derived from the experiences of Western economic history. The emergence of capitalism and the advance of the industrial revolution gave a distinctive form to Western developmental thinking. Development and economic growth became synonymous with progress and higher levels of civilisation. Growth was seen as a natural process which could be nourished through the application of correct and timely inputs. Likewise it could be impeded by bad conditions, but once these constraints were removed the process would continue. Development in the Third World was expected to be an imitative process in which the less developed countries gradually assumed the qualities of the industrialised nations.

Development was seen essentially as a question of increasing gross levels of savings and investment (both internal and external, private and state) until the economy reached a take-off point into self-sustaining development. Economic growth was a simple matter of applying appropriate levels of investment after taking into consideration the rate of population growth, the capital: output ratio and the desired rate of growth. A combination of domestic savings, international investment and international aid would provide the fuel to drive the process through 'stages of growth' which would ultimately bring the benefits of modernisation to the entire population.

But what happened? The dualistic nature of underdeveloped economies soon became apparent: the coexistence of a relatively advanced or modern sector with a backward or traditional sector. It was felt that various traps, vicious circles and barriers to development were to be found in the traditional or backward sector. It then became necessary only to reduce population growth, improve health, introduce new seed varieties, and then growth and development would occur so long as investment was sufficient.

And yet the optimism of the 1950s and 1960s could not be sustained. The empirical evidence could not be denied. More and more information accumulated which pointed towards a growing poverty complex: marginalisation, mass unemployment and recurrent starvation crises. The 'green revolution' was only one experience which confirmed the universal observation that what was taking place in many countries during the development decade was growth without development but with poverty, which in the 1980s has lead to negative growth and the debt crisis.

Dependency theory of underdevelopment

> The problem is that the actual volume of exports by the developing world has increased by over 30% in the last 20 years, whilst their value, in real terms, has increased by only 4%.
>
> *Susan George*

The dependency theory of underdevelopment was formulated by a number of Latin American economists and social scientists. The theory questioned the assumed mutual benefits of international trade and development asserted by European and American proponents of modernisation and growth theories. They undoubtedly reacted to North American economic dominance in Latin American countries, and were strongly involved in the development of so-called neo-Marxist thinking.

The theory maintained that the central nations benefited from trade whereas the peripheral nations suffered. Latin American nations were dualistic societies consisting of a proportionally large traditional agrarian society and a small, modern, urbanised society. The former was in many ways feudalistic, and the latter capitalistic. The urbanised centres were themselves developing at the expense of the rural peripheries. The unequal relationships between the centres and the peripheries led to the development of the former and to the underdevelopment of the latter.

The central argument of dependency theory is that socio-economic dependency (neo-colonialism) generates underdevelopment, i.e. the development of underdevelopment. Some of the reasons elaborated for the development of underdevelopment were: long-term trends in the terms of trade favoured the centres; the balance of economic and political power was at the centres; and finance and technology were controlled by the centres. In order to reverse this situation, the dependency doctrine stressed industrialisation by import substitution, planning and state interventionism in general, and regional integration.

Several governments emerged which were deeply influenced by dependency theory: Allende's in Chile, Manley's in Jamaica, and Nyerere's in Tanzania. Only Nyerere's survived, and it has obviously been economically unsuccessful. Dependency theory has been seen to be inadequate even by some of its earlier proponents. On the theoretical level it had failed to construct its own theory of development. As Hettne (1982) has pointed out:

> So much stress was put on the external obstacles to development that the problem of how to initiate a development process, once these obstacles were removed, was rather neglected. In fact one gets the impression that the development perspective implied in dependency theory was the modernisation model applied to an isolated national economy.

Industrialisation through import substitution was difficult because of the small size of internal markets and the need to import technology and other factors of production, especially petroleum products, which required large amounts of foreign exchange. Planning and state intervention created, in many cases, paralysing bottlenecks and inefficiencies. Regional integration has been agonisingly slow or non-existent.

The impact of the Latin American dependency theory has been substantial. It led to a critical examination of the modernisation theory and undermined the idea of progress as a more or less automatic and linear process. It led to the replacement of the idealised and mechanical vision of development by a more historical method. It stimulated dependency analysis in other areas of the Third World as well as the debate on the New International Economic Order (NIEO). It led to a necessary analysis of the particular conditions affecting the development process in the Third World and the many unforeseen contradictions that characterise this process.

Global interdependence
The response to the decline of the dependency theory was not a simple return to classical modernisation and development through growth, but rather towards attempts to define a more universal approach to development incorporating the complex relationships between both central and peripheral development, in other words theories stressing global interdependence.

The decade of the 1970s was a period which, to a large extent, shattered the optimism and confidence of theoreticians and leaders in the industrialised countries as well as in the Third World. The major economic event was the oil crisis of 1973 and the subsequent price increases of the late 1970s. Also significant were the American debacle in southeast Asia, the sub-Saharan droughts, and the wave of right-wing military coups in Latin America. The oil crisis clearly showed the vulnerability of Western industrialism, the unsustainability of natural resources and especially cheap energy, the power of transnational companies, and the decreasing capacity of nation-states to control their own economies. By the end of the decade the economies of the oil-importing countries of the Third World were in tatters. At the same time the industrialised countries were experiencing high inflation together with continued unemployment.

Throughout the 1970s, global interdependence became more and more obvious and resulted, of course, in a proliferation of new development strategies. Two of the more publicised ones, arising out of the debates on global reform of the late 1970s and early 1980s, were the demands for a New International Economic Order favouring the developing nations, and the Brandt Commission report *North–South: A Programme for Survival* proposing a massive transfer of financial resources to the poor countries.

Ironically, in the 1980s the world has seen the results of just such a massive resource transfer of petro-dollars to selected Third World countries through Western commercial banks, bilateral and international lending institutions. Rather than leading to balanced economic development in these countries, this transfer has developed into the world debt crisis which has yet to be resolved.

Another development

> In order to determine whether a society is developing, one must go beyond criteria based on indices of per capita income (which, expressed in statistical form, are misleading) as well as those which concentrate on the study of gross income. The basic, elementary criterion is whether or not the society is a 'being for itself', i.e. its political, economic and cultural decision-making power is located within.
>
> *Paulo Freire*

The theoretical debates of the early 1970s led to an increasing concern among some observers with the question of how development *should* take place rather than limiting discussion to theories about how it actually takes place. This is termed a normative approach in contrast to the positivist approaches exemplified in the modernisation and dependency theories. The significance of normative approaches is that they focus on the content of development rather than the form. Such approaches are concerned with the purpose and meaning of development rather than limiting discussion to questions relating to the mobilisation of the productive forces of development such as labour, capital and trade.

The Cocoyoc Declaration adopted at a symposium in Cocoyoc, Mexico, in 1974 is an important example of the normative approach. The subject of this meeting was resources and development and the majority opinion of the participants was that mankind's predicament is rooted primarily in economic and social structures, and behaviour within and between countries. It was declared that a process of growth that did not lead to the fulfillment of basic human needs was a travesty of development. This implied more than just basic physical needs; it also included concepts such as freedom of expression and self-realisation in work. Furthermore, there was a need for the rich to reconsider over-consumptive modes of living which violate the 'inner limits' of man and 'outer limits' of nature.

Although normative theories risk being labelled unrealistically utopian, they are nonetheless valuable if we accept that policies and actions are influenced by ideas as to what we would like to see happen. These trends in development theory have been actively promoted by the Dag Hammarskjöld Foundation,

Sweden, and the International Foundation for Development Alternatives (IFDA).

'Another development' theorists believe that development should be: *need-oriented*, geared to meeting both material and non-material human needs; *endogenous*, stemming from the heart of each society; *self-reliant*, implying that each society relies primarily on its own strength and resources; *ecologically sound*, utilising rationally the resources of the biosphere; and based on *structural transformation* as an integrated whole. The direction of this structural transformation is indicated by the normative content of the other four points. This implies that there is no universal path to development. Every society must find its own strategy.

The basic needs approach

By 1970 many observers had discovered that economic growth in the aggregate did not necessarily eliminate poverty. This led to a formulation of the basic needs approach which was adopted by the International Labour Organisation (ILO) in 1976. The meeting of the basic human needs of poor people became an important element in alternative development strategies. The ILO defined basic needs to include several elements. First, they include certain minimum requirements of a family for private consumption: adequate food, shelter and clothing are obviously included, as is certain household equipment. Second, they include essential services provided by and for the community at large, such as safe drinking water, sanitation, public transport, health and educational facilities.

There has been considerable discussion as to just what are the basic needs. Proponents of the various growth models were attracted to the idea of meeting basic 'material' needs and included various social indicators in their growth models. The most influential proponent of this basic needs approach is UNICEF, the United Nations Children Fund, which concentrates its activities on health, water supply and sanitation programmes. Adherents of 'another development' naturally emphasised satisfying basic human needs not only among Third World poor but also within affluent societies.

The discussions on meeting basic needs have been useful in creating awareness of the fact that growth does not necessarily benefit the poor, but the question of how these needs can be met has still not been resolved. The following statements eloquently elaborate on this question:

> A Basic Needs program that does not build on the self-reliance and self-help of governments and countries is in danger of degenerating into a global charity program. A NIEO that is not committed to meeting basic needs is liable to transfer resources from the poor in the rich countries to the rich in the poor countries.
>
> (Streeten, 1979)

How many still believe that development means building schools or wells rather than supporting processes of social change and self-reliance?
First International FFHC/AD Consultation, FAO, Rome

Ecodevelopment

Western thought has consistently placed man in the centre of the universe. The natural environment was there for man to conquer, exploit and develop for his sole benefit. Modern economic thought has been dominated by a concept of unlimited growth based on the exploitation of unlimited resources and technological development. However, other value systems have seen man as only a small part of a much greater natural order. The contrast in thinking between the American Indians and the European immigrants to North America illustrates these philosophical differences. The Indian saw land and all natural resources as something he was given on loan – his God permitted him to use the land so long as the Indian respected its sanctity. All living creatures had a soul. The Indian even went so far as to ask forgiveness of the bear after having killed him. For the European, the land, its resources and all living creatures were his to purchase or take and, thereafter, to exploit. Yet, the European went so far as to question whether the Indian had a soul!

The economic and ecological crises of the last decade have, to a large extent, brought an increasing awareness to the importance of man's relationship with the general environment – that human actions have ecological ramifications. The recent international conferences on the ozone hole and the greenhouse effect illustrate this concern. This increasing awareness has led to a school of thought called ecodevelopment. The concept of ecodevelopment arose partly as a result of the limits to growth debate instigated by the Club of Rome and the 1972 UN Conference on the Environment. Ignacy Sachs (1974), one of the main thinkers within this school, has suggested that:

Ecodevelopment is a style of development that, in each ecoregion, calls for specific solutions to the particular problems of the region in the light of cultural as well as ecological data and long-term as well as immediate needs. Accordingly, it operates with criteria of progress that are related to each particular case, and adaption to the environment plays an important role.

Within the normative approach of alternative development thinking, ecodevelopment recognises the outer limits to unfettered economic growth and exploitation of the environment. We have already seen that basic human needs represent a form of 'inner' limit, i.e. the minimum of what is acceptable. Ecodevelopment is therefore a developmental philosophy that aims to make efficient use of the natural and human resources of a specific region in such a way that provides in the minimum for the basic needs of the people living there while at the same time maintaining a viable ecological environment.

Recent Trends in Development Thinking

We have looked briefly at some of the conflicting theories and schools of thought relating to development. Unfortunately, few theories and strategies die when their weaknesses and deficiencies are exposed by new thoughts and strategies. We live in a world today which is cluttered with 'isms', 'ologies' and declarations of principle. Where does all this leave the poor peasant and his family? Or the 'poor' fieldworker trying to do his or her best to help individuals and groups to struggle up from the depths of poverty?

In recent years the questions of equity and equality in the distribution of the benefits from development have become key elements in the ongoing debate on development theories and practice. Edouard Saouma, Director-General of the FAO, has expressed this concern in his foreword to *The Peasants' Charter*:

> The rural poor must be given access to land and water resources, agricultural inputs and services, extension and research facilities; they must be permitted to participate in the design, implementation and evaluation of rural development programmes; the structure and pattern of international trade and external investment must be adjusted to facilitate the implementation of poverty-oriented rural development strategies.
>
> Growth is necessary but not sufficient; it must be buttressed by equity and, above all, by people's participation in designing, implementing and evaluating rural development programmes and policies.

Another area of increasing interest is the relationship between development and social transformation. More and more students and practitioners of development are beginning to see a need for changes or transformations in existing economic, social and political structures and relationships if development is to genuinely benefit the poor and disadvantaged. Some observers emphasise the need for changes at the local level between the poor and officials, landowners, moneylenders, etc. Others argue for national or international changes. These concerns are reflected by the following researchers:

> It is becoming clearer that community self-help which contributes effectively to economic and social development can only prosper if accompanied by profound transformations in the social and economic structures of the countries involved.
>
> (Stavenhagen in Pearse and Stiefel, 1979)

> There can be no fixed and final definition of development, merely suggestions of what development should imply in particular contexts. Development necessarily involves structural transformation which implies political, social and economic changes.
>
> (Hettne, 1982)

> Rural development takes place in a political context and it means nothing but a social transformation in rural areas by which poverty will be eradicated through attacking the existing power structure. This has not been conspicuous in past development thinking which has assumed a social framework that will change without conflicts. Transformation means that

those without power must gradually gain this to achieve some basic needs at the expense of those who already possess considerably more than basic needs.

(Bengtsson, 1979)

A third area of increasing concern is the difficult relationship between autonomy and interdependence. Autonomy is the capacity of individuals, communities and nation-states to make independent decisions. Working against autonomy are the increasing levels of social, economic and political interdependence at all levels of global society. Without significant autonomy there can be no genuine growth with equality. Teddy Brett (quoted in MacDonald, 1981) has noted that, 'Development is a change process characterised by increased productivity, equalisation in the distribution of the social product, and the emergence of indigenous institutions whose relations with the outside world are characterised by equality rather than by dependence or subordination.' There has been increasing awareness in recent years that development is not a question of things – schools, clinics, roads, dams – but one primarily of people and social, economic and political relationships.

Obviously there is more to development than changing positions within an international division of labour and the production and distribution of material goods. Development concerns people, it effects their way of life and is influenced by their conceptions of the good life, as determined by their cultures.

(Hettne, 1982)

Finally, the role of rural women in development has emerged as a major area of concern which has, until recently, been scandalously neglected both in theory and practice. This is of such importance that it deserves a separate section later in this book.

In closing this brief review of modern theories of development, it might be appropriate to reflect on the following quotation which questions the very concept of development as seen through Western eyes.

Another myth in our language is projected through the word development. Intertwined with the myth of 'technology', it has many of the same connotations. In addition, its general use implies a value judgement, i.e. that good, desirable social development is synonymous with economic growth, a linear process of social change ending in the model of the modern western consumer society. . . .

The myth of development has devastating effects at the local human level. Use of such terms as 'un-developed' and 'under-developed' is outrageous. Those who have worked closely with people in the Third World cannot avoid seeing how it hurts to be called under-developed, to be told – explicitly or implicitly – that what you do is a mistake, that what you have done is inferior, and that you do not really know what you should do.

(Fuglesang, 1982)

Development from Below – People First

The previous sections have briefly presented some of the prevailing theories and strategies relating to macro-development, i.e. development at the national or regional levels. We have already seen that rural people are affected by national policies and by international economic and political conditions over which they have little or no control. Does this mean that development cannot occur in rural areas unless all of the macro-level policies and relationships are conducive to local development initiatives? Certainly not. If that was the case it is doubtful whether Europe and North America would be developed today.

What, then, does development mean at the micro-level of the village, township, county and district? Certainly it must involve people of varying socio-economic status, varying occupations and skill levels, varying levels of education, varying levels of ambition, awareness and enlightenment. All people live within some form of social framework consisting of social, economic and political structures. Historically, development has always involved changes or transformations of these structures.

These changes will not all occur at once, nor will they ever cease; no society not totally isolated from the modern world remains completely static. There will be progress and there will be setbacks. Development must therefore be seen as a process evolving gradually over time.

Development will necessarily involve the use of physical, financial and human resources. The use of resources will depend on who controls the available resources and how decisions are made affecting their use. Some resources may come from external sources; this implies a degree of control by outsiders. This raises questions of self-reliance. Can resources be mobilised internally? What degree of outside control is tolerable?

These questions and others were discussed in training workshops by several groups of rural development workers in three widely separate rural areas of Uganda. The following definitions of human, political, economic and social development are, to some extent, universal but they are included here to illustrate the kind of thinking that development workers should be doing before they intervene in a situation of rural poverty and stagnation.

Human (personal) development

It was felt that development in any meaningful sense must begin with, and within, the individual. Unless motivation comes from within, efforts to promote change will not be sustainable by that individual. The individual will remain under the power of others. One group of rural development workers developed this definition:

> Human (personal) development is a process by which an individual develops self-respect, and becomes more self-confident, self-reliant, cooperative and tolerant of others through becoming aware of his/her shortcomings as well as his/her potential for positive change. This takes place through working with others, acquiring new skills and knowledge, and

active participation in the economic, social and political development of their community.

Economic development

Any productive economic activity involves the mobilisation and management of some combination of all or most of the factors of production. These factors are land and/or raw materials, labour (skilled and unskilled), capital, energy, tools, machinery, plant, management and entrepreneurship. Capital comes from individual savings or someone else's savings in the form of credit, shares or taxation. Management represents the skill of organising and controlling the factors of production. Entrepreneurship represents the willingness and initiative needed to identify opportunities, invest capital and take the risk of failure or success.

One of the simplest forms of productive economic activity is the peasant woman planting and cultivating some of last season's seeds using a simple hoe. Even this simple activity entails some management skills and entrepreneurship: management of her time, foresight in saving seeds, the decision as to when to plant; entrepreneurship in the decision to plant her seeds rather than eat them, and the willingness to risk crop failure rather than flee to a city slum.

Management and entrepreneurship can be exhibited either on an individual basis or collectively in a group of two or more persons. As we shall see later it can be advantageous for poor people to organise all or part of the factors of production on a cooperative basis.

Economic activity, if it is to lead to development, must be carried out on a sustainable basis. This means that the returns to the activity must be greater than the costs: it must be profitable. The back-side of production is marketing – there can be no cash profits without available markets. It also means that some of the surplus produced must be reinvested in the same activity or in profitable new activities. If this sequence of saving, investment and reinvestment fails, then the process of development will stagnate or reverse. Of course, at some point in time there may be limitations to continued growth. This is, however, not one of the problems confronting poor people in the Third World today. Having considered these aspects of economic activities, a second group of development workers formulated the following definition:

Economic development is a process by which people through their own individual and/or joint efforts boost production for direct consumption and to have a surplus to sell for cash. This requires that the people themselves analyse the problems, identify the causes, set their priorities and acquire new knowledge. It also requires them to organise themselves in order to coordinate and mobilise the effective application of all the factors of production at their disposal. This means that they must plan, implement and manage their own economic activities. The higher income that accrues through increased savings and investment can be used to satisfy a wider range of the people's wants enabling them to realise greater well-being. However, continued progress requires the reinvestment of part of this surplus.

Political development

All people live within some form of political structure whether formal or informal. This political structure may or may not benefit the individual or the general public as a collective entity. If development, in its widest sense, is to truly benefit the people, then the political structure must be responsive to their needs and aspirations as well as protect their rights and their property. Political development was therefore defined by another group of Ugandan development workers in this manner:

> Political development is a process of gradual change over time in which the people increase their awareness of their own capabilities, their rights and their responsibilities; and use this knowledge to organise themselves so as to acquire real political power in order (1) to participate in decision-making at local level and to choose their own leaders and representatives at higher levels of government who are accountable to the people; (2) to plan and share power democratically; and (3) to create and allocate communal resources equitably (fairly) and efficiently among individual groups. Hence it may be possible to avoid corruption and exploitation, realise social and economic development, political stability and peace, and create a politicised population within the context of their own culture and their own political system.

Social development

In this context social development refers to those investments and services carried out or provided by a community for the mutual benefit of the people of that community whether as a village, a district or a nation. These might include health services and facilities, education, water supplies, energy, transport systems, communications. Such services and investments could, of course, be provided by private individuals or companies, in which case questions of equity and regulation arise. Most societies have therefore chosen what for them is a suitable degree of public involvement in investment, operation and regulation.

Unless a society opts for completely unregulated private involvement in the social sectors, social development activities cannot be established and sustained without an adequate degree of political development. Resources must be mobilised through taxation, public bonds and expropriation, to cover investment costs and provide operating funds. Management and accountability systems must be in place to insure effective operation and to avoid corruption. For example, in Third World countries underpaid health personnel often sell scarce drugs on the open market at premium prices.

Likewise social development is dependent upon parallel and sufficient economic development to provide the resource base from which investment capital and operating funds are allocated. No social development activity is without cost. Without an economic base to cover these costs, social investments will collapse. As Dr Burton Singer of Yale University's School of Medicine says, 'If you want to improve the health status in underdeveloped lands, you can't do it without transforming agriculture and economic development.'

The relationship between social, economic and political development can be illustrated as two columns representing economic and political development and a girder representing social development where the girder is dependent upon the support of the two columns which in turn rest upon a foundation of personal (human) development (see Figure 2.1).

Figure 2.1
Building Development

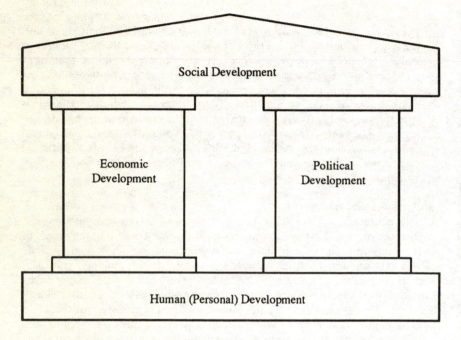

Unfortunately, too many governments and aid agencies either forget or ignore this basic relationship. The Third World is today littered with clinics, hospitals, training schools, water systems, community centres, and other social institutions which are dilapidated or in a terminal state of decline. Many of these institutions have been rehabilitated one or more times, often by the same agency that built them. This situation will continue unless external agencies are willing to continue providing operating funds and in some cases supervision (this is open-ended charity and paternalism – most agencies see the futility of it), or until local communities and nations develop the necessary political structures and economic bases to support social development activities on a self-reliant basis.

Taking these factors into consideration, rural development workers in Uganda formulated this definition of social development:

Social development is a process of gradual change in which people increase their awareness of their own capabilities and common interests, and use this knowledge to analyse their needs; decide on solutions; organise themselves for cooperative efforts; and mobilise their own human, financial and natural resources to improve, establish and maintain their own social services and institutions within the context of their own culture and their own political system.

The above examples of definitions of personal, economic, political and social development illustrate one way of defining development. To a large extent, they are generalised definitions, nonetheless other development workers would benefit from formulating their own views on development. Perhaps the failures of so many development projects can be traced partially to the lack, on the part of development agencies, of a clear concept of what development actually means.

Development is obviously a complex and slow-moving process involving people on the one hand and the factors of production and organisation on the other. It is obviously not a simple matter of an investment project here and a training programme there. Governments and development agencies would do well to realise this. Perhaps the whole concept of development projects and programmes is wrong. Perhaps development workers need to settle down to working patiently over time, directly with people, facilitating and supporting initiatives arising from the ambitions and priorities of individuals, groups and the community at large. Perhaps then we would begin to see the emergence of sustainable development processes powered by people themselves.

3. Self-Reliant Participatory Development

> The problems of the rural poor, in the final instance, cannot be solved by anyone but themselves, and all solidarity efforts must be aimed at strengthening their own capacity for independent action.
>
> (Sethi, 1983)

What is a Community?

Most Westerners and many development workers have an urban background with little sense of local community. They live and work in an urban or suburban environment, and most have grown up and received their education in an atmosphere of openness and relative freedom to pursue their own interests. Very few have lived for any length of time in small, relatively closed, rural communities or villages. The same can also be said of the urban, educated elite in Third World countries.

Because outsiders have so little experience of it, they tend to romanticise village life. They would like to believe in a community of friendly, warm-hearted natives living together in harmony, oppressed by their poverty, and perhaps also their ignorance, but working together and trying to make the best out of a difficult situation. Literature and history books, for the most part, strengthen this image of the harmony and friendliness of rural village life. Our brief visits to poor villages in the Third World as tourists, either holiday or development tourists, reinforce this impression. We are received with garlands, smiling faces and friendly handshakes; we experience festivals, dancing, weddings and other occasions where the whole community appears to be participating. Wouldn't it be nice to live in such lovely harmony with our friends and neighbours instead of the hectic, competitive, disassociated urban life to which so many of us are addicted?

This mental image of village life has determined to a large degree the approach to development work in rural areas. Without much analysis, a harmony model of community development has been adopted. Everyone is interested in the common good. With a little training and sufficient funding, the villagers will come together, work together, and everyone will benefit.

This model is, however, increasingly being questioned by social scientists and development researchers. Poona Wignaraja has called for a demystification of the harmony model of rural community life. He states emphatically that rural communities in the Third World are not homogeneous entities. The situation may be more harmonious where land reform has occurred or in a tribal society in which land is communally owned and traditional societal values continue. But even here a great deal depends on the extent of previous civil disruption and of the penetration of colonial and other external interventions which have created contradictions, eroded communal bonds and values as well as equality of access to resources.

Sharp contradictions among different groups with conflicts of interests exist in most Third World villages. Accordingly, there are dominance/dependence relationships even at the village level which need to be understood. These relationships give power to the dominant (the landlord, the trader, the moneylender, the bureaucrat) and enable them to exploit the poor.

The divisions among the poor themselves, and the inhibitions of the poor to taking economic, social and political initiatives to improve their lives, further compound their difficulties and prevent them from benefiting from the technocratically-evolved aid packages.

Rural communities are composed of individuals and groups with different and often opposing interests. Every village or complex of villages has its bigger than average landowners, its merchants and moneylenders. Even though many of these no longer live in the villages, they have their agents and families. Some have been exposed to modern education and use it to their advantage. Even village chiefs and headmen are now appointed by the government. Teachers, government agents, cooperative officials all have their positions of power and influence, and are concerned with maintaining their relatively privileged status.

And the poor, who are they? Here again we tend to see the poor as a homogeneous group with common interests. But some have land, others are landless and live solely by their labour. Some are fishermen or work in the forests. Others are petty merchants or craftsmen. Many are producing the same products and competing for the same limited markets. Others are competing for scarce, and often seasonal, work in the fields or on the plantations, on the roads or in the forests. Furthermore, do poor women have the same needs and interests as poor men? The disunity of the poor favours the rich.

Savale and Bhasin recorded discussions among poor tribal peasants at a participatory workshop in India. The local participants, who were going through a process of conscientisation, realised that their fights with each other, and many of their customs and habits, work for the benefit of the exploiters. When they launch legal cases against each other, both parties lose out to the police, lawyers and others. When they spend large amounts of money on marriages, the main benefit goes to the moneylender and trader. In fact, their marriage becomes a festival of the rich because often both husband and wife become bonded to the moneylender due to the loan taken for the wedding. Too much drinking leads to quarrels, ill-health, and profits for the others. Their superstitions are also used by the exploiters to fleece them.

Rural class structures

Every rural society has some form of socio-economic class structure. Rural development workers would therefore be wise to analyse the structure in the area where they will be working before they try to promote development activities.

A group of rural development workers in Uganda evolved the following analysis which proved useful in most farming areas of the country:

Labourers: men and women who lack access to land, and who must survive by working for others as hired/indentured labourers.

Poor Peasants: have insufficient land and/or livestock to meet their needs; often work as part-time labourers for others; never hire others but often join in mutual help 'digging groups'.

Middle peasants: have sufficient land/livestock to meet their own needs; normally would not work as hired labourers and would seldom hire others to work for them.

Rich Peasants: have more than enough land/livestock to meet their own needs as well as marketable surpluses; never work for others, but often hire others to work for them.

Wage earners/artisans/professionals: have a high level of interdependence on others, e.g. employers, customers, clients, etc. In many Third World countries, professionals such as teachers, nurses, and extension workers in government service are extremely poorly paid and usually must find additional sources of income.

Capitalists: are those having sufficient capital to invest in productive assets and to purchase the necessary factors of production, e.g. commercial farmers/ranchers. *Petty capitalists* are shop owners, taxi and lorry owners, etc. *Bureaucratic capitalists* have acquired their capital through corruption or favouritism; they use their influence to get a land title on which they get a bank loan for commercial/productive investment.

Poor and middle peasants are often called *subsistence farmers* while rich peasants are sometimes called *transitional* or *progressive farmers* on their way to becoming *capitalistic commercial farmers*.

Once having identified the various socio-economic classes in a community, the rural development worker must analyse the relationships between the classes and quantify the numbers of men and women (or families) belonging to each class. Of course, people as individuals are not so easily classified because the transition from one class to another is quite blurred in practice. But the exercise is necessary in order to understand the community and how it works.

Community development

Despite the fact that the realities are otherwise, the commonly accepted approach to rural community development has been to establish projects which treat the village as a more or less harmonious unit. It has not been good practice to give special consideration to specific groups within the community.

The researchers of the Participatory Institute for Development Alternatives (PIDA) report that practically all rural development initiatives in Sri Lanka, whether governmental or nongovernmental, have attempted to work with total village communities without recognising the basic contradictions or conflicting interests that exist within communities. These agencies apparently assumed that either rural communities are harmonious socio-economic entities, or that the conflicting socio-economic interests (hence the power structure) could, for all practical purposes, be ignored. However, some agencies intentionally avoid disturbing the status quo as a matter of deliberate choice. The PIDA researchers pessimistically conclude that, given the differentiation of the rural society into rich and poor, elite and non-elite, and the dominant–dependent or unequal nature of the socio-economic relations that exist between these two groups, even a so-called neutral intervention would adjust to the dynamics of power relations and end up serving the dominant interests.

So-called community development projects seem to have been trapped in their own nomenclature: since we are carrying out a community project, we have to treat the village as a whole entity. But after 35 years of community development work in the Third World this assumption is being called more and more into question.

The Community Development Movement in India, a nationwide programme started in 1952, was perhaps the best known of these attempts. Gerrit Huizer (1984) has reviewed the studies of the movement undertaken by A. R. Desai. The programme implicitly accepted the assumptions that individuals, groups and classes in a village community have common interests which are sufficiently strong to bind them together. It also assumed that the interests were sufficiently common to create general enthusiasm, and that conflicts of interests were sufficiently reconcilable. These assumptions proved to be unrealistic. In fact, the better-off benefited most from the programmes and a growing disparity and inequality became visible in the rural areas.

It was generally accepted in community development circles that working through the established traditional leaders in the villages, generally the better-off, would automatically benefit the whole community. This did not prove to be the case, and the approach was, therefore, called 'betting on the strong'. After several consecutive evaluations it became obvious that the better-off, mainly the dominant landowning groups, benefited from the extension work and other projects, rather than the majority of the poor peasants in the community. Huizer concluded that the 'harmony model' of community development ironically enhanced and sharpened the potential for conflict at the village level.

Working within communities

Given the negative results for the poor arising from the harmony model of community development, what changes need to be made in our approach to working with the poor? Obviously, we must find a way to ensure that the organised and powerful elements in the community do not appropriate the benefits of development activities. To do this we must discriminate in favour of the poor. This can be done by consciously directing our efforts to smaller, more homogeneous groups such as fishermen, landless labourers, potters. This must, however, be done slowly and carefully. A large sudden influx of money and other resources will make such a discriminatory approach explosively disruptive. Unless the poor can build up an adequate institutional framework to support and protect their activities, they will again be overcome by the more powerful.

Many, but not all, local development organisations in the Third World, especially in Asia and Latin America, have adapted their rural development work along these lines. Unfortunately, few international agencies have yet used their considerable influence on development policies to promote a move in this direction.

Oakley and Winder (1981) discovered a characteristic common to all the participatory projects that they studied in India and Latin America. They found that the social development work is based upon group (as opposed to community or village) development. Group work and group development are basic to the educational process. Oakley and Winder believe that this emphasis upon the formation and development of clearly identified peasant groups reflects the current dissatisfaction in rural development practice with the aggregate community or village as the object of any development initiative.

As indicated above, the poor themselves are very often disunited and in competition with each other. Their difficult situations have taught them to distrust outsiders, local elites and each other. This distrust often results in an apparent resistance to change. Is it possible to break through this passivity and defensiveness?

Huizer (1971) reports that in a study regarding peasant life in Latin America, it was shown that the distrust and passive resistance of peasants towards development efforts is not an inherent characteristic of peasant societies, but a reaction to the fact that most development efforts benefit those who are already better off, while the peasants continue to live under a system which has been characterised as the 'culture of repression' or 'internal colonialism'.

It can also be shown that the peasants are quite able and willing to participate enthusiastically in programmes or movements that are clearly designed to solve their grievances and to benefit them, instead of the better-off. Distrust, if its reasons are discovered and placed in a social context, can, in fact, be utilised to arouse peasants to take organised action as a starting point for radical change. The participatory efforts in the projects studied were directed against those whose power and influence was justifiably distrusted.

The privileged groups in rural communities do not take lightly to the idea of the poor improving their positions in any way that lessens their own wealth or power. They and their reactions to projects directed specifically towards assisting the poor cannot be ignored. However, instead of a trickle-down approach to development, it might be appropriate to adopt a trickle-up philosophy. Income and employment-generating activities must be directed at the poor if they are to benefit. The privileged will manage on their own, and adopt tactics that attempt to co-opt some of the benefits of these activities for themselves. However, there will be a whole range of development activities within the spheres of health, education and infrastructure that will also directly benefit the privileged as well as the poor. So long as the poor are not in any way excluded from the benefits or further exploited as a result, then such 'community-wide' activities are justified, and useful in reducing conflict and tension.

Previously, most development planners and social scientists attempted to avoid social conflict and tension. This approach was blind to the hidden conflicts and tensions in rural society. There is now a growing awareness among development workers that social transformations bringing economic advancement for the poor are almost certainly accompanied by conflict. Development workers, instead of fearing conflict, are beginning to appreciate conflict as a possible creative force in promoting change and development.

It would be nice if harmonious communities still existed (if they ever did) but we are living and working in the real world in which individuals or groups co-operate, compete and exploit – when it is to their own advantage. Our policies and actions must take the real world into consideration.

Social and Cultural Change

> Culture is how people structure their experience conceptually so that it can be transmitted as knowledge (information) from person to person and from generation to generation.
>
> (Fuglesang, 1982)

Each of us is very much defined by our social relationships and our cultural traditions. In Western societies, and to an increasing extent in the urban centres of the Third World, the individual functions as a separate member of society. In these individualistic societies, a person has greater freedom to choose his or her social relationships and to participate or not in cultural traditions. Modern societies are pluralistic in the sense that different forms of social relationships are tolerated, and several cultural traditions exist together, intermingle and hopefully enrich each other. Relationships and traditions in modern societies are changed or transformed relatively rapidly.

In isolated rural communities, social relationships are generally rigidly defined and cultural traditions strong and relatively static. The individual is an integral part of the society, and may not even perceive himself or herself as an individual in the Western sense. Freedom of the individual is clearly subordinate to the interests of the family, the clan and the community.

Social relationships are established and cultural traditions maintained through ceremonies and social events. They are given intellectual expression through beliefs, usually religious, and legends, myths and tales either written or oral. There may or may not be formal carriers or transmitters of these beliefs and customs such as priests or monks, elders, age-group societies, shamans and traditional healers. Individuals are indoctrinated with these beliefs and initiated into formal social relationships through various life-phase ceremonies connected with birth, name-giving (baptism), coming-of-age (confirmation), marriage, old-age (retirement) and death. Societies throughout the world have developed innumerable variations on these themes, and made the science of anthropology so fascinating and important for our understanding of peoples and their cultures.

The behaviour of individuals and groups and their response to external impulses cannot be understood completely without an intimate understanding of their social relationships and their cultural traditions. Societies use these relationships and traditions to minimise conflict. They set the rules for interaction between individuals and groups. They determine how new information will be processed and how decisions are made.

Verhelst maintains that the African peasant is not a *homo economicus*; he makes decisions according to a precise rationality that encompasses elements other than the cost–profit relationship (but not necessarily excluding the latter). If the relational and communal dimensions are safeguarded, and if his security is not threatened, if other elements such as his value system are not brought into question, if, furthermore, the advantages to be gained from an innovation have been well established, the African peasant is perfectly willing to change his techniques and increase his productivity.

Development workers must be intimately familiar with the social and cultural systems in which they are working in order to successfully promote change. New ideas and new activities will only be adopted if they do not create more conflict with accepted beliefs and traditions than is tolerable. If new ideas are presented in terms which are familiar and recognisable to the existing system, they will more easily be identified as useful and acceptable.

Development workers should be aware that their work among the poor will undoubtedly lead to changes in social relations and cultural traditions. It is essential and urgent to realise that insulting statements about traditional ways of life and condemnation of people's customs are counterproductive in any process of social change. Traditional values should instead be recognised and appreciated for their special contribution to a better future. Development workers should therefore respect the beliefs and traditions of the poor, while at the same time help them to analyse how these beliefs and traditions either provide them with emotional and economic support or contribute to keeping them in a state of poverty and oppression. The poor will make changes when they see that such changes are to their advantage.

Case Study 1 – Changing marriage customs

The Bhoomi Sena (Land Army) Movement in the Palghar District of Maharashtra State, India, is an indigenous movement which bonds the Adivasis (tribals) and other poor groups in the region into a united force.

Traditionally, poor Adivasi peasants borrow large sums from the moneylenders for extravagant marriage celebrations which often put them in debt for life. In the Bhoomi Sena area, however, after many years of struggle these peasants had formed their own farmers' associations (Tarun Mandals). In their efforts to improve their economic situation, one of these associations took up the problem of the finances required for such marriages.

The Tarun Mandal analysed the expenditure pattern of three or four recent marriages and discovered, to their surprise, that a large part of the expenditure was not on themselves, but on the *sawkars* (the moneylenders). It was a strange system: borrow money from the *sawkar*, spend it on buying materials from his shop, feed him with that food and then, as soon as the marriage is over, start working for him as a bonded labourer, often for life!

When the Tarun Mandal put these facts before the people, one old man exclaimed: 'How can this be called our marriage; this is *sawkar*'s wedding!' It was unanimously decided to eliminate all items which concerned the *sawkar* and to reduce the expenditure otherwise.

However, as the bride and groom could come from different villages, it was realised that there would have to be other Tarun Mandals in other villages which also thought along these lines. They arranged a match between a girl from the village and a Tarun Mandal member from a neighbouring village. Both the Tarun Mandals helped out in kind and with money. All the poor in the two villages participated in the ceremony with great enthusiasm. The couple – who would not now become bonded labourers – took the oath of never becoming slaves again, of unity with the poor, and of equality between husband and wife with full respect for each other.

More marriages of this type followed. The Tarun Mandals have made an important contribution towards changing exploitative social traditions.

(From de Silva et al., 1979)

Existing social relationships and cultural traditions will, to some extent, affect the decisions made by interest groups regarding their choice of development activities and how these are implemented. Development workers should help groups to become aware of these factors and to make their decisions on the basis of a conscious evaluation of what to change and what to retain. Haque and his colleagues go so far as to suggest that social and cultural activities can deliberately be used to reduce intra-communal conflicts to a level where joint economic activities would be feasible.

These decisions can be facilitated by helping the group and the community to examine the new ideas and activities, as well as the expected social transformations, in ways that can easily be related to existing customs and traditions. This analysis can often be carried out by using traditional forms of cultural communication such as dance, drama, story-telling and puppets.

Fuglesang proposes that new information should be presented in forms familiar and appropriate to people's ways of expression. Proverbs, riddles, tales or whatever form is customary should be adopted and adapted as the means of communication. He feels that it is easier for a village community to turn its eyes to the future if it starts by looking at its past. He has never met a community which is not interested in the history of its people and the ways of the ancestors. How did people do it in the old days? Why did they do it like that? What are we doing now? Why are we doing it like this? What is the situation today? How can we do it better? Fuglesang believes that when people are aware of the changes they have experienced in the past, the prospect of new change becomes more meaningful and acceptable.

Integrating local cultural traditions with participatory development is a powerful tool for helping the poor become better aware of their situation and helping them to find culturally acceptable solutions to their problems.

Development as social transformation

Development is more than the provision of social services and the introduction of new technologies. Development involves changes in the awareness, motivation and behaviour of individuals and in the relations between individuals as well as between groups within a society. These changes must come from within the individuals and groups, and cannot be imposed from the outside.

SARILAKAS is a Philippine NGO working with independent groups of poor producers. Rahman in his study of this agency was particularly impressed by the transformation of previously external-delivery oriented people into vibrant collectives actively engaged in deliberating upon their problems, setting priorities and seeking solutions, taking action to realise them, and in improving their skills and knowledge of their rights and privileges.

This transformation was further reflected in the development of individual personalities. The timidity and shyness that characterised many of them previously is now gone – each individual now comes forward to greet a visitor, insists on shaking hands with the visitor, and proudly introduces himself or herself as 'I am so-and-so, a member of this organisation'. According to Rahman, a sense of pride and dignity in belonging to the organisation, and hence pride and dignity in oneself, is visibly present. Genuine transformations such as these in individual and group behaviour take time to develop, but they are nonetheless essential for a sustainable, self-reliant development process.

Social transformation, and hence development, will not take place unless there is consensus among the group attempting to carry out the transformation. Through internal dialogue the group must sort out the options available to it and choose those that are consistent with their own social framework. New ideas and new behaviour cannot be imported unmodified. Changes must be socially acceptable to the group as a whole. This group cohesiveness is essential as there will always be individuals and groups within the community as a whole who will try to prevent social transformations being introduced.

Those wishing to provide technical advice and assistance to groups trying to implement development activities must first try to gain an understanding of the social realities within which the groups are functioning. This understanding will then make it possible to help the group to find its own consensus from which group behavioural change can proceed. These changes will lead to social transformations that again open new possibilities for further development. This process is a far cry from the mechanical show-and-tell approach to development.

So-called integrated development programmes are still popular among many development agencies, but in practice these programmes are more multi-sectorial than truly integrated. Such programmes consist of sectoral activities such as health, education, water supply and agriculture. Each sector is usually planned by sectoral experts who are primarily interested in seeing the people organise to implement 'their' activities.

However, as Rahman (1985b) points out, rural people live an organically linked multi-sectoral life and, left to themselves, do not usually restrict the work of their organisations to activities in limited areas. Organisations of the poor will initiate action in any area in which they consider that action will best promote or protect their interests.

To illustrate this natural multi-directional approach to development activities on the part of people's organisations, Rahman reports that in the Rural Action Project in India, the rural poor started small consumer stores on a collective basis, goateries and joint cultivation. They improved drinking water sources, stopped drinking and gambling, and built huts for primary schools. In one village they challenged an oppressive landlord who was usurping assets of the poor such as livestock, extracting free labour from the poor, and molesting their women. In other places the people took steps to reduce exploitation by moneylenders and middlemen by building their own group savings funds and collective marketing arrangements.

Support to development activities must not be limited by our own sectoral thinking and budgetary code systems. We must follow where the people lead. People's lives are composed of many inter-related parts which form an integral whole. A transformation or change in one sector cannot be achieved without simultaneous changes in other sectors. These changes in themselves will open new possibilities or needs for change in other sectors. Participatory development is not a patchwork quilt of different coloured components, but a finely woven textile of many coloured threads. These threads are woven together by the people; and the pattern is determined by their own needs and priorities.

The rural poor will generally attempt to first solve those problems which they consider to be the most urgent within the limits of their own resources and capabilities. They are not in the least concerned with trying to classify these problems as economic, social or political problems. Agencies which genuinely wish to help people must be willing to respond to these needs.

Experience indicates that most groups will first choose activities which can help them to remove the constraints on their economic development. Once they have achieved success in this area they will often decide to move on to areas which affect the quality of their lives such as water, sanitation, curative and preventive health. These decisions will be based on their own perceived needs and the complexity and expense of the interventions required to solve these problems. Additional activities can be added when the people feel the need for them and have the money and time available to implement them. The rate and direction of the expansion should be decided by the people rather than by an external agency's need to spend programme money.

What is Self-Reliance?

Self-reliance has become another piece of jargon in development circles similar to 'basic needs', 'awareness' and 'participation'. Aid agencies, however, all too often flood their projects with expensive inputs, project vehicles and buildings, foreign experts and highly paid local staff while at the same time talk about making the people self-reliant. You cannot make people self-reliant; people become self-reliant. It is more a question of attitudes than money and materials. Too much money and materials from external sources can easily prevent the emergence of self-reliance.

People must feel and believe that it is their own efforts that are driving the development process. They must feel that they themselves are contributing the maximum of their own human, financial and material resources, and that assistance from outside is only for what they cannot yet manage themselves.

Correct attitudes must be encouraged from the very start. Field staff must be instilled with the idea that they are not to do things for the people; that their job is to help people to do things for themselves. In no way should promises or indications be given that the project will 'give' anything to anybody. The approach should be one of: we can help you to analyse and understand what your problems are and how they can be solved; we can also help you to acquire the skills and knowledge that you need to carry out what you have decided to do; but, it is you who must decide and act: we can't do it for you.

Self-reliance requires a wide variety of knowledge and skills. People need to learn how to form and manage their own organisations. They need to learn how to use their organisations to gain access to resources and services and to prevent exploitation. They need to learn how to acquire and adapt new knowledge and technologies for improved agriculture and other income-generating activities. They need to learn how to establish and manage these activities.

People must have confidence in their own knowledge and skills, in their ability to identify problems and find solutions in order to make improvements in their own lives. This can best be done starting with small groups and small problems. As their self-confidence increases, they can move on to bigger and more complex activities. This evolvement of self-confidence, leading to self-reliance, can be easily destroyed by outside agents pushing the process too quickly.

Self-reliance is doing things for one's self, maintaining one's own self-confidence, making independent decisions – either as an individual or within the context of a collective group to which each member has voluntarily allied himself or herself. Self-reliance comes from within, but is directed outwards. Self-reliance is based on social relationships. Like-minded individuals come together and voluntarily pool their efforts and their resources in small groups; small groups ally themselves with other small groups working towards the same or similar goals; these may form associations which can further the interests of the members in interactions with external entities such as merchants, exporters, banks and government departments. Decisions and actions taken at all levels are based on self-confidence and self-determination.

This is true self-reliance. It can be learned, but it cannot be given. No government and no development agency is ever going to 'develop' a rural region; it can only be done by the people themselves perhaps with the assistance of government and other development agents.

It is important to understand that self-reliance is not intended to lead to complete self-sufficiency, i.e. the ability to manage completely on one's own without interaction with others. We are not here dreaming of the isolated family farm where all the basic needs are met through the farm's own production. Very few communities, even in the remotest parts of the Third World, are able to maintain complete self-sufficiency, nor do they want to. And those few communities, which both want to remain isolated and are able to attain self-sufficiency at a level acceptable to themselves, should be left alone.

Self-reliance in the economic sense is the ability of a family, community or nation to produce some or all of its basic needs as well as producing surpluses with which to trade for those commodities and services which it does not produce efficiently itself. Self-reliance must not be confused with self-sufficiency. No individual can, over time, be completely self-sufficient. There are few communities today, and none of any size, that are self-sufficient. There are no such nation-states. Interdependence between people and communities is essential. Global interdependence is a fact of life, whether we like it or not. The development of self-reliance begins within individuals through a process of human development or conscientisation. Outside attempts to promote self-reliance which ignore these processes will ultimately fail.

Human development

> Self-depreciation is a characteristic of the oppressed, which derives from their internalisation of the opinion the oppressors hold of them. So often do they hear that they are good for nothing and are incapable of learning anything – that they are sick, lazy and unproductive – that in the end they becomed convinced of their own unfitness.
>
> (Freire, 1972)

Many, although not all, poor people have a low opinion of themselves and of their own ability to change their situation for the better. Because of this low opinion, and perhaps also out of fear, the poor do not assert themselves. They remain shy, passive and withdrawn. Their dependency relationship with others who are stronger diminishes their self-confidence and initiative.

The poor, if not oppressed by the more powerful, are oppressed by their own limited knowledge and poverty. Their lack of knowledge and information prevents them from competing successfully for their fair share of resources and keeps them from effectively utilising the few resources that they do control. Although often aware of their limitations, they do not know how to acquire knowledge or gain access to information.

No development activity, whether initiated by outsiders or by the poor themselves, can hope to succeed unless it contains a strong element of human development. In simple terms, human development involves the strengthening of the personality and the acquisition and internalisation of knowledge and information.

If the poor are to manage and control their own development, then they must gain self-confidence, learn to be assertive, have faith in their own abilities and trust in their comrades. They need to develop a self-image which says: together with my comrades, I can succeed in doing this. They must build on their present knowledge, replace false beliefs with new knowledge and develop new skills and abilities. These inner developments provide the basis for external development. According to Fuglesang (1982), 'No one should decide in advance what the village community needs to know. Ask people, very often they know what they need to know.'

As part of the planning for any new development activity, the people must learn to discuss among themselves, and with others – especially development workers – what they already know about the activity, what skills individual group members have and how these can most productively be utilised. They must investigate what knowledge and skills they need to acquire and how this can be done. In other words, they must set up and carry out their own personal development plan. Development workers can help them considerably with this during the early phases of their development, but in terms of their own long-term development effort, this process must become internal. Equally as important as the acquisition of new skills and new knowledge is the ability to judge oneself what one needs to learn, and to find ways to do this. Learning how to learn is fundamental to self-development.

Quite often when discussing new skills and new knowledge people think almost exclusively of technical skills and knowledge, such as how to select seeds and fertiliser, how to repair a machine, how to administer a vaccine. Equally important are human skills – skills in communication, organisation and management. People must learn how to express themselves in public, analyse and verify information, make decisions and resolve conflicts. They must learn how to constructively criticise their companions, acquire and use power, maintain channels of communication, keep accounts and use money wisely, and avoid such common problems as favouritism, nepotism, gossip, manipulation and autocratic leadership. Constructive participation also requires a certain minimum of mutual trust, honesty and concern for others.

Working in small groups provides an ideal classroom for developing these skills. From modest beginnings the group members can learn with the assistance of development workers to manage their own affairs, develop self-confidence in working with others and in dealing with the external environment. The acquisition of technical skills without these fundamental human skills will not lead to successful development activities.

Poor people, as well as some development workers, are often socially and culturally conservative. Their dependence on others and their precarious economic position have often kept them from following new lines of thought. Skills and trades have for various reasons been monopolised by certain individuals or groups. The poor, as well as some educated people, believe that these are skills that are beyond their reach. In one development project, the poor as well as the project staff insisted that only skilled bricklayers could lay bricks although anyone can learn this basic skill.

Such blinkered thinking does not usually run very deep. Often it is merely a matter of 'we never thought of that'. Sometimes there are strong cultural or religious restrictions, but often these are imposed by the powerful to maintain privileged positions or static social structures. Development workers should encourage groups to 'think the unthinkable', to ask themselves, why are things this way? Can we change them? Sometimes it is only necessary to demonstrate what is possible, and then what previously seemed unchangeable is transformed overnight.

This is especially true of the situation of women. They are usually more restricted in their freedom and range of choice. Yet poor women, and their men, cannot afford the luxury of discrimination. Being poor, and often destitute, women are frequently among those who are most willing to defy tradition and to try new ideas, learn new skills and take new chances. We should encourage new lines of endeavour for women – and for men.

Kamla Bhasin (1979) has observed that in the Gonoshasthaya Kendra workshops in Bangladesh young rural women were trained in woodwork, metalwork and shoemaking. They have proved that Bengali women can be equal to men in their mastery of these skills. When the male carpenter who was training the girls was asked how he felt about it, he replied, 'In the beginning I found it odd teaching girls. Some of my friends also made fun of me. But now I know that girls are even more hard-working and responsible than boys.'

Conscientisation

Perhaps the greatest contribution that development assistance can make is to help the poor regain their confidence in themselves and in their ability to fight their way up from poverty. Yet most development assistance does exactly the opposite. It teaches the poor that they are helpless; that foreigners and strangers are needed to do things for them; that they are ignorant and backward. Unless these processes are reversed, development assistance will continue to fail.

However, self-confidence cannot be taught, it must be acquired. Self-confidence is acquired through positive experience, through small successes reinforcing each other. Self-confidence can be promoted through expressions of confidence and encouragement. It is destroyed by attitudes of superiority and negative criticism. Development workers must avoid attitudes and comments which reinforce feelings of inferiority. They must show that they appreciate the poor as individuals and respect their knowledge and judgment. Development workers who do not have a fundamental belief in the abilities of the poor will not be successful.

Kamla Bhasin (1980) suggests that development workers should constantly ask themselves: am I increasing the confidence of the poor, their faith in themselves, and their self-reliance, or am I making them instruments of my own plans of action, imposing my own ideas on them? There is a tendency to do the latter among development workers who come from university backgrounds, are well-spoken and use standardised terms. This makes people who do not understand such language feel small and inadequate; instead of increasing their confidence there might be the opposite effect. Paulo Freire has pointed out: 'One cannot expect positive results from an educational or political action programme which fails to respect the particular view of the world held by the people.'

In his important book *Pedagogy of the Oppressed*, Freire compared traditional classroom and training-course education to the banking system, in which the students are the depositories or receivers and the teacher is the depositor. Instead of communicating, the teacher issues communiques and 'makes deposits' which the students passively receive, memorise and repeat. He called this the banking concept of education in which the students are restricted to receiving, filing and storing the deposits.

Freire proposed that the ultimate goal of true education could be achieved through problem-posing education. In this form of education the separation of teacher from student found in banking education was replaced by dialogue between the teacher–students and the students–teacher. The teacher is no longer merely the one who teaches, but one who is himself taught in dialogue with the students who, in turn, while being taught also teach. They become jointly responsible for a process in which all grow.

In comparing banking education to problem-posing education, Freire maintained that banking education treats students as objects of assistance while problem-posing education makes them critical thinkers. The banking method emphasises permanence and becomes reactionary; problem-posing education – which accepts neither a 'well-behaved' present nor a pre-determined future – roots itself in the dynamic present and promotes change. According to Freire:

> It is not our role to speak to the people about our own view of the world, nor to attempt to impose that view on them, but rather to dialogue with the people about their view and ours. We must realise that their view of the world, manifested variously in their action, reflects their situation in the world.

There is something about modern education that seems to promote intellectual arrogance. This is true whether the student is European, African or Asian. We seem to believe that the only type of knowledge is that which has been acquired in school or through reading or, at a more sophisticated level, through scientific experiment. Those who lack these privileged experiences are considered ignorant. Fuglesang proposes that the significant feature of European culture is not only its scientific and technological achievement, but that it also exudes disrespect for other cultures as well as insensitivity to the miraculous multiplicity of life and human behaviour.

Yet, is it possible to consider as ignorant and without knowledge a Kalahari desert bush woman who can name over one thousand plants and knows their usefulness? Is the Bangladeshi farmer, who works with 20 or more native rice varieties carefully adapted to different depths and quantities of water, ignorant?

Our intellectual arrogance has prevented us from building on what the people know. Their knowledge, unlike much of our own, is based on personal experience and the accumulated experiences of their forebearers. This knowledge, if wisely used, can provide a foundation for wise and successful development and, when given proper respect, can provide the basis for the acquisition of modern scientific knowledge as a complement to their own experiential learning.

This process of problem-solving education is often called conscientisation. Conscientisation as formulated by Paulo Freire means the stimulation of self-reflected critical awareness in people of their social reality and of their ability to transform that reality by their conscious collective action. A self-reflected critical awareness is achieved by 'looking into one's self' and using what one hears, sees and experiences to understand what is happening in one's own life. From this understanding arises an inner conviction that you yourself, together with like-minded others, can do something to change your lives – to transform reality. It is important to realise that conscientisation means something which occurs within a person. It cannot be imposed from outside.

Conscientisation is a process in which the people try to understand their present situation in terms of the prevailing social, economic and political relationships in which they find themselves. This analysis of reality must be undertaken by the people who can decide what their important needs and experiences are, and not by experts. From this analysis the people themselves may be able to take action against the oppressive elements of their reality. This involves the breakdown of the relationship between subject and object, and constitutes the essence of true participation. Those who have been considered objects for development – poor men and women – become active subjects in their own development. If this is taken seriously, it means a very deep change in many relationships: between husband and wife, men and women, teachers and pupils, governments and their citizens, and between development agencies and the poor.

Development workers cannot effectively promote conscientisation and human development in others unless they themselves are open to personal development. They must try to avoid falling into the trap of over-confidence in which they understand everything and know automatically what to do in any situation. Such attitudes will not only lead to errors, but will also destroy the positive relationship between them and the people. If development workers feel that they only need to bring the people up to their own level of consciousness, then this will lead to an unequal relationship in which the development workers attempt to dominate, to indoctrinate, the people. In such situations there can be no dialogue and no genuine learning – conscientisation will wither and die away.

What Do We Mean By Participation?

> Participation by the people in the institutions and systems which govern their lives is a basic human right and also essential for realignment of political power in favour of disadvantaged groups and for social and economic development. Rural development strategies can realise their full potential only through the motivation, active involvement and organisation at the grassroots level of rural people, with special emphasis on the least advantaged, in conceptualising and designing policies and programmes and in creating administrative, social and economic institutions, including cooperative and other voluntary forms of organisation for implementing and evaluating them.
>
> *The Peasants' Charter*, FAO

The poor have not participated in sharing in the benefits from the massive development efforts of the past three decades, neither in proportion to their numbers nor their needs. The interest in analysing the question of the participation of the poor in development is indicated by the number of special international programmes which have been established during the past 10 years. The question of participation by the poor has been closely linked to other development issues. The value of participation by the poor for development stems not only from such idealistic considerations as basic human rights or 'the rejection of authoritarian and paternalistic alternatives, but also from the inherent strength of participation as a means of articulating genuine needs and satisfying them through self-reliance and mass mobilisation.' (D. P. Ghai *et al.* 1977)

Participation of the rural poor in their own development has been measured as a key factor in the success of projects. Cohen and Uphoff (1977) cite a study by Development Alternatives, Inc. based on an evaluation of over 50 rural development projects. This study found that local participation in decision-making during implementation was even more critical to project success than such participation in the initial design. Project success was measured in terms of increases in farmer income and agricultural knowledge as well as in self-help capacity and probability of project benefits becoming self-sustaining. Accordingly, local action taken by farmers to complement outside management and resources accounted for half the variation in overall success rankings, and farmer involvement in decision-making in the implementation phase was one of the two factors found to be most significant in promoting overall project success.

Participation is an essential part of human growth, that is the development of self-confidence, pride, initiative, creativity, responsibility, cooperation. Without such a development within the people themselves all efforts to alleviate their poverty will be immensely more difficult, if not impossible. This process, whereby people learn to take charge of their own lives and solve their own problems, is the essence of development.

However, as with many other important concepts within the field of development, the word participation has become a catchword. Participation is 'in' – you can't be an approved member of the development jet set these days without dropping a reference to participation into your speeches, scholarly papers and conversations on development theory and policy.

Unfortunately, participation, even when taken beyond mere rhetoric, is often felt to be sufficient, for example, when villagers turn out on request to dig irrigation channels or build roads merely to participate in the labour element of project implementation. Participation in project design and decision-making is all too often limited to a few village meetings where the project is explained and the people are asked to give their comments, and where the few comments made are by the school teacher in a language unintelligible to the majority.

Participation, if it is to really release the people's own creative energies for development, must be much more than the mere mobilisation of labour forces or the coming together to hear about pre-determined plans. Participation must be more than a policy statement – there must be a genuine commitment to encourage participation in all aspects and at all levels of development work. One of the leading researchers in the field, Professor Orlando Fals-Borda, refers to participation as a philosophical approach to development rather than a policy. He points out that even General Pinochet of Chile believed that his government was participatory and warns that we should not deceive ourselves by the official or common definitions of the concept of participation. Paulo Freire has written that:

> Attempting to liberate the oppressed without their reflective participation in the act of liberation is to treat them as objects which must be saved from a burning building; it is to lead them into the populist pitfall and transform them into masses which can be manipulated.

It is becoming more and more apparent that the first step in achieving genuine participation is a process in which the rural poor themselves become more aware of their own situation, of the socio-economic reality around them, of their real problems, the causes of these problems, and what measures they themselves can take to begin changing their situation. This process of awakening, raising of levels of consciousness, or conscientisation, constitutes a process of self-transformation through which people grow and mature as human beings. In this sense participation is a basic human need.

You have by now noticed that the word process is frequently used when discussing the concept of participation. Where there is genuine participation, mistakes will be made; there will be failures and there will be progress – a few steps forward, a step or two back. Participation is essentially a 'learning by doing' exercise – plans are made, action is taken, results are studied, lessons learned and new plans and action take place. This step-by-step process is often referred to in the literature on participatory development as praxis which means practice as distinguished from theory.

Mohammed Anisur Rahman maintains that participation is a process whose course cannot be determined from outside – it is generated by the continuing praxis of the people, by a rhythm of collective action and reflection. Rahman (1983a) believes that this is what makes the process the people's own as opposed to the people being mobilised, led or directed, by outside forces:

> Praxis, and hence participation, is a continuous educative process – a process of progressive conscientisation. Through collective self-reflection on their experiences and problems, people become more aware of the dimensions of their reality and of what can be done by themselves to transform it. With this awareness they decide upon and take collective action, and analyse its results to promote their awareness (knowledge) further. Thus they move on with progressively advanced knowledge of their evolving reality.

In the debates on the meaning of people's participation there has been much discussion as to whether participation is a *means* used to achieve development – or an *end* in itself, *i.e.* by establishing a process of genuine participation, development will occur as a direct result. The proponents of the second view often maintain that development for the benefit of the poor cannot occur unless the poor themselves control the process through the praxis of participation.

The English researchers, Oakley and Marsden (1984), point out that until recently the notion of participation as a means to achieving development has dominated development practice. According to them, the two main vehicles for implementing this notion of participation were (1) community development programmes which were aimed at preparing the rural population to collaborate with government development plans; and (2) the establishment of formal organisations (cooperatives, farmer's associations, etc.) which were to provide the structure through which the rural people could have some contact with, and voice in, development programmes.

Oakley and Marsden concede that some economic development was achieved as a result of the above strategy, but they maintain that the evidence suggests that only a few achieved any meaningful participation and benefit by this means. In their view, this strategy has not resulted in meaningful participation of the poor in development. In fact, it is a strategy which has resulted in our current situation: confronting the issue of the lack of meaningful participation in rural development.

Oakley and Marsden believe that participation is an end in itself, and is the unavoidable consequence of the process of empowering and liberation. The state of achieving power and of meaningfully participating in the development process is, in their view, the object of the exercise. They feel that there need not be any notion of fixed quantifiable development goals. According to them, the major effort should be concentrated upon the empowering process.

There has been frequent use in this discussion of words such as empowerment, control, liberation. These are strong and active words. Some people are frightened by their use because they generate images of revolution and violent change. Perhaps we should look at a few more such statements before deciding how 'dangerous' participation is.

We are left in no doubt that meaningful participation is concerned with achieving power: that is the power to influence the decisions that affect one's livelihood.

We cannot conceal the fact that the practice of empowering challenges established interests and seeks to confront those forces which oppose the rural poor's access to the means of development. Established bureaucracies do not charitably concede participation. This participation must result from the unrelenting processes from below.

We conclude that the meaningful participation of the rural poor in development is concerned with direct access to the resources necessary for development and some active involvement and influence in the decisions affecting those resources. To participate meaningfully implies the ability positively to influence the course of events.

(Oakley and Marsden, 1984)

The following definition of participation is used by the United Nations Research Institute for Social Development (UNRISD):

Participation involves organised efforts to increase control over resources and regulative institutions in given social situations, on the part of groups and movements of those hitherto excluded from such control.

(Pearse and Stiefel, 1979)

Participation in this context leads to greater control by the poor over their own life situation. Through the acquisition of knowledge and awareness they become better able to understand the causes of their poverty and are in a better position to mobilise and utilise the resources available in order to improve their situation. This in no way implies violent revolution, but it can involve conflict in those situations in which the poor are denied rightful access to resources.

A key element in this process in which the poor gain greater control over their own lives is collective effort, i.e. organising to carry out activities in like-minded groups. It is generally accepted that participation is meaningless outside the collective context. Poor people must come together and pool their human and material resources in order to attain the objectives which they set for themselves. Participatory development implies a collective process of self-improvement.

Participatory development, however, is a complicated process with no clear-cut guidelines and no straight pathways to success. Studies by the ILO (Rahman, 1984a) have identified five basic issues which make participatory development difficult:

(a) Participation will develop in different ways in specific situations dependent upon the problems faced by specific groups of the poor and the specific factors inhibiting their development. The promotion of people's participation according to neatly defined standard 'development objectives' may actually inhibit people's initiatives rather than promote them.

(b) The poor need to be approached as a specific group and their economic situation must be improved if participation is to be successful. This will, in most situations, automatically imply conflict with more well-to-do elements in differentiated rural societies.

(c) There is a complex relationship between self-reliance and the need for external assistance. Participation requires self-reliance, and is surrendered by dependence. However, the promotion of participation in initially non-participatory, dependent situations often requires some initial external assistance. This dilemma must be approached with extreme sensitivity if the process is not to result in new dependencies.

(d) Participation requires organisation. Yet organisations easily become centres of formal power controlled by the few. Maintaining 'people's power' requires that the poor retain genuine control over their own organisations.

(e) Participatory processes seldom begin spontaneously. Such processes are generally initiated by a leadership whose vision is external to the perceptions and aspirations of the people concerned. Resolving this contradiction implies going beyond mere mobilisation for the support of an 'externally' defined cause.

The resolution of these issues is essential for the achievement of self-reliant participatory development. These issues will be discussed more closely later in this book, hopefully in a manner which will help the reader to find workable balances in practice.

Participatory action research

> The people do know their problems. After all they are their problems, they live with them. How can it be that they do not know them? If they do not express their views openly it is because they have no power of an organisation behind them. They know they are weak and their frankness will mean further exploitation.
>
> *Indian farmer* (quoted by Bhasin, 1979)

The first step in involving poor people in participation in their own development is what is most often called Participatory Action Research or PAR which is a process of conscientisation. The preliminary objectives of PAR should be: (1) to increase the development worker's understanding of the local situation; and (2) to increase the insight of the local people, especially the poor, into what factors and relationships are the root causes of, and contributing factors to, their poverty.

Traditional pre-project studies are directed almost exclusively to the first of these objectives. A team of outside researchers arrives with the intention of gathering scientifically neutral facts about the people and their situation. They usually come armed with a detailed questionnaire concerning family situation, employment, income, education, health, etc. The investigators interview a representative selection of individuals or families. The data collected is then subjected to a quantitative analysis. The information derived from this aggregation of individual data is then assumed to provide a picture of the society as a whole. This approach treats people and families as units and society as a quantitative sum of the situations of these units. As Gianotten and deWit (1983) have observed:

> This application of quantitative techniques has led to an over-simplification of reality and to an abundance of quantitative analyses not related to history or evolving social relationships. This is like taking a snapshot of the runners halfway through a foot race – the snapshot tells nothing about how the runners arrived at their relative positions or where they will be in a few seconds' time.

Participatory action research, however, starts from the principle that it is not possible to separate facts from values and social relationships. Instead of looking at human beings in the abstract, it tries to set them in a social and historical context. It upholds the view that human intelligence is active, selective and creative. In traditional social research, values do not form part of the sciences, but of the ideology of the investigator. For participatory action research, science is a social activity in which the investigator becomes part of the reality being investigated. Comstock and Fox (1982) have given eloquent expression to this point: 'Participatory research subordinates technical knowledge to human values.'

The relationship between the investigator and the groups being investigated is therefore a fundamental aspect of participatory action research methods. Not only is it necessary for the people themselves to participate in the analysis of their own reality, but the investigator must share this reality in order to understand it. It is not possible to get a correct understanding of social realities by coming into an area, collecting answers to pre-determined questions and then retiring to statistically analyse the data collected.

Participatory action research demands an unusual degree of awareness and humility on the part of the investigator. Gerrit Huizer (1984) suggests the need for an awareness of one's own limitations and of one's relative ignorance of local problems compared with that of the people involved. Having accepted this relative ignorance, the researcher must try to learn from the people through empathy and friendship what their problems, needs and feelings are. Finally, the researcher must be conscious of the fact that he or she is working with certain values which may differ considerably from those of the local people.

Participatory action research takes place in time as part of the analysis-action–reflection process where the people are both the subject and the object of the research; where the investigator not only shares this reality, but in fact participates in it as an agent of change. Participatory action research is thus an active research with a clearly defined purpose of creating knowledge to be shared by both the people and the investigator, knowledge that leads to action and, through reflection, to new knowledge and new action.

Rahman (1983a) asserts that traditional field research on rural poverty by external researchers is based on a subject–object relationship which 'assumes and asserts the myth of the incapability of the people to participate in the research as equals'. He maintains that this humiliates the people, and alienates them from their own power of generating knowledge relevant for transforming their environment by their own initiative. Traditional research in this view 'makes them wait upon elite researchers to come and find the facts about them, to write about them and make policy recommendations for outsiders to solve their problems. This helps perpetuate domination of the people not only because of their economic dependence, but also of their intellectual dependence on privileged elites.'

The basic tool of participatory action research is dialogue, an interchange and discussion of ideas based on a process of open and frank questioning and analysis in both directions between the investigators and the people, both individually and in small groups.

Shanmuganathan (1984) has succinctly summarised the essentials of the dialogical approach to participatory action research as follows:

- It is based on a participatory principle which eliminates through effective dialogue the distinction between the researcher and the poor although the external researcher may draw his or her own independent inferences from the research;
- A basic premise is that the rural poor's perceptions of their own conditions are different from the perceptions of outsiders however sympathetic they may be. It is the perceptions of the rural poor that should form the basic point of reference for any analysis. These perceptions can be identified and understood only through intimate and continuous dialogue and joint reflections;
- A convergence of perceptions between the concerned outsider and the rural poor is possible only through such a dialogical process which is essentially action-based.

The following is a dialogue with a tribal (Adivasi) poor peasant in India quoted by Rahman (1983a). Lakshmi and Swaraswati are the Hindu goddesses of prosperity and knowledge respectively. Sawkar is the money-lending landlord or trader.

Question: Do you know who is Lakshmi and who is Swaraswati?
Adivasi: Yes.

Question: Who is Lakshmi?
Adivasi: Rice; clothes; hut.

Question: And Swaraswati?
Adivasi: Sawkar's knowledge.

Question: If you could have only one of them, which one?
Adivasi: Swaraswati.

Question: Why?
Adivasi: If everyone has knowledge, then no one can cheat others. Then only can we have true equality.

Poor people know that it is a lack of knowledge that not only keeps them from developing themselves, but also provides the advantage which the wealthier and more powerful have over them. Although they may feel that it is textbook knowledge which may enable some of their children to escape from poverty into secure professions, they know that it is practical knowledge that they themselves need – knowledge about sales, prices, weights and measures, credit, accounts, applied research, technical skills, disease control. Participatory action research provides a means for them to gain knowledge and to use it to improve their lives. Rahman (1984b) sees the intimate relationship between internal knowledge and self-improvement as a key to participation:

> For participatory action, by the people, the people must develop their own knowledge. This is not to suggest intellectual autarky for the people; but one must stand on one's own knowledge to be able to trade with others' knowledge as equals; only then can one participate rather than becoming dominated.

In traditional research the results – the new knowledge – are normally presented in elaborate academic reports which are not easily accessible even to the well-educated. But with participatory action research, as Orlando Fals-Borda (1981) has indicated, 'There is an obligation to return this systematic knowledge to the communities in which it was gathered because the people involved continue to be its owners and guardians.'

Participatory action research emphasises this obligation to return knowledge to the people and encourages the people themselves to preserve this knowledge in forms available to other poor people. Rahman (1985b) maintains that the people should be encouraged to document, store and disseminate in their own language their on-going experience for progressive advancement of their collective knowledge based on their collective effort. They should also be encouraged to use their own cultural traditions (story-telling, drama, ballads) to document and disseminate their knowledge, and to take their experiences to other groups and villages. In this way, research becomes an effective means of expanding development efforts into other communities. The local participants in the process thus become agents of change.

However, as Comstock and Fox (1982) have emphasised: 'The object of participatory research is not only to generate liberating knowledge and practice, but also to initiate a permanent process of action and reflection which leads communities to undertake further analyses and struggles on new issues.' Participatory action research is intended to increase the people's knowledge of themselves and their situation and, with this knowledge, gain greater control over their own lives through action emerging from the research. Without action by the people themselves, research becomes an exercise for the benefit of the researchers only. As Comstock and Fox point out:

> The validity of the results of participatory research can be gauged first, by the extent to which the new knowledge can be used to inform collective

action and second, by the degree to which a community moves towards the practice of a self-sustaining process of democratic learning and liberating action.

Participatory action research is essentially an on-going process of analysis–action–reflection. This can best be summarised in the form of a diagram (see Figure 3.1).

Figure 3.1
Participatory Action Research

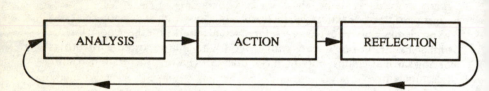

A true development process is based on a continuous series of analysis–action–reflection–action. Beginning with awareness and analysis poor people must mobilise their own resources and link into sources of external credit and technical assistance in order to initiate an action. When the action has been taken, the results are reflected upon; these reflections lead to a new analysis and to new action; and the development process hopefully continues.

Participation of women in development

> Chinese men have to carry the burden of three mountains: oppression from outside, feudal oppression and the burden of their own backwardness. But Chinese women are burdened by four mountains; the fourth one being the Chinese man.
>
> *Mao Tse-tung*

In nearly every single rural community females are in a majority, especially among the adults. Adult men are in a minority either because they have migrated to find work or have been eliminated through their propensity to succumb more easily to the natural and unnatural perils of growing up impoverished.

Not only are women a majority in rural society, but they are responsible for well over 50% of all productive activities, even in those households where adult men are present. In African households carrying out subsistence or near-subsistence agriculture, women have been measured as doing over 80% of agricultural labour. In most cultures they are responsible for planting, weeding, watering, harvesting, transporting and storing of crops. When their men are not present, they also have to do the clearing of land and the preparation of the soil.

Of course women also bear the full responsibility for household chores. Together with their children, especially their daughters, they must obtain the food, firewood and water to keep the household functioning. The fetching of firewood and water over ever-increasing distances has become a major time-consumer for most families in the Third World. Food preparation is both time-consuming and tedious – peeling, shelling, pounding and cooking with primitive tools and methods. Other chores like washing and mending clothes and marketing require the time and energy of the females in the household.

Evelyn Hong of the Consumers Assocation of Penang reports (in *Ideas and Action*, No. 158, FAO, 1984) that rural women in Malaysia work 15 to 16 hours a day, either in the field or their rubber gardens. They gather fruits and vegetables, look for fuel (which sometimes takes two or three hours), fetch water, cook, bath the children and feed them, prepare feed for, and feed, pigs and chickens. The other major task is food preparation comprising husking, drying the padi grains, milling or pounding them, winnowing and storing the rice. Apart from these activities, women are engaged in weaving mats, making sunshades and making rice wine.

In addition to their main roles as housewives and farmers, more and more rural women are becoming the income-earners in their families. They are wage labourers whenever there is a seasonal need for their hands, heads and backs. Needless to say, as casual labourers they have no security and receive low wages – almost always lower than men receive for doing the same work. Not only are poor rural woman overworked – their lives a never-ending drudgery – but they are burdened with frequent pregnancies which sap them of their energy. Infant mortality rates are high, health services are lacking or require long hours of travelling and waiting. They have no time nor can they afford to be sick, although they often are.

In light of this litany of hardwork and deprivation, women in the Third World would be assumed to be the prime target of development assistance. Yet the period of colonial government, followed by several decades of development assistance, has left women not only untouched, but by general opinion worse off than their grandmothers. Development planning and development programmes have been formulated by men for men; the needs of women have essentially been ignored. Changes in land-use rights have deprived them of their customary right to cultivate and control the land. The introduction of cash crops has strengthened the Western male concept of ownership. Subsidies and extension advice have gone almost exclusively to men. Women are, in many cases, not entitled to join official cooperatives; they are denied credit. They have been systematically excluded from agricultural projects involving mechanisation. Because their work is largely unpaid and unrecognised, their efforts are not included in national statistics and they fall outside the scope of national development planning.

Although the Women's Decade (1975–85) has significantly increased the understanding of women's needs and problems, this has not yet resulted in significant changes in development priorities. Women's needs are still too often seen as separate and marginal. The increased interest in supporting 'development programmes for women' has resulted in the establishment of women's bureaux and women's departments within the ministries of labour, social welfare and community development. Development agencies have hired women as special advisors for 'women in development'. The current fad is to have a 'gender officer' who presumably will convert the men as well as motivate the women.

Yet so long as these programmes remain segregated from the major development programmes in agriculture, irrigation, forestry, small-scale industries, they will not effectively assist women. Development programmes for women must recognise that women's needs and problems are an integral part of rural poverty. There is no area of rural life in which women do not constitute a major portion of not only the problem, but also the solution. Any rural development programme that does not place emphasis on women has not comprehended rural realities. Any rural development programme that does not include the active participation of women will be a programme benefiting primarily a privileged minority: men.

Based on need, women should be the prime target for rural development assistance. There are other equally good reasons for emphasising women in development. We have already touched upon the key role of women in subsistence agriculture – in Africa this is often a question of whether or not the family will starve. However, in addition to women's key roles in rural economies, there are other characteristics of rural women which make them better suited as recipients of development assistance.

Not only is the rural woman in the Third World more hard-working than the average man, but she is also more reliable. Money that comes into her hands is used almost exclusively for the benefit of her family. She does not usually drink nor does she smoke. She normally pays back loans. Yet, she normally has no access to official credit. In the words of one rural development worker:

> Women are more open to change than men. Women instinctively listen to the opinions of others as this has been part of their upbringing. When women are convinced of the need for a change, they will fight far more courageously for it than men.
>
> *Aruna Roy*, Social Work and Research Centre, India

Any rural development programme that does not give emphasis to women's participation in development is making things more difficult for itself. What then needs to be done? How can rural development programmes address the needs and problems of women? How can they take advantage of women's special qualities? Obviously, participation is central to the problem, but participation must be understood in terms of participation in economic production, ownership in the means of production as well as participation in decision-making.

Kamla Bhasin (1977) has observed that the participation of women in development has to be seen in the larger context of involving the poor in a self-directed process of development; yet because of their particular problems, special efforts need to be made to integrate women into such a process. She recommends that instead of *making* women take part in something which is planned for them, their active participation should be sought in economic production and in decision-making at all levels of society from the domestic to the international policy-making level.

Bhasin recognises that although participation in economic production is basic to improving the lot of women, by itself it is not enough. In addition, it is important for women to participate in political decision-making as it is politics which determines the direction and pace of most development plans. Ultimately, Bhasin calls for an all-round transformation in the consciousness of both men and women if women are to participate fully in development. Such a transformation is needed because our socio-cultural norms, the mass media and the patterns of education all presently tend to perpetuate a passive unequal role for women in social, economic and political affairs.

Is it the role of international development agencies to fight for women's liberation in the Third World? Wouldn't that be cultural imperialism at its worst? It isn't necessary to campaign for women's liberation; it is necessary that agencies make sure that their programmes and projects do not make the situation of women worse. For example, mechanisation of agriculture has provided jobs for some men, but often at the expense of a large number of female agricultural labourers without providing them with other alternatives for earning an income.

The second crucial step is to ensure that women genuinely do have at least equal opportunity to participate in development projects with men. If rural women have genuine opportunities for participating in their own development, then they will take care of the when and how of women's liberation.

> Women should participate and contribute on an equal basis with men in the social, economic and political processes of rural development and share fully in improved conditions of life in rural areas.
>
> (*The Peasants' Charter*, FAO)

A third and equally important step in promoting women's participation in development is the recruitment and training of women to work at all levels of development agencies. It is particularly important that women are well represented among development workers as they are better able to understand the special situation of rural women and to establish contact with them. The importance of female staff members was underlined in the Programme of Action of the World Conference on Agrarian Reform and Rural Development:

> Establish special recruitment and training schemes to increase the number of women in the training and extension programmes of development agencies at all levels, including professional fields from which women have been traditionally excluded. (*The Peasants' Charter*, FAO, 1981)

Throughout the remainder of this book, the reader should constantly strive to overcome the culturally ingrained tendency to think in terms of men rather than women. There is nothing in the self-reliant participatory development methodology which is not applicable to rural women. Indeed, the methodology appears to be particularly effective when put into the hands of women.

Participatory Development and the Time Factor

> The tree is not uprooted with the first gust of wind. Persistence is needed for everything. Everything takes time.
> *Saying of a Peuhl woman*, Mali (quoted by Léger, 1984)

The poor have patience: they wait for the rains; they replant when the first rains fail; they replant again when the birds and rodents have eaten their seeds; and they wait again for the harvests. They wait in offices and by the roadsides. They know that things take time, and that they take more time for the poor. They also know that taking time can produce better results. A consensus achieved after many hours of discussion maintains not only unity of purpose but also essential feelings of belonging.

> We don't have time; we don't have time to talk; and we certainly don't have time to listen; and we don't take time to understand.
> *Aruna Roy*, fieldworker in Rajasthan

Development workers don't seem to have very much time or patience. Perhaps it's all a result of the invention of the jet engine – if we can get there in only 10 hours, why do we need 10 years to develop the place? On a more serious level, we do seem to want results amazingly quickly. It is, however, doubtful that the development process can be compressed to meet our ambitions. We used to talk about three-year projects; now we talk about five-year projects; but perhaps we should be talking about 20-year programmes. How many rural areas have developed in one generation?

Our priorities are often such that development workers feel an enormous pressure to produce visible results as quickly as possible: a grade school here, a wide road there, here a dam, there a well, and everywhere a clinic! But we are working with people; people with their own urgencies, priorities and time scales. It is their development that is the measure of success, not the school buildings and the roads which soon deteriorate.

Development workers have to learn to be patient in their work with people. They have to wait for the people themselves to become fully aware of how they can alter their situation by taking responsibility for their own organisations and acting collectively to make changes. Development workers should patiently work to strengthen these organisations rather than trying to get things done quickly.

Perhaps we need to change our priorities. Perhaps we should think less about projects and more about long-term programmes. Is it really too long to work 20 years in one single district, if that district has a population of 100,000? Do we believe that donors need a new project every five years? We are talking about development processes, and these require time in order to grow strong and viable.

> A great deal of heartbreak which in the past has too often turned over-optimistic idealists into later cynics, would be avoided if those who wish to help in development could learn to be content to do good slowly.
>
> *Geoffrey Masefield*, Oxford University (quoted by Bunch, 1982)

After three decades of foreign aid programmes in the Third World, the number of cynics may be growing. Hopefully, the idealists are being replaced by realists: people who take the time to analyse together with the poor what is wrong, and what can be done to right these wrongs; people who realise that we cannot develop poor areas, but that the poor themselves can initiate a development process if given long-term support for their own efforts.

> If you try to pluck away all of the feathers in one go it will be painful for the chicken. The chicken will scream, shout and resist. It is easier to remove the feathers one by one although it will take longer.
>
> *Asian change agent* (quoted by Bhasin, 1976)

In working with groups of the poor, development workers need to remember that ingrained ideas and behaviour patterns cannot be changed all at once. Behavioural change takes time. Change must be a gradual process, a process in which the ideas and behaviour of both the poor and the development workers will most probably change over time.

Poor people who have never had the opportunity of participating in a democratic process require time to learn to formulate and express their ideas, participate in open debate, take collective decisions and follow-up with cooperative action. Mistakes will be made, but these can be turned into lessons leading to better decisions in the future. As Roland Bunch (1982) states, 'Democracies take more time than dictatorships, but they allow the participation that is the essence of development.'

We somehow expect near miracles of poor people. We expect people who are struggling every day to eke out a bare existence to suddenly be able to come together, give up their individual needs, forget their fears and suspicions, and work for the common good of their group or community. We know that individuals cannot develop on their own, but we seem to forget the long process of awakening, organising and patiently learning to adjust to the dynamics of democratic group activities. We could easily make the decisions for them, but it is the learning of the collective decision-making process that is the ultimate goal.

It is important to remember that the development process evolves in stages. Starting from the initial contacts and familiarisation stage, through mobilisation and conscientisation, the poor plan and carry out their first collective actions. These first activities are small steps in a long journey towards broad-based organisations of the poor. Although some activities will fail, these failures provide lessons through reflection and analysis which make it possible to attempt the next step. As their experience matures, so too should the ambition and scope of their activities become greater and more complex.

There is, however, a risk of back-sliding and even disintegration if a certain momentum is not maintained. Unless a group moves on to a new problem after having made an advance, negative forces such as individualistic ambitions may inhibit a forward-moving process. If, for example, a group has successfully initiated collective purchases of agricultural inputs, their further development may stagnate unless they go on to attack the next problem which may be usurious credit or monopolistic marketing.

People's participation in development activities should be seen not only as a means to an end, but an end in itself. However, once a successful participatory development process is initiated, it should become a continuous process with no visible end to it. The only thing that should end is the intervention of the development workers who should withdraw as soon as the people themselves can maintain the development process on the basis of their own initiatives.

Although development work primarily concerns people, it is amazing how impersonal it often is. We seem to forget that poor people everywhere actually have a history that stretches far back in time long before the start of *our* project. We seem to think that there was nothing there before we arrived. Likewise, we don't seem to give a moment's thought to the idea that these people and their children's children are most likely going to be right where they are long after our project has been terminated and we have gone home or moved elsewhere.

We desperately need to expand our vision. Our short interventions will only have been a success if the children's children of today's poor also benefit from what we did. The only way we can achieve this is to help the people alive today to acquire the skills to keep their own development process alive for future generations.

This section ends Part I. This has been the theoretical section of this book. As in participatory action research, action without analysis will normally lead to less than satisfactory results. As development workers we need to first analyse the causes of poverty in each particular circumstance; we need to be familiar with various theories of development and we need to understand what development is from the point of view of the rural poor; we need to understand communities, the meaning of self-reliance and genuine participation; we need to understand the processes involved in human development, conscientisation and participatory action research; and finally we need to appreciate that development requires social transformations that can only take place slowly over time.

Hopefully, an understanding of the theoretical basis of self-reliant participatory development processes will make our actions more meaningful for the rural poor. Part II – Action – will hopefully explain how development workers can become agents of positive change – change agents, and how change agents can work with groups of the rural poor to assist them in starting their own development processes.

Part II
Action

4. Agents of Change

What Part Can Development Agencies Play?

> Like many other social phenomena, many so-called policy-makers and planners do not take participation seriously. Appropriate lip service is given but no serious consideration. Furthermore, and more important, most large financing agencies are administratively ill-prepared or simply do not want to change operational styles to attempt to foster more participatory development. To them participation takes too much time to organise and costs too much in terms of administration. This, I believe, is worth researching.
>
> *Duncan Miller* (quoted in Cohen (ed.), 1980)

Self-reliant participatory development processes normally require an external catalyst to facilitate the start of the process and to support the growth of the process in its early phases. The provision, training and support of external change agents is a role that should be natural for development agencies. Many small local agencies throughout the Third World have adopted this role. International agencies should not hesitate to financially support such initiatives.

Is there a more direct role for an international development agency in facilitating self-reliant participatory development processes? Or, using development jargon, what are the agency inputs to such processes? Here are some suggestions:

1. *Familiarisation*: The more time spent by the field staff in living with the people, getting to know them and their community with all its socio-economic relationships, the better able the external change agents will be to facilitate the development process.

2. *Awareness-building*: Often called conscientisation – the process of discussion, reflection, questioning and analysis together with the poor so that they become increasingly aware of their own world and how it works. The people must be encouraged to continue the analysis–action–reflection cycle.

3. *Facilitation*: Once the people are aware of their situation and the root causes of their problems, they may want to act. Agency staff can then act as

enablers or facilitators, helping to make it possible for them to do something they have decided to do on their own.

(a) Agency staff should not encourage people to do something they probably would not do on their own initiative.

(b) Agency staff should not try to organise people, but wait for people to decide to organise themselves and then assist them in this process. Bringing them together for informal discussions can be the first step in this process.

(c) Agency staff should not implement projects, but should assist groups of people in carrying out their own projects.

Once this preliminary process has started, then the role of facilitation can assume more practical aspects:

4. *Organisational training*: Agency staff should encourage people to organise themselves into groups. In conjunction with these groups, agency staff should assist in arranging informal, practical training in group dynamics, simple book-keeping and accounting, adult literacy, banking, letter and proposal writing, etc.

5. *Leadership development*: Again in conjunction with people's groups and on the broadest possible basis, informal practical training opportunities should be provided for leadership development and the planning, implementation and evaluation of projects and activities. These training programmes should in theory be available for everyone so that the leadership base is as broad as possible.

6. *Technical training*: Based on needs and priorities defined by the people themselves, training opportunities in various skills should be arranged either internally or externally. Training should be available for all who are interested or, if this is practically impossible, those who have been trained should share their knowledge. Insofar as possible the people themselves should participate in the planning, implementation and financing of these programmes so they can in future arrange their own programmes.

7. *External linkages*: In addition to technical training, people's groups will need to be assisted in establishing linkages to external agencies such as government offices, banks and co-operatives, and voluntary agencies so that they too can get access to available funds, materials and technical resources. Part of this work is helping people to acquire the skills and self-confidence required to establish and maintain such linkages.

8. *External legitimacy*: Development agencies, especially international ODA and NGO agencies, have certain advantages in establishing good working relationships with officials at all levels of the host country government. It is imperative that people's groups are assisted in establishing and maintaining acceptance and legitimacy with local officials.

9. *Exchanges of experiences*: People's groups should be assisted and supported in arranging visits to, and exchanges with, other similar groups, projects, training and research centres. The intent of these experiences is to expose people to alternative ways of doing things, of organising and of solving problems, as well as to expose them to alternate technologies and new ideas. Through broadening their horizons, they will also hopefully see their own

situation and problems in wider terms than just their own locality.

10. *External funding*: A special case of external linkages. Wherever possible external funding for people's activities should be obtained by the people themselves through existing sources of credit and grants. This funding should come in addition to each group's own savings. When necessary in the early phases of group activities, agencies can provide direct loans or grants in modest amounts.

11. *Support and encouragement*: The continued presence of agency change agents living and working in the communities and sharing the experiences and problems of the people is often a decisive factor in encouraging people's groups to persevere in their early efforts to improve their own lives. Agencies should maintain their presence in the area over at least five years, preferably more.

Why have external change agents?

> Only those amongst you are welcome who can help us think of our problems on our own, and bring to us information that is useful to us, and are yourselves willing to learn a lot from us.
>
> *Member of the Bhoomi Sena movement,* India
> (quoted by Rahman, 1981)

Only rarely do participatory development activities arise from within poor groups without any form of outside stimulus. If this were not so, we would be seeing much more development than we do. The following observation provides the rationale for this:

> A truly participatory development process cannot be generated spontaneously, given the existing power relations at all levels and the deep-rooted dependency relationships. It requires a catalyst. The catalyst or change agent who can break this vicious circle is a new type of activist who will work with the poor, who identifies with the interests of the poor and who has faith in the people. (Wignaraja, 1984b)

As we saw in the previous chapter, self-reliant participatory development is concerned with people and social relationships. The primary role of change agents is to release the creative energies in people. Change agents are not, however, free agents; they work within an organisational structure and with a leadership. The organisation and the leadership must also be people-directed. An organisation trying to promote participatory development cannot be bureaucratic and have a rigid hierarchical structure; in such an organisation, 'participation' would merely be a catchword without genuine meaning. Unless the leadership is genuinely committed to democratic participation within the organisation, it cannot promote participation among the poor.

Participatory development cannot be initiated by the traditional kind of extension agents who try to deposit, transmit or extend their 'magic' formulas to others as if development is a one-way process. We need a new breed of change agents who, first and foremost, care for people as human beings, who treat them as subjects and not objects or recipients of change, who steep themselves in the aspirations, problems and the wisdom of their own people and who therefore actually follow the people – like Mahatma Gandhi who said, 'There go my people and I must follow them for I am their leader.'

D. L. Umtali (quoted in Bhasin, 1976)

For those agencies which are committed to promoting participatory processes, this chapter and the following one represent the first steps in establishing a successful self-reliant participatory development programme. Not only are they the first steps, but also the most important steps. This chapter deals with the selection of change agents. The next chapter discusses the training of change agents and the choice of organisational form and leadership style for the programme as a whole. The choice of change agents, organisational form and leadership style is crucial: mistakes at this stage may very well make it impossible for a programme to succeed.

In the broadest sense of the phrase, everyone working in development is essentially a change agent, i.e. someone who is attempting to promote change. However, not all change is for the good. If we are to assist poor people in changing their situation for the better, then the role of the change agent becomes critical. We are therefore looking for a very particular type of change agent. The work of a change agent must, however, be carried out within an atmosphere of mutual trust:

It is necessary to trust in the oppressed and in their ability to reason. Whoever lacks this trust will fail to bring about or will abandon dialogue, reflection and communication, and will fall into using slogans, communiques, monologues and instructions. (Freire, 1972)

What is a Change Agent?

Change agents should be like waves on a sea; made of the same water, but which rise up above the water according to the needs of the situation and merge into the water again when the need is over.

Filipino peasant (quoted by Bhasin, 1976)

A change agent is a person who initiates a process of change. Change in itself can be either good or bad. The direction which this change will take should be decided through interaction with the people with whom the change agent is working, rather than unilaterally by the change agent acting alone or on behalf of outside interests.

The term is open to endless discussions. Many different designations are presently being used for the village level development worker. Organisations using a 'directive' approach to development often use such words as extentionist or instructor. Some agencies use more neutral designations like rural development worker or community development coordinator. It is more common for participatory organisations to use terms such as animator, motivator, cadre, action researcher, mobiliser, facilitator or change agent.

Although some may associate the word agent with shadowy figures spying on innocent people, the term change agent is not only short, but precise and accurate. For this reason, as well as the fact that a considerable portion of current literature on participatory development uses it, the term change agent will be used throughout this book. If you are uncomfortable with this, then animator or facilitator are worthy substitutes.

Although this book is concerned primarily with working directly with the rural poor, change agents can operate at different levels:

1. In the rural villages or the urban slums where they work directly with the people. This is the so-called grassroots level. They may be from the village itself, in which case they will be called village change agents, but most likely they will be someone from the outside who works with the people to start the process of change through conscientisation. These can be governmental or non-governmental workers.
2. An intermediate level can be defined in which governmental or non-governmental personnel who are genuinely committed to participatory change provide support to grassroots level change agents by coordination, fund-raising, information, research, support activities, etc.
3. At the international level in the U.N. agencies and in non-governmental international organisations there are individuals trying to support projects and movements which genuinely help the people and, as such, these persons are also change agents.

Change agents at the grassroots level

> There can be no doubt that the change agent is a critical element in the process of participation and that the critical dimension is his/her role with the group in building up its organisational base, its internal solidarity and its potential actively to intervene in the development process. (Oakley and Marsden, 1984)

Change agents may occasionally emerge spontaneously from within rural communities. These are unusual persons who begin reflecting on problems and eventually involve others in specific participatory activities. Dr. James P. Seawell (1984) reports being approached for technical assistance by an exceptional villager in Zimbabwe. The American Friends Service Committee eventually built a successful participatory programme on the initiative of this one person without involving outside workers directly in the fieldwork. Such village change agents may or may not have very much formal education.

More and more frequently idealistic secondary school-leavers or university graduates are returning to their home communities to work with their people. Through work or study they may have been exposed to ideas of people's participation and conscientisation. Although natives, they will need to re-establish their acceptance among their people. Their experiences outside as well as their physical absence may have led to alienation. They will need to be very careful to avoid talking down to their people.

Isolated village change agents will face considerable obstacles in their efforts unless they can obtain outside support in the form of ideas, information and legitimation. Development agencies should be quick to identify and support these change agents whenever they emerge. However, village change agents are most often identified first by outside change agents, and then encouraged and assisted to work with their own people.

Change agents coming from outside a community will be completely frustrated in their development efforts unless they gain the acceptance and confidence of the poor people with whom they are trying to work. It is perfectly natural to question the motives of outsiders who suddenly turn up with the expressed purpose of 'helping you'. It has been correctly pointed out that these educated, well-fed and well-clothed outsiders are precisely the same kinds of persons who have been exploiting the poor in the name of religion, welfare, business, politics.

The process of becoming accepted is non-specific. It will depend on the community and its previous experiences with outsiders, and on the personalities and attitudes of the external change agents. They will need to live among the people, make friendships, share burdens as well as joys, and gradually establish that they are honest, well-meaning and have no ulterior motives for personal benefit. Village change agents must also gain acceptance for their work because all too often people from the same community have exploited the faith and power that was vested in them. The process of being accepted by the people might be a little longer for a new person coming from outside, but it is basically the same process for all kinds of change agents.

External change agents, and especially the donor agencies supporting them, are generally in a hurry to get started with specific development activities. They will quite often begin conscientising and organising the people before they have been genuinely accepted by the people. This will be very detrimental to their efforts because the work will not have a foundation of trust and confidence. There is, of course, no rule for deciding how long it will take to become accepted. Oakley and Marsden report a case study in which a female change agent (animateur) spent nine months observing Brazilian fisherwomen at their work, and being observed by them, until the women gradually began speaking with her and inviting her into their lives. This interaction eventually led to a genuine process of awakening and mobilising by the fisherwomen for their own rights and welfare.

The Role
Change agents have basically two roles. The first is as facilitators of human development or conscientisation. Once this process of critical awareness

building has begun among a group of rural poor, then the role changes to one of being an organisational and rural business consultant.

A group of experienced change agents in Asia worked out the following elaboration of these basic roles (Bhasin, 1976):

1. It was felt that change agents should work *with* the people and not *for* them because people have to be the subjects and not the objects or targets of change. To work with the people, change agents should be able to identify with the people – but to do this is a difficult process which requires tenacity, dedication and sensitivity.

2. Change agents should *work mainly with vulnerable groups* who have benefited the least or have actually been harmed by previous developmental efforts. Thus it is the poor and oppressed people, the peasants, tenant farmers, small fishermen, landless labourers and especially poor women, with whom change agents should mainly be involved.

3. The most important role of change agents is to *initiate a process of critical awareness-building* (conscientisation) among the rural poor. They should set in motion a dialogue on the realities of the local situation and so enable the people to identify their own needs and problems and express what kind of changes they want, how they would like to see them come about. It was emphasised that change agents should not impose their own ideas on the people. The process of identifying problems and finding solutions is extremely important, and the people, not the change agents, must determine the pace and direction of this process. Economy of time or effort should be no argument for change agents to impose their own views and ideologies on the people.

4. Change agents must *assist the people to appreciate the advantages of working in groups*, because it is only through group action that the poor stand a chance of increasing their bargaining power and control over their own lives. Change agents should not become the driving force behind such groups. They should be merely spark plugs with the people playing the role of combustion engines. Any activity initiated and sustained by the change agents only might appear to have force for some time, but would peter out sooner or later.

5. Change agents should *promote the broadest possible participation* through the emergence of numerous and varied small groups based on the interests of their members. Groups sharing similar objectives can be encouraged to work together as people's organisations. Change agents should ensure that no disadvantaged groups are left out of the conscientisation process. For example, in some communities the women might be left out or remain outside such efforts to discuss and organise. In such cases, the change agents must initiate discussions on this very issue before going on to other issues.

6. Change agents should *assist groups during their establishment phase* to analyse and make decisions regarding their rules and objectives, decision-making, leadership and financial controls. This role implies that change agents be skilled in the task of social organisation – enhancing people's participation in decision-making, identifying and mobilising resources,

establishing simple book-keeping systems, etc. Even if not technical experts themselves, change agents can, and should, enable people to acquire specific skills of a technical, social or political nature that will lead to greater self-reliance.

7. The *encouragement and development of leadership skills* among as many group members as possible is another necessary role for change agents, so that they may withdraw after some time without fear of the movement or process collapsing.

8. Change agents should also *assist and encourage groups and communities to establish external linkages* between themselves and development agencies, government departments and institutions, commercial enterprises, banks and credit institutions. Through these contacts, information, resources and specialised services could be made available for development activities. Here again, it must be the people who decide whether or not they want outside help, and in what quantity and on which conditions they are ready to accept it. Change agents can also *encourage and assist groups and communities in communicating their needs and grievances* to officials at higher levels of the political and administrative hierarchies.

9. In addition, the change agent may also have special expertise in fields like agriculture, health and appropriate technology. They should *share this knowledge and experience with the people*, but in a manner which maintains their dignity and self-reliance.

10. Another important role which change agents can play on the basis of their knowledge of macro-issues is to *provide a wider perspective*, a macro-analysis, of the structures and problems of society to help the people to better appreciate and understand their own problems and how these are related to larger issues.

11. Change agents should *encourage groups and communities to establish links between themselves and other groups or organisations* struggling with the same issues or similar issues. These links may help to avoid the danger of being isolated, crushed or co-opted.

12. Change agents have to *realise that genuine people's organisations and movements have to start as people's movements*. It is the people themselves who must be the driving force of a movement from the beginning. In fact it cannot be otherwise. Activity initiated and led by outsiders might appear impressive for some time, but eventually one would find that this was a deceptive appearance. Increased and continuous participation of the people has to be regarded not just as a means of achieving certain ends, but also as an end in itself. It is the participation of the people that will act as an internal safeguard against new oppressive vested interests which might emerge from inside the new organisations.

13. Change agents should also constantly *review and assess their own role, behaviour, relationships with others and performance as change agents*. In this reflection and assessment they can be helped by outsiders working elsewhere. It is better to reflect in a group than alone. Such sessions of self-examination and questioning are vital to the role of change agents.

They should also encourage the people to express openly opinions and criticisms of their work.

14. Change agents should also *play the role of militant observers* religiously noting down whatever they observe, the problems they face, the how and why of the process of change as and when they experience it. For change agents and programmes to be replicable, and for evolving realistic policies, it is essential to know more about happenings at the grassroots level. By writing about their experiences, change agents should be able to reverse the flow of information from top-down to bottom-up.

Change agents can play their role effectively only if they have adequate knowledge and understanding about the community with which they are going to work. They should study and analyse the socio-economic conditions, the value systems and the cultural traditions. It is also very important to know about the open as well as hidden conflicts within the community and its leadership patterns. This of course requires patience and sensitivity.

Change agents and their work

Change agents have to integrate with the people. They have to become one of them by living with them. Long-distance operation of organising people does not work. (Bhasin, 1979)

Judging from the various roles expected of change agents, we certainly are asking a lot from them. Obviously, this type of work requires a very special type of dedication. Not only is the work very demanding, but the working conditions will be hard, irregular and uncomfortable. Are we asking too much?

External change agents are usually attached to an agency or a programme. Together they form a team of change agents. These teams can vary in size from five to 25 members, and ideally should be equally divided between male and female members. In the field, the indvidual team members work alone or with a partner. These mini-teams should live in the immediate area of their work, preferably at the village level. There are few office hours for this kind of work, and change agents should do their work with little consideration of time. Evening work, when it is easier to meet with peasants in their communities, is common, as are weekend group meetings or training sessions. The work is long, hard and unpredictable and can never be fitted within a more conventional urban work routine. This type of work situation is quite different from that of the typical development worker who lives in town, uses a motorcycle or vehicle to visit the work area, spends almost as much time in the office as in the field, and usually resents the occasional weekend work activity.

Characteristics of change agents

Change agents must listen more than talk, learn more than teach and facilitate more then lead. (Bhasin, 1976)

What qualifications or characteristics should change agents have? Which are essential? Which are desirable? What would disqualify a person? What attitudes are essential? Desirable? What aptitudes are essential? Desirable? These are some of the more important questions which need to be answered in order to select change agents who will be willing and able to live and work with poor people over extended periods of time.

The same group of experienced Asian change agents reflected on these questions and developed the following thoughts:

1. Change agents should have *respect for and faith in the people* with whom they are working. They should believe in the potential power and age-old wisdom of the people. A faith in people should be their guiding force.

2. They should go to the people *as learners and not as teachers*. They should be ready to be criticised and corrected and also to change themselves. People will not hear speeches, pontifications. They are fed up of do-gooders and talkers. You have to go to the people to learn from them, to be one with them. You have to show by doing, not by lecturing. You have to help people regain their dignity, which they have lost because of the oppression in our societies.

3. Change agents should be *humble, honest, dedicated, patient and sensitive.*

4. Their *life styles should be simple and reasonable*. Their dress, material possessions and their language should not be too different from that of the people. If they are assigned a motorcycle or motorcar, they should minimise its use. Cars, and even motorcycles, tend to alienate change agents from the people. The use of automated forms of transport gives them a different sense of time and space, and this can create gaps instead of bridges.

5. They should try to *know the people*, their socio-economic, political and cultural situation and problems. Change agents should also have an idea of the macro-issues and structures in order to be able to see the local problems in the correct perspective. Ignorance about larger political and economic issues could result, in the long run, in working against the people. They should not minimise the importance of theory because just as theory without practice is lame, practice without theory is blind.

6. They should be well *acquainted with the management of conflict*, since their work might lead to conflict situations within the community. People should be made aware of possible conflict situations that might arise so that conflicts may be anticipated and properly handled. The local people are usually aware of this, whereas change agents sometimes get carried away with their own idealism and do not pay attention to the serious consequences of their work.

7. Change agents should have the *capacity and humility to withdraw* as soon as the people are ready to manage their own affairs. They should aim at becoming dispensable and not to perpetuate their role and position.

Only half in jest, someone also said that change agents must also be saints! Certainly not everyone is either suitable for or inclined to do this type of work. The key word is commitment. This, coupled with the right attitude towards the capabilities of the poor and an aptitude for working with them as an equal, are the basic ingredients. The rest can be learned.

Common weaknesses and inadequacies

This same group of experienced change agents discussed their own weaknesses as well as those of others in their approach to their work:

1. Sometimes change agents tend to be very *paternalistic* in their approach. They consider the village people to be like children who do not have a comprehension of issues and solutions. As a result of this they become authoritarian and directive. They impose their own ideas on people. Such change agents fail to develop the leadership potential of the people. Many times the development workers do all the talking while the village people just sit and nod their heads.

2. In their enthusiasm to do things well and to achieve quick results, some change agents start *doing everything themselves*. They become like over-protective parents who do not trust their children to do anything. This may also be due to the unconscious desire of change agents to become indispensable, to remain forever important for the community.

3. Most change agents tend to *emphasise projects more than long-term programmes*. Development of people and strengthening of genuine people's organisation often remains a secondary concern. Quantifiable material development becomes more important. 'There are heaps of people who call themselves social workers, but who in fact harm the people. Their main fault is that their approach does not instill in the people a quest for social justice.'

4. Many change agents have an *inadequate understanding of macro-issues* and of the different political forces at work. Their analysis of the problems at times is superficial because of which they fail to attack real issues. Toilet construction projects were cited as possible examples of misplaced emphasis. A peasant who was being pestered to construct a toilet by a do-gooder was quoted as saying 'Child, I will make a toilet, but tell me if I do not have enough to eat, what will I put in it?'

5. Often change agents do not know about the activities of other change agents; thus they cannot learn from the experience of others and *fail to coordinate and cooperate* with them.

6. Some people start *doling out material goods* to people, thereby creating further dependencies. These are the worst kind of do-gooders.

Because of their own impatience as well as the external pressures from their agencies and funders, many change agents exhibit one or more of these weaknesses which collectively might be designated the cardinal sin of development work: *Doing things for people, rather than helping people to do things for themselves.*

Formal Qualifications

The role of the change agent is primarily one of working with people's groups in such a way as to enable them to better control their own situations. This has been called the pedagogy of empowering. Oakley and Marsden (1984) argue that the selection of change agents is critical in that unless a change agent possesses certain necessary characteristics such as humility, commitment, sensitivity and self-confidence, he or she would be inappropriate for the work involved. With regard to skills, they maintain that a change agent needs the ability to communicate, both verbally and non-verbally, and to analyse and diagnose the context of his or her work with the rural poor.

So far the discussion has primarily concentrated on personality characteristics, and this is how it should be. But what about more formal qualifications such as age, education, work experience and origins?

1. Teams of change agents should be composed of young men and women between the ages of 25 and 45. A combination of vigour and life-experience is advantageous. Too much previous exposure to overly structured jobs is often disadvantageous.
2. They must speak the language of the people with whom they will be working, and preferably belong to the same ethnic group or, at the least, be familiar with the culture. They should preferably be from rural backgrounds.
3. They should have socio-economic backgrounds and/or personal values which would facilitate integration with the rural poor.
4. They should have analytical abilities, but not necessarily academic qualifications or a knowledge of foreign languages, a usual prerequisite for employment.
5. They should not be looking for long-term secure careers leading to status positions in the urban centres.

We are looking for correct attitudes, suitable aptitudes and commitment. Of all the change agents that I have personally recruited and trained, some of the very best were ordinary farmers, fishermen, traders, teachers and housewives who had no more than a secondary level education.

Recruitment of women

We have earlier discussed the importance of women in development, the special difficulties which they face, and the need to ensure their participation on their own terms. Experience has shown that female change agents are in a far better position to work with poor rural women than male agents.

However, many development agencies have relatively few females working in their field staffs. It is not uncommon to find rural development programmes in which a large amount of money is spent annually and having large local field staffs with few or no females except handicraft instructresses, health personnel, and day-care centre attendants. The organising of women's groups for productive activities is often attempted by the male staff members.

Special efforts must be made to recruit women as change agents. Agencies must set goals and quotas. Female candidates must be selected separately from male as the men will almost always have more experience and better formal qualifications. Agencies must accept that female change agents may require greater leave time for pregnancies and family illnesses and, if necessary, compensate through hiring even more women. It is a question of will – no excuses should be accepted.

Training programmes for change agents should always include women so that the training groups 'not only talk about them but with them; and the women learn to participate on equal terms with men, and the men learn to listen to the women and realise the importance of their role in development'.

Recruitment and selection in general

We appointed the man who seemed least remote from the realities of farming. He left us after a few weeks, saying he couldn't stand working such long hours in the sun.

Dr. Z. Chowdhury (quoted by Bhasin, 1980a)

The first step in the process of recruiting and selecting change agents is to set down on paper a list of the desirable qualifications that you require. The second step is to discuss and decide how the selection will take place. Finally, you must decide how you will make it known that you are looking for candidates.

Finding candidates is the first step in the selection process. This can be done through advertising in the national or local newspapers and radio, but this may well miss a lot of good candidates living in your rural programme area. Notices can be distributed to schools, churches, government offices. Local officials should be consulted and requested to spread the word through their administrative areas. If your programme has been operating for some time, then candidates should be known already.

Traditionally, staff are selected on the basis of an interview lasting maybe an hour. For candidates who are unknown to you, this is totally unacceptable when selecting change agents. Some people do very well in an interview situation, but they may not actually have any of the important aptitudes for working with people for which you are looking. Others may do very poorly in an interview, yet be excellent at working with small groups of poor people.

An interview, of course, saves time especially when you have a large number of candidates from which to choose. But remember, you are making choices that will be decisive for the success of your programme. You cannot afford not to spend a considerable amount of time on the selection process.

The two most important characteristics that you are looking for are: (1) the ability to work well in a team as well as with small groups of poor men or women; and (2) the individual's attitude towards the poor and to the idea that the poor are capable of developing themselves given the opportunity. The selection process must in some way test these characteristics.

Mosharraf Hossain (1982) reports that one of the most respected NGOs working in Bangladesh, Proshika, uses a distinctive approach to the recruitment of their 'Kormy' (change agents). Proshika is convinced that the involvement and dedication required of these agents can only be measured through continuous observation and evaluation in the field situation. A prospective Proshika Kormy has to work in the field for at least six months as a volunteer. During this period, he or she does not get any remuneration. The volunteers work under the instruction of other Kormy and independently encourage the formation of groups of the marginal and landless peasants. Proshika does not support these groups until the volunteer becomes a Proshika Kormy. On the recommendation of the local Kormy, the apprentice is selected for appointment.

This is a rather extreme approach. It may well be the most effective, but perhaps not always practical – especially when starting up a new programme. A modified approach would be a one- or two-week workshop in a rural situation. The teams would live in the villages and work in small groups of three or four. Each team could be given a problem area to investigate such as marketing of products, informal and formal credit facilities or water supplies. This investigation should include bringing small groups of villagers together to informally discuss the problem area being investigated. The candidates should keep a journal of their activities and findings. They should also come together with your selection team and with the other candidates to present and discuss their findings. By observing each team in the field and during the discussions, you will get a fairly good picture of each candidate's strengths and weaknesses.

Some key points to remember: All written work and discussions should, if at all possible, be in the vernacular of the individual candidate. It may prove necessary to re-organise the teams if one person is too dominating (grounds for disqualification?) or if there is too much discord in the team. Female candidates should most likely be grouped together in all-female teams; they should also work with women's groups, but not on traditional women's problems such as child-care or health problems. Find out what the women are most concerned about, and concentrate on these problems.

If you still think that you can't afford the time and effort to hold a field selection workshop, then the absolute minimum would be a one-day workshop where each team of candidates is given one or more group exercise with which to work. Exercises could be prepared on topics such as:

• Present your own experiences with working with poor people? What have you learned from these? Reply to questions from your fellow team members.
• How would you go about setting up a farmers' association?
• How would you go about setting up a village cooperative store?
• How would you approach the question of women in development?

These group exercises should be designed so that you can observe how each candidate functions in a group situation, how well they can present and defend their own ideas, how well they cooperate, and how well they participate without dominating. Although the solutions to the case studies will be interesting, remember that you are primarily concerned with each person's behaviour and personality.

The Staying Power of Change Agents

According to Harsh Sethi (1983), many NGOs in India were founded and staffed by semi-radicalised middle-class youth who were dissatisfied both with the official attempts at planning and the political attempts at transformation.

They brought with them their own hopes and aspirations, a desire to make an immediate and spectacular impact upon their societies. Unsurprisingly, this rarely happens, both due to the complexity and vastness of the problems and to the very ephemeral and transitory nature of voluntary activity. The idealism soon flags, and the process starts of either returning to the conventional fold, or wanting more radical solutions via political parties. The fact that many of the leading cadres are urban, middle-class youth with professional skills and contacts permits them a relatively easy re-entry into the world of secure jobs. They leave, creating in turn a major problem of staff instability.

This is only one side of the problem of keeping change agents long enough to justify the time and money involved in training them, as well as avoid the damages caused by too rapid a turnover of field staff. The more common problem is avoiding young people, especially university graduates, who use these positions as stepping stones to more permanent positions in government bureaucracies or private enterprises. A special problem is often young, unmarried women. They will normally be under considerable pressure from their families to either marry or get a position, usually teaching, with the government. Although we certainly cannot condemn young people for wanting to ensure their future careers or for respecting parental wishes, these are not the type of staff members we are looking for.

In many respects, bright young rural men and women from the less well-to-do village classes who have the ability, but lacked the opportunities, for higher training will make the most dedicated and long-lasting change agents. For them, village development often becomes a calling rather than a job – and this is exactly what we are looking for in change agents. Many experienced change agents have identified an earlier exposure to the problems and realities of village life as one of the main factors responsible for their deciding to dedicate themselves to rural development, and saw this as a turning point in their lives.

In light of these findings, it would be worthwhile to consider an organisational investment in exposure programmes whereby promising young women and men are given an opportunity to live and work alongside experienced change agents for a short period during their education. In this way a pool of possible candidates can be built up. As a development programme progresses, the change agents working in the field will identify village change agents, men and women who voluntarily work with their fellow villagers. Some of these may have the skills, commitment and freedom of movement to become full-time professional change agents. Ultimately, what will keep men and women in the field as full-time change agents is their own commitment together with the support and encouragement they receive from each other and their supporting agency and funders.

5. The Training and Support of Change Agents

The best way to teach about 'bottom-up planning', people's participation and decentralisation is by practicing these very ideas in a training programme. If training is top-down, rigid, paternalistic, the change agents will learn the same attitudes. To bring out creative and innovative qualities in them, trainees should be given the maximum responsibility possible.

Change agent trainee (quoted by Bhasin, 1976)

Participatory Training

The previous chapter looked at the very special role that change agents play in participatory development. The importance of commitment as well as the attitudes and aptitudes of the individual change agent was underlined. It was stressed that the change agent works essentially as a catalyst, and his or her success is dependent on an ability to understand socio-economic relationships and to work constructively with people.

In this chapter the question of the training process for change agents will be discussed. You may have noticed in the previous chapter that many of the researchers and practicing change agents quoted in the text maintained that there could be no formal training for this work. This is correct in the sense that change agents cannot be trained solely from textbooks or manuals, nor in the classroom or at a training centre.

However, there are effective training methods for developing in change agents an understanding of their work and the skills needed to carry it out. The following sections will attempt to create an understanding of participatory training for change agents, but it is impossible to prepare a manual for trainers.

The methodology described has been practised in various forms for over 10 years. A series of programmes have been conducted throughout Asia by Kamla Bhasin, Programme Officer, FAO Regional Change Agents Programme. A number of training programmes have been conducted in Sri Lanka by the staff of the Participatory Institute for Development Alternatives (PIDA) and the Sri Lanka Change Agents Programme. Eleven extensive training programmes for change agents have been conducted by the author in Uganda during the past six years. The following sections are based primarily on the writings of those connected with these programmes as well as on personal observations of the training experience.

Training of change agents takes time and is an on-going process. It is essentially a personal experience depending on the commitment and participation of each trainee. There is no training course, no syllabus, no textbook. The only essential equipment or teaching aids are pencils, field journals, flip-overs and blackboards. The initial intensive training experience should last at least three months and preferably six months. It cannot be over-emphasised that this type of training is a process – it cannot be condensed or shortened. It requires commitment by the organisation and by the training coordinators.

Traditional training programmes

Most existing training programmes for extension workers or for development workers tend to have the following features:

- There are clear distinctions between those who give and those who receive knowledge, and there is little participation of the trainees in planning and running the training programme. Certain organisations do use terms like 'dialogical', 'non-directive' and 'participatory' training, but these concepts are often only presented in lectures and have little real meaning.
- The lecture method is still the most common way of disseminating knowledge. The higher the status of the person delivering the lecture, the less discussion there is. Out of respect for the speaker, trainees often dare not ask questions.
- Training in social skills concerned with communicating and working with people are often neglected or dealt with in an academic rather than practical or experiential manner.
- Most training programmes avoid dealing with vital questions such as the social, economic and political structures in a country or an analysis of the causes of poverty and disadvantage. Hence, they fail to make change agents critically aware of the importance of analysing and understanding these forces and how they affect the lives of the people with whom they are working.
- Training programmes are usually conducted at special centres often in the capital city and far removed from the lives of poor people. Thus the training is largely theoretical and the change agents do not have the opportunity of experiencing genuine solidarity with the poor.

Traditional training programmes emphasise the transfer of technical skills and knowledge from the trainers to the trainees. The content, methodology and the setting of the training are all determined by the trainers. The trainers decide what skills and knowledge to transfer to the trainees who become passive recipients and objects of training. The trainees do not participate in organising the learning process. They take no responsibility which lies solely with the trainers. This type of training is essentially undemocratic, hierarchical and non-participatory. Kamla Bhasin (1980a) has rightly observed that:

> After going through such a training the trainees could be expected to adopt the same attitudes in their own work. They would assume the role of trainers *vis-a-vis* the people and work in an authoritarian, undemocratic and anti-people way.

Objectives of participatory training

Training should not only help in the search and acquisition of new skills and knowledge, but also help the participants to acquire and strengthen values like justice, equality, honesty, truthfulness and solidarity amongst oppressed groups. (Bhasin, 1976)

The following are the main objectives of change agent training programmes:

- Change agents should acquire a clear understanding of their role as change agents working in a community.
- They should develop their social and human skills in communicating and working with poor people.
- They should develop their understanding of group dynamics, and the importance of 'analysis–action–reflection' in the self-reliant participatory development process.
- They should develop their ability to criticise others constructively and sympathetically, and to handle criticism of themselves.
- They should develop their skills in identifying and analysing the issues and problems that confront them as change agents working with poor people (poverty analysis).
- They should increase their understanding of the connections between local community structures and problems (micro-analysis) and national/international policies and structures (macro-analysis).

Methodology of participatory training

The most important and valuable aspect of this training is the participatory aspect. I had never experienced this before. This has given opportunity to all of us to increase our speaking power, self-confidence, and our ability to analyse. The field for participation was open. Everyone has taken advantage of this according to his or her capacity.

Change agent trainee (quoted by Bhasin, 1979)

The methodology of participatory training consists essentially of two things: (1) group discussions in which the primary role of the training coordinator is to ask questions; and (2) field studies carried out by small teams of trainees and forming the basis for the next round of group discussions. The training should be conducted so that maximum use is made of situations and experiences as learning opportunities. The programme should take the local community as its frame of reference and not be dependent on imported theories. Emphasis should be on dialogue and discussion rather than on lectures.

Change agents are expected to initiate a process of participatory development. They are expected to help people develop a critical awareness of their development situation which will lead to self-directed and self-determined action for change. The training process should therefore equip them for such a role. Change agents therefore need to acquire skills in areas such as awareness building, promotion of participation, analysis of local situations and group dynamics. They need to develop a sensitivity to local needs, customs and habits, limitations and opportunities. If they fail in this they will become alienated from the people and end up being barriers rather than catalysts of participatory development.

The methodology for such training has by definition to be participatory and non-directive. It needs to be experiential, i.e. based on field experiences, and dialogical, i.e. conducted through dialogue and discussions. Change agent training should take place in two environments: fieldwork by small teams living and interacting with the poor in their villages, and discussions among the trainees and coordinators. The emphasis should be on self-training and group-learning through continuous interactions between the participants, villagers and the training coordinators. Learning thus takes place within the real world and arises out of real situations rather than being presented as a package of accepted knowledge by the trainers. Direct exposure to the realities of rural development will enable the change agents to identify issues and problems, develop solutions within the context of an on-going dialogue, and initiate actions which reflect the realities within which they are working.

Living and working together provides an opportunity to experience the problems and possibilities of cooperation and collective action. This will be a positive experience if an atmosphere is created in which the participants feel free to express themselves openly and honestly. Opportunities must be provided for frank reflection and analysis of whatever the participants consider important, including the training itself, and an honest, if painful, process of self-searching, criticism and self-criticism. Regular and on-going evaluation of the training programme within such an atmosphere should be carried over into the change agents' own working situations.

It should be self-evident that the persons coordinating this type of training experience cannot be dominating and directing. They must see their role as facilitators and catalysts rather than trainers in the traditional sense of that word. The approach to participatory training of change agents is essentially identical to the approach taken by change agents in promoting participation among poor people. Through the training experience they come to understand the analysis–action–reflection process of participatory development. The training coordinator acts as a change agent among the trainees.

Structure of the training programme

A major expectation of participants was not only to learn and evaluate, but also to share, i.e. sharing in the informal and semi-formal sense. (Bhasin, 1976)

The basic training programme should extend over a period of at least three months and can well last as long as six months; 20 weeks is an appropriate length. The training schedule can be organised into periods of fieldwork followed by training workshops for group discussions followed by a short break. Fieldwork periods should last about two weeks and workshops five to 10 days.

The training programme can begin with a one-week orientation programme in which everyone gets to know each other, personal case studies are presented and discussed, training needs are identified and discussed, personal expectations from the training can be reflected upon, and the practical structure of the training programme can be discussed and organised. Time can also be taken to organise the fieldwork.

The fieldwork must, of course, be carried out among the poor in suitable villages. These villages should either be in an area where your organisation is presently working or in an area selected for future work. Only in exceptional cases should fieldwork be done where there will be no follow-up – this would in effect be using villagers as guinea pigs.

Training workshops should be held at a quiet, rural site preferably near the villages where fieldwork is to be done. The choice of site will be limited by the desire to have communal living arrangements. In many areas of the Third World suitable boarding schools or rural training centres may be available.

The number of participants on this type of training course should be between 10 and 20. Fewer than 10 is not sufficient to ensure adequate breadth and depth of discussions. If there are more than 20, discussion either becomes cumbersome or some participants tend to remain quiet. The ideal seems to be 12 to 15 participants. It is very important that the group be more or less equally composed of men and women otherwise discussions will probably not be based on a realistic understanding of the village situation.

Participation is best learned in practice. The trainees should, as far as possible, identify their own training needs, and plan and carry out the training programme. The learning experiences should be directly related to the actual problems of poor people, and solutions should be examined and discussed in terms of the real situation being studied. Through their own active participation in the management of the training programme, the trainees will develop their understanding of the importance of people's participation as well as their skills in identifying, analysing and solving problems.

For the training workshops, living arrangements should be communal, with everyone eating and sleeping in a residential complex. Some meals should be prepared by the participants although main meals can be catered to save time. Insofar as possible, participants should have responsibility for organising the menu, budget (based on a daily allowance), and rotational work groups for cooking, housekeeping, food purchasing and book-keeping.

Communal living is an essential part of the training process as it creates an environment conducive to participation, interaction and sharing. The informal discussions held at all hours of the day are often as enlightening as the more structured discussions. The training coordinators should share in all aspects of the communal arrangements as benefits a change agent. Communal living provides the participants with an opportunity of studying at first hand within their own mini-community the problems as well as the advantages of collective action.

Group discussions should be held in a quiet, well-ventilated room of adequate size for free movement. If weather permits, a large shade tree would provide an excellent setting. A discussion circle should always be used even when guests are invited. Coordinators should melt into the circle. Participants should become conscious even about such apparently simple and common-sense things like how one sits and how one addresses others. An atmosphere of equality and mutual respect should be created.

With regards to invited guests who have come to participate in the discussions on specific topics, it is important to invite only those who are familiar with the methodology of participatory development, who realise the importance of fieldwork, and who have respect for fieldworkers as well as the poor. They should, if possible, be willing to share the living and working arrangements with the trainees.

Training programmes should, if at all possible, be held in a language which all the participants feel comfortable with – normally their mother tongue – otherwise their confidence, participation and understanding will be greatly lessened. The training must be directly related to the local situation and this cannot be completely understood through any language other than the local language – even an official language may distort this understanding. If an official language must be used, then time should be taken to allow the participants to translate important terminology, book-keeping, etc. into their own languages.

The participants should structure the discussion sessions as well as their own fieldwork. A chairperson and a recorder or rapporteur should be selected at the end of each day for the next day's discussions. These roles should be held in rotation. Regular evaluation sessions and recapitulations should be organised, starting each day with a recapitulation and an evaluation of the previous day's work. Each group should evolve their own rules of conduct and be subject to self-discipline.

Note-taking is very important and should be practiced by every participant as well as the coordinator – both in the discussions and in the field. These habits must be developed so that the change agents continue taking notes while working in the field. These notes are an important source material for the analysis–action–reflection process.

Daily timetables can be decided after discussion and consultation. Programmes and timetables can be revised by mutual agreement from time to time, in accordance with what the group feels are its needs. Given responsibility, the participants will quite often plan longer and more demanding working days than the training coordinators find comfortable!

Participatory training programmes must be self-governing. They should reflect exactly the self-reliant participatory development principles and methodology. The objective is to expose the participants to an open, democratic participatory experience so that this becomes a natural foundation for their own work among the people. In all of this the training coordinator sets the example as to what is expected of a change agent.

When doing fieldwork, the participants should be given a daily living allowance and arrange themselves for sleeping and eating facilities. Insofar as possible, they should make such arrangements with a suitable family in the village in which they are working. Training coordinators should, when visiting these villages, stay overnight under the same conditions. Participants will in this way learn to respect and appreciate local customs and hospitality.

Training content: topics for investigation

> Structural analysis of the society one lives in and awareness of the interplay of social, economic and political forces at local, national and international level should be a part of the training. This should not become an academic exercise imposed from above, but evolve out of actual experiences of the participants. (Bhasin, 1976)

The content of a participatory training programme for change agents will emerge primarily out of the discussions on the trainees' own field investigations. In these discussions questions will naturally arise concerning poverty and its causes, dependency relationships, self-reliance, development, community structure, socio-economic relationships and power structures – all at the micro-level, i.e. relating to the village and immediate district. These discussions should be naturally linked to a relevant macro-analysis.

The following is a list of some topics which are suggested for discussion during a training programme. In most cases they will be taken up as a natural result of the fieldwork and analysis, but the training coordinator can, by posing appropriate questions, bring the group around to discuss topics which haven't yet arisen. It is useful at the beginning of the training programme as well as later to suggest to the participants that they set up their own list of relevant topics. Training coordinators can expand on this list as they find it is appropriate.

1. What are the problems facing the poor people of the field study area? What are the symptoms and what are the causes of these problems? Do these problems seem to be vicious circles? Can the causes be separated into categories? What are secondary causes, and what are the genuinely primary or root causes of their problems?
2. How are the micro-issues of concern to the community affected by national and international macro-issues?
3. What is a community? What socio-economic classes are found in our communities?
4. What does self-reliance mean in terms of our communities and our nation?
5. What is people's participation? How can a change agent elicit genuine people's participation?
6. Discuss the different strategies and approaches to development. What do we mean by human (personal), economic, political and social development? What do we understand by a 'self-reliant participatory development process'?
7. What is the role of tradition, culture and religion in development?
8. How can women's role in development be properly promoted?
9. Discuss the inner structures of organisations. What are the factors

contributing to the success or failure of small rural interest groups?

10. How does a change agent promote and support the formation of participatory organisations of the poor?

11. What are the roles of savings and credit in economic development? How can savings be promoted among the rural poor?

12. What are the roles of change agents? What weaknesses are common among change agents?

13. What role do images, lifestyles, funding, etc. play with regards to the relationship between the people and the change agent and his/her agency?

14. How can good relationships with government officials, local elites and the power structure be maintained at the same time that poor people are organising themselves in order to gain greater control over their own lives? How can organisations of the people be co-opted by outsiders?

Throughout the programme, time should be taken to discuss which topics need to be gone into in depth. There should be a clear understanding of why a particular topic needs to be discussed and especially its relevance for participatory development. These discussions not only increase the understanding of why particular topics or issues are being brought up for analysis and reflection, but also ensure that nothing irrelevant or well-known to the group takes time from more important issues. The participants should feel free to suggest that additional topics be taken up or that more time be spent on specific issues.

Training materials can be useful, but it is essential to be aware of their limitations. Reading materials can be used to introduce various issues so long as they present different points of view and encourage the reader to explore further, read more and reflect for himself or herself, and then make up his or her own mind. Reading material should be simply written, but with a good, rather than a simplistic, analysis. It should, if possible, be in the language of the participants. This means that time and money will need to be spent in preparing such material. If it cannot be made understandable in the local languages, then it is not going to have very much value for work in the villages.

Audio-visual materials such as films, video tapes, slide-series and sound cassettes are more effective than the written word and can be used effectively for educational purposes. However, these media often are used to communicate a prefabricated message intended to create a predetermined reaction and response. The message may be about family planning or radical people's organisation, but the approach is the same. The effort is seldom to stimulate thought and to make the audience question, analyse and reach its own conclusions. There is often a certain element of propaganda and manipulation in the use of these media. The producers have their own perspective which determines the presentation and the message. In this way they are manipulative and hence not educative in the real sense of the word. Audio-visual techniques can be used if they are not accepted on face value, but are used like case study material to be discussed and analysed. The advantage of these techniques is that they can present facts in a selective and effective manner and keep the interest of the audience alive. But if they don't lead to questioning, discussion and analysis they can easily be counterproductive.

Far better than pre-packaged teaching aids are role plays, skits and short plays written and staged by the participants to illustrate concepts, situations and experiences. Trainees can make their own wall-charts summarising their discussions. And unlike elaborate audio-visual aids, these techniques can be transferred directly into rural learning situations.

Participation of trainees in programme management

Training groups should try to function as democratically and with as much participation of each individual as possible. At least in this small group we should try to practice what we preach. Only by practicing it will we know whether what we preach is practical or not.

Change agent trainee (quoted by Bhasin, 1976)

Participation in the management of the training programme is perhaps the best way in which trainees can achieve a genuine understanding of such topics as group dynamics, communication and participatory democracy. By studying and reflecting on how the group functions, they will learn practical group dynamics. They will realise that everyone, including themselves, has weaknesses, hang-ups, defence mechanisms and idiosyncracies. Through trying to grapple with their own personalities, they will discover how difficult and sometimes painful the process of change can be. Hopefully, this will help them to sympathise with and relate to the people with whom they will be working.

Direct participation allows the trainees to discover how difficult it is to practise true democracy. They will see for themselves that even in small groups, undemocratic tendencies can easily emerge. They will learn how to prevent or correct such tendencies. As a result they will hopefully see the power of people's participation as well as experience how fulfilling and rewarding genuine participation can be.

Important personal skills and self-confidence can be developed through the participatory method. Each trainee takes his or her turn at leading the discussion as well as recording for the day and presenting the recapitulation the next day. Speaking and listening skills are developed as is the ability to pose questions which lead to more discussion and insight.

Through personal experience the trainees will discover how difficult and challenging it is to share leadership rather than always being led by one person. They will learn to recognise how unhealthy power relationships can easily develop even in small groups, and learn how to deal with these situations. All of these insights will have direct relevance for the participants in their work with groups of rural men and women.

The training coordinator must, especially in the beginning, ensure that every trainee participates in the discussions. This can best be done by asking direct questions or asking for opinions. The trainees should be encouraged to bring the less assertive into the discussions. This is an important part of their future work with groups.

Experience proves that it is difficult to achieve equal participation. Participants should be encouraged to practise self-discipline. The groups themselves should police their own discussions. Those with tendencies to speak too much should be encouraged to speak less, and those who hesitate because of shyness or lack of language skills should be encouraged to speak more. Groups should realise that they have failed if some people do not speak while others speak all the time. In the words of one training group, 'Those who did not speak at all, or who tended to dominate discussions, were referred to as oppressors: they oppressed others either by their silence or by too many words.'

Participatory training represents a great challenge to training coordinators. They must be willing and able to set aside their authority, their greater experience and knowledge in order to give the trainees the opportunity for self-development. But then, isn't this exactly what self-reliant participatory development is about? The example set by the coordinator is perhaps the single most important factor for determining the success or failure of the training programme and the subsequent work of the change agents in the field.

Personal case studies

> We are not only discovering others, but also ourselves.
>
> *Change agent trainee* (quoted by Bhasin, 1976)

Prior to the start of the training programme each participant, including the coordinators, can be asked to prepare a personal case study on themselves and their experience with rural development. The purpose of this case study is two-fold: (1) during the orientation week each case study is presented and discussed, and thus provides a good way of quickly getting to know one another; (2) by preparing the case study prior to the start of the training, each participant must reflect on his or her previous experiences and motivations.

Each case study can include information on the participant's background – family origins and situations, education, work and previous organisational experiences. Each can be asked to write down their views on rural and urban development problems, and how these might be solved, the problems they themselves have faced in the field, their motivation for becoming a change agent, their conception of the role of change agents, and their expectations for the training programme. Personal case study presentations are a very effective way of getting to know each other well.

> By talking also about personal matters and not being silent about them, it was emphasised that one's approach to work and performance as a worker was closely linked to one's lifestyle, beliefs and family life. (Bhasin, 1979)

Fieldwork in rural situations

The periods of fieldwork in villages are the prime resource for the workshop discussions and give the training programme direction. There should be at least five such periods if the teams are to really break through the surface and gain a genuine understanding of the situation. Teams should have three to four participants. Often it is most productive to have all-male and all-female teams, but this is by no means absolute. The composition of the teams should be discussed and decided upon by the participants.

Each team must organise its own fieldwork and establish eating and sleeping arrangements for itself. Teams should be visited regularly by the training coordinators and, if possible, include overnighting. In this way there will be more time to discuss with the team their work and progress, as well as establish closer bonds between the trainees and the coordinators.

The first two or three fieldwork periods will normally be needed for the teams to get an understanding of the socio-economic relationships in their field area. They should try to identify and understand the various production cycles, who is doing what and why, factors inhibiting improved production including secondary factors such as health and nutrition – in essence produce a 'map' showing who has what problems and why.

After getting a fair feel for the rural situation, each team should pick out one particular problem area which is important to a significant portion of the poor sector of the community, and work with these people on analysing this particular problem. It is at this stage that work with small groups becomes essential although informal group discussions should have been possible as early as the second fieldwork period.

It is vitally important that each participant take detailed notes of their meetings and conversations with the people as well as writing down their daily reflections on their experiences. This material is essential for later analysis and reflection in the group discussions. This is particularly true of numerical information such as sales and purchasing prices, interest rates and production figures.

Although it is not expected that small action groups evolve out of the trainees' investigations, this does often happen. This then presents a dilemma unless it has been decided to follow-up the work after the training programme ends. This has often been the case in practice.

Reflection, criticism and self-criticism

Before change agents can change others, they have to change themselves and their consciousness. They have to constantly try to shed their own contradictions, weaknesses, prejudices. In any organisation or group which is engaged in rural development, it is essential to have regular sessions of criticism and self-criticism. Only through such sessions can a genuine understanding of each other and of the work one is doing emerge. A thorough understanding of each other and sharing a common value system and an appropriate philosophy of work is the basis for strong team work. (Bhasin, 1980b)

It is of crucial importance for the success of the training programme as well as of the change agents' later work that habits of reflection, criticism and self-criticism are developed in the trainees. Throughout the group discussions, as well as within the team discussions, time should be taken to reflect upon the work and behaviour of individual trainees as well as of each work group and fieldwork team. Opportunities should be given to openly discuss these things, and everyone should be encouraged to look at themselves and their efforts self-critically. Coordinators should set an example by constructively criticising both the group's and individual behaviour and work, as well as exercising self-criticism and being open to criticism from the group.

This is not easy. In most cultures there is no tradition of permissible open criticism of others. Genuine self-criticism is equated with loss of face although some self-deprecation is tactically used to give a sense of humility. In many cases this will be the first time that participants openly criticise others and are criticised themselves in a group situation. The group should reflect also on the response of each person to such criticism. Many interpersonal problems arise not so much from criticising and opening-up, but from not speaking frankly and suppressing oneself.

A group of trainees working with Kamla Bhasin (1976) realised that criticism and self-criticism can be practised only among people who know each other well, who share a common concern and who have faith in each other. Criticism should be practised at the right moment, right place and in the right manner. Harsh criticism should be avoided because it can lead to the breaking up of the group. The aim of criticism and self-criticism should be to cure a sickness, not to kill the patient. One has to raise others up, not knock them down. That is why criticism should not be too hard. It should be mixed with praise and appreciation. While practising criticism and self-criticism, change agents should guard against subjectivism and arbitrariness. Before one criticises others, one should make sure that the criticism is objective and purely for the purpose of improving work. Personal criticism should be made only if it is related to the work. Criticism cannot be separated from self-criticism. If we want to criticise others we should first start with ourselves.

It is necessary for change agents, who often are quick to point out weaknesses in others and who readily prescribe changes for individual and community behaviour, to evaluate themselves, their behaviour and their own value systems from time to time. They must avoid becoming rigid, authoritarian and insensitive; their work and behaviour patterns must stay consistent with the philosophy of participatory development. Unfortunately, there are many development agencies with hierarchical structures, centralised decision-making and autocratic leadership which discourage constructive criticism.

It is important that reflection and mutual criticism be conducted in an atmosphere of support and understanding – an atmosphere of solidarity, but not of harmony. The goal is a new kind of unity based on rigorous group criticism rather than on the smoothing over of conflict in order to maintain harmony. On the other hand, relentless and merciless criticism leading to alienation of members must be avoided. Solidarity and criticism should be combined, with criticism leading not to disharmony but to improved unity.

Women and development training

> Two female participants felt that even those men who talked of change and removing injustices, etc. sometimes tended to be 'unliberated' in their attitudes towards women. Political radicals, they felt, could and often did behave as social reactionaries. (Bhasin, 1976)

As was mentioned earlier, there should be a more or less equal number of men and women participating in the training programme. It is equally desirable that there be at least one male and one female on the team of training coordinators. This is not only to ensure that female insights are brought to the important question of women and development, but also to ensure that the women are not intimidated into passiveness while doing the training.

But numbers are not enough. Very few cultures in the world, even now, treat women as equals to men. This is especially true of most Third World countries, and not only those with strong Islamic traditions. It is too much to expect that the male trainees, because of their commitment to working with the poor, will automatically be immune to the prejudices against women found in their own cultural backgrounds. Nor will the women be free of habits of quiet submission.

The male participants in one training programme:

> admitted that this was the first time they were interacting so intensively in a small group situation with women, and that too with very independent-minded women. One of them said he had been brought up in a way which denied women equality. For another it was the first time he had realised that women had as important a role to fulfil in development work as men. Another expressed his lack of confidence in relating to women in the group with whom he found it difficult to be as normal as he could be with the men.
>
> (Bhasin, 1976)

An important area of discussion during the training programme is not only the general question of women and development, but also the more specific question of how the participants relate to members of the opposite sex. Questions such as the following should be discussed openly and thoroughly: Which attributes should a woman have? Which should a man have? What are the male participants' reactions to the women in the group? The women's reactions to the men? What does the culture and its traditions say about male–female relations? Whose culture is this really? Whose traditions? How do the men react to being criticised by the women, and vice versa? Do women have as much pride as men? How do all these questions (and many others) affect the role of women in the training programme and in development in general?

One woman participant in a training programme (Bhasin, 1976) said she wanted to be treated as a human being first and then as a woman. People wanted to push women into stereotyped roles irrespective of whether or not they wanted to fit those roles. She said she felt stifled by this pressure: 'In the name of culture many other undesirable things were pushed down the throats of people. We had to realise that everything in our cultures was not good. There was a need to retain the good and discard the unjust features in our respective traditions.'

The use of words such as he/him/his when speaking generally, or chairman instead of chairperson, or man instead of humanity, deny women their own identity. Trainees should compile a list of such words. Should efforts be made to avoid using sexist words? Are there substitutes? This type of exercise can be invaluable in making us realise that we are all prisoners of culture and upbringing, and that we have constantly to reflect on our language, behaviour and ideas, and to change them if they are found to be outdated and unjust. If we continue to regard women in stereotyped terms, then we can hardly expect them to participate actively and to take a leadership role in development activities.

The role of the training coordinators

> Thank goodness the coordinator did not take on the sort of role we imagined a coordinator to perform as then we would have been turning to her for everything and would not have gained the objective of the programme.
>
> *Change agent trainee* (quoted in Bhasin, 1979)

As mentioned in the previous section there should, if at all possible, always be two coordinators, one male and one female, taking part in every training programme. The best way of seeing the role of the training coordinators is as change agents. The coordinators work with a group of trainees in the same way that it is expected that change agents will work with groups of poor villagers. The goal is to increase their awareness of their own situation and to analyse what can be done to improve their work. We want the change agents to be self-reliant while at the same time appreciating the power and usefulness of teamwork and collective action.

Every statement made and action taken by the coordinators should be intended to reinforce this image of a change agent. The coordinators will most likely become one of the most important role models for the change agents. If the coordinators always assume leadership roles and are directive and authoritarian, then these same attitudes will be transferred to the change agents in their work with poor groups.

It is important to reduce the distinction between trainers and trainees, resource persons and recipients, between those who give and those who receive, between subjects and objects. There can be no participatory training, nor for that matter participatory development, unless the traditional attitudes of the teacher are replaced by those of the friend and fellow seeker. Use of the word 'coordinator' instead of 'trainer' is one step in this direction.

From the very beginning of the training programme, the coordinators must try to minimise their role as the leaders of the group. This is the only way to maximise the participation of the trainees. If the group becomes dependent on the coordinators at the start and accepts their role as passive trainees, then it will be difficult to change this pattern later in the programme. This, of course, applies equally well to change agents working with groups of villagers. However, as Kamla Bhasin (1979) has observed on the basis of her own experience as coordinator on many change agent training programmes:

> For a coordinator to strike a balance between being a 'trainee' as well as 'trainer' is a very difficult business. It is almost the same as the dilemma of a change agent in a community. How much of an outsider should a change agent be and how much a part of the community?

The coordinators should try to merge themselves into the group according to the 'unity of trainer–trainee' principle. The coordinators should not make any decisions which the group could just as well make collectively or could be made by the functioning group chairperson.

How much should the coordinators participate in the discussions and debates? As a general rule, as little as possible. The coordinators are the change agents for the group, and should help the group to arrive at their own awareness of the problem being discussed. The coordinators can assist by asking questions intended to open up new avenues of discussion or point at areas that can be probed for greater understanding. If the analysis of a problem has been correct, then there will be no need for the coordinators to give the answer, nor will there even be a need for the coordinators to confirm the correctness of the conclusions reached by the group. However, if the coordinators feel that the group's understanding is incomplete, then discussion can be reactivated by posing appropriate questions.

The coordinators should be prepared when necessary to take the initiative in getting discussion started when reflecting upon progress of the training and the analysis of problems within the training group. In the early stages of a training programme, the coordinators must also ensure that there is equal participation in discussions and decision-making, but always encouraging the entire group to be conscious of this and to follow-up.

The role of the coordinators should not be too succinctly spelled out at the beginning of the training. The coordinators should play the role, and only in the event that the participants raise the question should it be discussed. However, it is almost certain that the question of the proper role of the coordinators will be raised by one or more members of the group. Most people are brought up and educated in an authoritarian way; it is often confusing and difficult for them to get used to a situation where there is no earmarked authority to lead, to direct. As one of the participants on an Asian Regional Change Agent Programme said: 'We are used to being dictated to and to dictating to others. We come from a working background where participation is little emphasised. That is why we are confused. But we have to get out of this confusion. This programme has made us aware of our own behaviour.' Another participant said that although in her organisation they had been talking about various participatory and dialogical approaches, they had not been practiced.

However, if the coordinators are to become more participants/catalysts than coordinators, then each participant must in turn become more of a leader or coordinator. If the discussions are going in the wrong direction, if everybody is not participating in the discussion, or if someone is dominating the discussion, then it is the responsibility of each participant to point such things out and to suggest corrective actions. In this way it can be hoped that a feeling of group responsibility, under shared leadership, will emerge.

The discussion of the role of the coordinators in the group should be an important learning process for the participants because the role of the training coordinators is very similar to the role of the external change agent working in the community. To a large extent the model which the coordinators present to the group will determine how the participants practice their role as change agents in the community – the power of example here is determinant.

It should by now be clear that participatory training is not the easiest way of doing things, neither for the coordinators nor the trainees. Everyone must constantly strive for constructive participatory democracy avoiding, on the one hand, anarchy and, on the other, domination by a few authoritarian individuals. In other words, this is very similar to the world in which the change agents will be working.

Summing up

> It was indeed a constant challenge to the whole group, and to the coordinator in particular, to function as a group where decision-making authority, responsibility and initiative was shared and where there was maximum opportunity for learning. (Bhasin, 1979)

This has been a long presentation of participatory training. Because this type of training is more of a methodology than a syllabus, it is hard to describe. One almost needs to participate in such a programme in order to understand and appreciate its effectiveness. Hopefully, the quotations from the several Asian Regional Change Agents Programmes will give a sense of the atmosphere of this type of training.

Participatory training is a process, and it is therefore important that the direction and progress of the programme are monitored frequently so that decisions can be made early to change course, speed up or go back and cover old ground. An on-going evaluation of the content, method of work and inter-relationships within the training group should be built into the programme. Each participant can be asked to write down his or her thoughts on the programme and then present them to the group for discussion at appropriate times.

Participatory training is not finished with the end of the initial training period. As we shall see in the next section, it is a continuous process.

Follow-up and Support

It should by now be fairly obvious that the young men and women who choose to do the work of village level change agents, and who are qualified for it, are a very special and, unfortunately, uncommon species in most societies today. The following comments made by young Asian change agents indicate their special situation (Bhasin, 1976):

> My parents did not want me to work in the rural areas. In fact my father does not even like the idea of girls working. So my decision to work, and that too in the rural areas, was a double catastrophe.

> My friends, professors and even some sisters in my nursing school thought that it was just part of youth's idealism and soon I would change my mind. I do not think they understood why it is imperative for us to turn our heads to the rural areas instead of building up all human and institutional resources in the city. My parents had the same reaction, but they recognised my right to make my own decision and despite their frustration they allowed me to do what I wanted to do with my life.

> What is the matter with me – everybody said. My parents and friends thought I was foolish. They told me that the university work had many more chances for my progress. What could I achieve by working in the rural areas?

These comments indicate that many young people who choose to become change agents in the rural areas receive little support from their families and friends. In some cases the disapproval is so strong that young people have been forced to break their ties with their families. Needless to say, this can create considerable social and psychological problems.

From the above descriptions of their personal situations, and from our knowledge of their often very difficult work situations, we can see that there is a great need for follow-up and support of each individual change agent. They need support, encouragement and guidance from those who are close to them. This is essential if they are to maintain enough psychological strength to be able to do their work well, to develop their capabilities, and not least, if we are to retain their services.

Md. Anisur Rahman (1985b) has over a long period of time been associated with numerous change agents in many different situations. He summarises the problem as follows:

> The hardship of their work, the test of doing pure catalytic work in which

fulfilment is to be sought in not establishing one's own image but in liquidating it, the hazards arising from confrontations with rural power groups, often the police, etc. and the opening up of softer job opportunities – all together contribute to a rather high rate of cadre drop out, as high as 50 per cent in some cases.

He goes on to point out that it had been the practice in all of the initiatives he reviewed for change agents to continue to meet among themselves periodically for review and sharing of experiences.

Group discussions and training workshops
The most important tool for providing change agents with support and opportunities for personal development are group discussions and training workshops. Field teams of change agents should sit down at least weekly to discuss together their problems, opportunities and work progress. If these teams are organised into project groups, then all of the teams composing one project staff group should come together at least once a month for a training and review workshop. In addition, there should be regular meetings for change agents and coordinators from different projects as well as programme managers.

Some people feel that all these meetings and workshops are just taking valuable time from productive development activities. It can be seen in a different way: Is it more productive to let the change agents get on with their work, fighting their frustrations and problems alone, possibly losing their sense of direction, giving up for lack of moral and intellectual support? In other words, getting nowhere fast. Is it not better to reach the goal even if it takes more time? In the end it might actually take less time.

It is equally important that change agents be given regular opportunities to improve their specialised skills as well as learning the basics of other specialised skills. Every change agent should over time acquire a basic understanding of health and nutrition, agriculture, marketing and accounting. This training can either be organised internally or externally with the assistance of outside training institutions.

Unfortunately, many development agencies tend to forget that their fieldworkers need regular opportunities to gain additional knowledge and understanding of new ideas and trends in the field of rural development. New discoveries are constantly being made not only in technical areas such as health, agriculture and rural technology, but also in rural sociology. Agencies should therefore ensure that change agents are given opportunities to attend seminars and training courses. Reading materials on various development subjects should be circulated among the staff, and study groups can be established using these materials as a focus of discussion. This will not only improve individual knowledge and skills, but will also strengthen the sense of unity among the staff, which is the basis for effective development.

The need for wider contacts

There is one further area of activity which should be considered with regard to the development and strengthening of change agents. We have so far looked at group discussions, workshops and additional training within a national context. In an age of ever-increasing inter-dependencies, national situations are influenced by trends and movements within regions as well as international developments. Change agents are not working in a vacuum; they should participate in national and regional 'sharing experiences'.

Throughout the world today there are many development organisations promoting self-reliant participatory development. Most of these are local or national non-governmental organisations; unfortunately, there are still very few First World and international agencies promoting genuine grassroots development. In recent years there have been several regional workshops which have brought together change agents from these organisations. These sharing experiences have proven very valuable, not only for strengthening existing organisations, but also in promoting the evolution of new participatory programmes.

Although these efforts have been supported by international organisations and programmes such as the ILO/PORP, FAO–FFHC/AD, IIED and IRED, they themselves lack funding because of the tendency of many donors to support only specific national projects rather than regional and international efforts. Serious development agencies should therefore support and participate in these activities. Such an involvement will undoubtedly strengthen country programmes as well as give invaluable inspiration to field staff.

Consequences of staff development

One should not assume that all this activity to strengthen and support the change agents will not have its effect on the organisational form and leadership style of programmes and even agencies. Participatory development and participatory training have a dynamic of their own which of necessity must lead to greater openness, straightforwardness and democratic decision-making and policy development. If attempts are made to stifle these developments, then the participatory process will whither and die – not only within the organisation, but also in the community groups. The two processes are totally interdependent.

The observations of Mary Racelis Hollnsteiner (1978), a leading UNICEF executive with long experience in participatory development, support this reasoning:

> Staff development and training become very different when practicing participatory development. Once the staff becomes aware that they need to promote participation, and what that means operationally, it does not take much for them to start saying: 'How can we preach it if we do not practice it?' A grassroots development begins in your own organisation and making that come about can provoke some very creative tension.

Agencies genuinely committed to participatory development should consider some form of staff council or worker representation in their policy and decision-making bodies. Trust in the people is a myth unless we trust the maturity and good sense of our own fellow workers.

Career development

Because of the nature of the work – long hours, evening meetings, weekends, remote localities, simple living conditions – there will always be a fairly high turnover of change agents. The work of a change agent does not make family life any easier. No matter how understandable, these drop-outs represent a considerable loss of training and experience. Although not totally avoidable, efforts should be made to provide career opportunities for the best and most dedicated.

Often, however, it is not the work itself that causes someone to drop out. Those change agents who are genuinely dedicated and committed will continue as long as they feel that their efforts are appreciated, that they are judged on their work with the people rather than for the organisation, that their opinions are respected and listened to, that there is fairness and no favouritism within the organisation, and that they have a fair opportunity of being considered for promotion. A good organisation keeps good people. As Kamla Bhasin (1980a) has noted:

> Usually the careers and the promotions of village level workers have depended on what their superiors thought of them. Too much effort is too often put into producing short-term visible results that impress visiting higher-ups. If the peasants were to judge the performance of the field staff, if the promotion of these people depended on reports written by the village people, then none of these corrupt practices would go on.

Staff support and development are probably the most important area of concern for programme managers after the initial selection and training of change agents. There is no use recruiting the best possible people for training as change agents if they are not given enough support for them to want to continue working.

Organisation and Leadership

> To work with people is easy because they have a sense of humour. The biggest obstacle to working with a bureaucracy is that its very nature is against humour. (Fuglesang, 1982)

Fifteen years ago a group of change agent trainees in Asia visited together with Kamla Bhasin (1976) 13 national and international projects throughout Asia. Their conclusions on the basis of their own experiences and observations are listed below. My own observations confirm that very little has changed in the intervening years.

1. Organisations working for rural development and change often fail to reflect on and analyse their own structures, ways of functioning or human relationships. In many of the organisations visited, there was hardly any discussion on these issues.
2. Both government and non-government organisations often function in rigid, authoritarian, top-down, centralised and undemocratic ways.
3. Policy decisions are often made entirely by the people on top. Decisions are often handed down to the workers as orders which have to be carried out. Fieldworkers become conditioned to always look 'heavenwards' with their hands stretched out for orders. This has two main defects:

    (a) It does not let fieldworkers feel involved and responsible in shaping the policies and direction of work. It also does not let their initiative and drive develop. Worse still, they develop similar patronising attitudes towards the village people;

    (b) The decisions which are made do not reflect the real field situation because those who set the policies do not have recent field-level experience. The group felt that fieldworkers should be represented on the policy-making bodies of development agencies and institutions.
4. The directors and managers tend to be paternalistic; they tend to treat fieldworkers as their children, who always need to be guided. These big people tend to be like Banyan trees, all embracing and royal, but underneath which little else can grow. Some of them suffer from a 'founder syndrome'. Some of these people refuse to realise that although they pioneered certain changes and programmes a few decades ago, their ideas have now reached a dead end.
5. The salary differentials within organisations are sometimes too large, leading to different lifestyles and lack of solidarity. The salary differentials are most glaring (up to 40–50 times) in projects where there are both local and foreign experts. The buildings which they put up sometimes do not reflect their ideals of simplicity and austerity.
6. Training programmes for their own workers are often rigidly structured with little scope for participation from trainees. There are lectures on people's participation but little practice of the principle.
7. Very often there is a lack of a common understanding of the aims, objectives and ideology behind the tasks at hand. People are sometimes hired only to do a particular job.
8. All these characteristics contradict the very principles which many organisations claim to pursue and propagate. The best way to propagate ideas is by practising them.

Two years later another group of experienced fieldworkers visited projects in four other countries of Asia (Bhasin, 1979). Their summary was as follows:

It was sad but revealing to see how each level of authority bosses over those below it. A person who was most quiet and subservient in the presence of his or her boss would suddenly become bossy *vis-à-vis* his or her own subordinates. In some of the organisations the lines of authority were so clearly drawn that there was no possibility of teamwork. One wondered how such agencies could successfully implement participatory programmes for bringing about egalitarian social change.

We found that hierarchies are so deeply entrenched in our societies that they make nonsense of the now fashionable terms like 'people's participation', 'starting from below', etc. So long as your superiors, and not the people you are supposed to serve, write your annual reports and supervise your work you can forget about the people.

The above observations are, unfortunately, all too typical for the majority of development projects and programmes in the Third World (as well as all types of organisations in the industrialised countries). They indicate a tendency towards top-down policy formulation, centralised decision-making, one-way communication, authoritarian leadership and undemocratic and hierarchical organisational structures.

An organisation which genuinely desires to promote self-reliant participatory development among the poor must try to turn all of these characteristics around or otherwise fail. A participatory organisation will be characterised by mutual consultations with regards to policy formulation, decentralised decision-making, two-way communication, non-authoritarian leadership, and an informal and democratic organisational structure. Andreas Fuglesang (1982) has expressed this in the following way:

> Vertical, hierarchical information systems maintain order by exercising authority. These systems are combinations of limitations which inhibit the flow of information through vested interests, with the end result of producing limited decisions for action.
>
> Horizontal, self-organising information systems introduce order without authority and have an infinite capacity for new combinations, by communication through shared interests which motivate a high creative potential. Such systems are capable of coping with complex and unpredictable environments by producing optimal decisions for action.

Fortunately, more and more development organisations, most notably Third World NGOs, are experimenting with participatory forms of management. One of these is Proshika, a large NGO in Bangladesh. Mosarraf Hossain (1982) reports that participatory decision-making plays a crucial role in their rural development management. Meetings at the headquarters or at the development centres are characterised by an atmosphere of easy informality in which the participants actively discuss questions before reaching decisions. Hossain contends that: the rural poor have their own problems and distinct perception of these problems. An organisation which understands poor people's problems cannot develop into a bureaucratic organisation. When it does, it alienates itself from the poor.

Another Third World NGO, also in Bangladesh, is Nijera Kori which is trying to help the rural poor, both women and men, to organise to assert their rights and create a better existence for themselves. Nijera Kori's field operations are divided into geographical divisions. There are four levels of decision-making. The first is, of course, the independent primary group or organisation of the landless, artisans and women in the villages. Representatives from these groups and Nijera Kori workers of the area form a district level coordination committee. In this committee 50 per cent of the members are expected to be women representing women's groups. The representatives of district coordination committees form a regional committee.

Major decisions are made by a central committee of four representatives from the regional committees, one from the central secretariat, one central organiser, one central trainer and two specially elected women. This central decision-making authority is, like all other committees, composed both of full-time workers and representatives of the rural poor. Nijera Kori emphasises democratic decision-making. All policy decisions, as well as personnel matters, are decided by the committees. Committee members are elected to take on specific responsibilities for management, organisation and training.

Nijera Kori emphasises democratic decision-making. All policy decisions, as well as personnel matters, are decided by the committees. Committee members are elected to take on specific responsibilities for management, organisation and training.

These examples are both from indigenous organisations working very closely with the rural poor. But what about international agencies, both large and small, governmental and non-governmental? Usually a resident representative functions as the sole decision-maker. Is it impossible for such agencies to manage through participatory processes? How can fieldworkers promote participatory organisations when they have no say at all in their own organisations?

Organisational style and image

Once upon a time there was a representative from a European donor agency (DONOR) who was making his first inspection trip to a project in Africa which his agency was supporting financially. The project was being implemented by a well-known international private voluntary organisation (PVO).

Unfortunately, the co-directors of PVO were on their home leave at the time, and as they were the only paid employees of PVO, they wrote to DONOR and gave him instructions as to how he could proceed out to Mondoro District where PVO was working. DONOR hired a Land Rover with a driver and they drove the 150kms south from the capital to Mondoro. They came to a group of men working on a bridge-dam in a dry river bed and asked where the PVO project was. The men said that they hadn't heard of that project, but they could ask at the school which was up the road.

When they came to the Nyundo Primary School, DONOR went over to a group of women sitting in an open shed under the sign 'Zhakata Adult School of litteracy (sic), farming, dressmaking'. The women were obviously learning about poultry-keeping from a man who turned out to be from the Veterinary Service. No, they hadn't heard of the PVO project, but ask the men over at the workshop. The workshop turned out to be two commercial workshops, four men making sisal/cement roofing sheets and two men in an arc-welding workshop. But, 'No, sorry. Try over at Watykoka. Those people are building a clinic, maybe they know where your project is.' After taking a drink at a water-tap (which he was surprised to see), DONOR drove on to the Watykoka Village Clinic, but the villagers there hadn't heard of the PVO project either.

To make a long story short, DONOR never did find the PVO project. After returning home, he wrote to the PVO directors again and expressed his surprise at not having found the project. Although he had seen a lot of interesting village activities, he had not seen any PVO signboards nor had any one heard of the PVO project. Either the driving instructions were wrong or they had made a wrong turn somewhere!

The PVO project had been working three years in Mondoro with volunteer 'village change agents' working with groups of men and women in the villages. Since the first group had built the Nyundo Primary School, committees had formed in 18 surrounding villages. In addition to the schools and clinics, groups had established poultry and sewing cooperatives, adult literacy classes, built roads and bridges and water supply schemes. PVO had also given loans and arranged training for the establishment of small commercial workshops. But there were no PVO signboards and no PVO project office. The people had never thought of the projects as anything but their own!

Do we really need signboards? Do we really need the 'DONATED BY PVO' in big letters on a white-washed village school with the attractive agency symbol painted above it? Aren't we really saying, 'Here we are. See how good we are'? Aren't we also depriving the villagers of their self-respect?

If the villagers have built a school, and if the villagers want to put up a sign, then of course they should. If we have done our job of participatory development properly, then the people will see it as their school. They might then put up a sign which reads, hopefully in their own language: OUR VILLAGE SCHOOL, BUILT BY THE PEOPLE OF OUR VILLAGE with the assistance from the Government, of Our Country and PVO.

Signboards are only the most conspicuous advertisement of an external presence. There are many others, and each of them contributes to setting the staff and the organisation apart from the people we are supposedly working with. We should always ask ourselves: Does this set me or the organisation apart from the people?

Vehicles represent another prominent class division, especially the country director's expensive sedan or Land Cruiser (Range Rovers are too expensive for us!): 'But we need to be representative especially when meeting with government officials.' Do we really need to play that game? Why not leave it in the capital city? 'But visitors can't be rattled to death in a pick-up?' Why not? 'But we need a pick-up to go into town to buy fertiliser.' Really? What does a group of poor farmers do? What are they going to do after we leave? 'But it takes so much time otherwise.' Is it really time that is the problem? Think about it. 'Does it set me apart from the people?'

Project compounds are lovely, especially those with flowers, white-washed bricks, fences and watchman. 'Here we are. Keep out!' Are they really necessary? Often these compounds are very comfortable for the staff. Sometimes they have their own cooks and servants – often local villagers. But aren't cooks and servants the prerogative of the richer classes? Must the project staff live apart from the people?

There are many other seemingly small things that in reality can set us apart from the poor: the clothes we wear, our behaviour during our free time, our language. Local staff should never speak a foreign language in the presence of villagers unless, of course, speaking to a foreigner. Foreign staff and visitors should not speak only to those who speak their own language, but should take the time, and insist, that everything be translated. Language is the greatest divider of all.

Full-time employment, salaries and benefits are things the poor hardly dare dream about, even for their children. Salary structures in many NGOs are higher than in government or corresponding sectors. Harsh Sethi (1983) has observed that a high lifestyle rarely goes well in working with the poor and has noted that 'the more discerning within the NGOs have often described themselves and their colleagues as "Comprador Development Bourgeois"'. In the least, we can avoid displaying our wealth to those less fortunate with whom we are working.

Respect for people

> I have noticed that when Lute Mirla goes to see her sister, she stops for a while among the trees at the brink of the bush a good distance from the hut, calling out loudly, 'Hodi! Hodi!' Among the Bembas it is polite to notify those inside of one's arrival, thus avoiding embarrassment and giving them time to prepare for the visitor. I have also noticed that the extension worker does not always do that, but then of course he is educated and knows better! (Fuglesang, 1982)

It should go without saying that we should always respect and, whenever possible, follow the customs and behaviour patterns of the people with whom we are working. Outsiders are generally received with a good deal of respect by villagers. Unfortunately, this can easily lead to a reinforcement of feelings of inferiority. Md. Anisur Rahman (1985a) reports being introduced as a 'very learned man' at an inauguration ceremony in a village of a programme of group-based bank credit for the rural landless. His observations on this experience are sharp:

> What a deadly wrong start: to create (or strengthen) the inferiority complex among the people at the very beginning of their coming together to cooperate. As for the truth, I know that all my learning would be of no value if I were thrown into the village to make a living – I can neither cultivate nor build a hut with my own hands, and would have to learn from the rural poor how to do these things and survive. I also know that the rural poor are

developing through their own organised efforts and struggles. Give them the inferiority complex, and then they will only wait for deliveries from outside which will be the sole purpose for organising.

Visits and visitors to project areas are always difficult. Unfortunately, they cannot be completely avoided – which probably would be best from the viewpoint of participatory development. When agency programme managers or other agency employees visit, no special arrangements should be made by project staff. Project staff should avoid making special arrangements for external visitors, unless perhaps for government dignitaries if this is expected. Nor should they instruct or request villagers to make such arrangements. They should, however, in every case inform the people as to who is coming and why they are coming. It is, after all, their village. If the villagers wish to make special arrangements for receiving visitors, this should be accepted. Discussions can be held in an attempt to meet the needs and wishes of all parties concerned.

In many areas white visitors, including agency staff, create special problems, the biggest of which is raising expectations. White people are rich, and it takes a great deal of awareness and self-assurance for poor people not to expect benefits as a result of a visit. This type of thinking perpetuates dependency relationships and weakens the people's evolving self-reliance. If at all possible, white people should keep out of project areas until the people have built-up self-confidence in their own abilities to change their situation.

Profile

Foreign agencies and donors seem to suffer from the schizophrenic personality of the munificent do-gooder righteously indignant at the inefficient utilisation of his money, and the liberal who is trying to atone for the collective miseries that his ancestors inflicted upon an unwary people. Along with the few who are genuinely concerned are many more, arrogant about their superior knowledge and skills, all set to transform the world in their image.

As important is the pressure of being in business. Charity and development are part of a market activity, and a rather big one at that. These markets, like all others, require constant nourishment, so that with their expansion the importance of the aid-giver grows. The neo-colonial impulse that permeates through this business has not even been discussed. (Sethi, 1983)

The biggest problem for a foreign aid agency is to maintain an image of solidarity with the poor. The biggest handicap is the relatively easy availability of money, not only for vehicles, offices and housing but also project funds. It is essential to maintain a low profile. Although this is difficult, it can be done; it is a question of attitude on the part of staff members, especially expatriates and home office personnel.

Harsh Sethi goes on to argue that many worthwhile local projects have been ruined as a result of easy availability of foreign funds. He goes so far as to welcome greater restrictions on foreign aid to local NGOs unless the aid is earmarked to support the change agents. This negative viewpoint is not based on moral objection to aid, as such, but to his feeling that aid, particularly in the form of funds, 'represents an easy way out'. He feels that aid 'reduces the need and, therefore the effort, towards self-reliant solutions and, in the long run, there is no short cut to social transformations.'

In this work you have to constantly fight your enemies, and the greatest enemy is yourself.

Change agent (quoted by Rahman, 1983a)

6.   Getting Started

We cannot work with all of the poor. Therefore, we must work in those areas where we have the greatest opportunity of substantially and inexpensively improving the poor people's situation. (Bunch, 1982)

Questions relating to the selection of programme countries are outside the scope of this book. Within programme countries experience has shown that initial suggestions for new projects and project areas come from many different sources. In this book we are concerned with self-reliant participatory development processes, and are therefore less interested in the selection of a new 'project', but rather a new 'programme area', i.e. an area which is considered suitable for the initiation of such processes.

'A project is an artificial construct which does not express the local reality or the daily struggle of the rural people.' This conclusion was reached by the participants who attended the Second International FFHC/AD Consultation held at FAO, Rome in 1983. The conference was attended by representatives of donor agencies from 11 countries and representatives of local NGOs from 19 developing countries. The theme of the consultation was 'What sort of support can be given by non-governmental organisations to people's organisations in the rural areas of the Third World?'

The consultation concluded that projects with their predetermined objectives, time plans and budgets, have all too often been the main link in the chain of dependency and divisiveness stretching from local communities, through local and international NGOs to donor governments via co-financing arrangements. Projects fail to recognise development as a process – a process that can only be sustained by people's genuine participation in their own development. It was recommended that NGOs and donor governments support programmes and processes rather than projects even though proportionally more funds would, as a result, be directed into 'software' and administrative expenditures such as educational and training activities as well as local salaries and support expenditures.

It is not possible, nor useful, to set up absolute, objective criteria for the selection of programme areas. The selection will in many ways be subjective in the sense that non-quantifiable factors will play a role in the selection process. However, it is necessary to evaluate a number of important considerations first. The following questions should be answered satisfactorily before making a final decision:

1. Is self-reliant participatory development work in the area approved by the national and local authorities?

2. Is the population in the area large enough to warrant a sustained intervention? Is there a relatively high proportion of poor and under-privileged within this population? This evaluation can be based on a rapid appraisal of the general standard of basic needs (food, shelter, water, sanitation, land, employment, health and educational services), physical quality of life (infant mortality, life expectancy, adult literacy) as well as income levels.

3. Do the poor and underprivileged genuinely wish assistance, would they welcome an outside intervention, and are they prepared to work for their own development? These questions, can only be satisfactorily answered after 6–12 months of living and working with the people. But, if the answers are negative, the intervention should be terminated.

4. Is there a reasonably good chance of promoting the emergence of a long-term, self-sustaining development process by the poor within a reasonable time-frame (say 10 years)? Are there resource bases for such a development process? Are there appropriate technologies available with which the people can utilise the resource bases? Is the area reasonably accessible? Will local and national markets be able to absorb increased production?

5. If the above questions can be answered affirmatively, is the agency willing and able to commit itself in terms of time and financial resources to a long-term sustained commitment to this particular programme area and the poor people living there?

Although in this book we are primarily concerned with rural development, the principles of self-reliant participatory development are applicable to the improvement of urban slum communities, the selection of which is primarily a political question to be resolved through discussions with local authorities.

Preparatory Studies

> Please tell your workers to come and work here quietly first for six months. Only then will we consider talking to them.
>
> *Sri Lankan peasant* (quoted by Bhasin, 1979)

Unfortunately, this is exactly what development agencies do not do. The traditional, almost obligatory, approach is to send in a team of researchers, often from the university or perhaps a consultancy firm, and sometimes even a team with a strong representation of white, European development experts from various disciplines. An expert on women in development is obligatory these days, and the social anthropologist is becoming a required fixture. All this is well and good, and certainly an improvement over the days when such teams were composed almost entirely of male technical specialists (engineers, agricultural specialists and economists).

These teams stay maybe a month, sometimes two. They hire interpreters and university students or young graduates who can speak the local language. They bring with them their well-tested questionnaires. They move around in their

Land Rovers. If they stay in the area overnight, they usually stay with the well-to-do, the elite. They collect their data and they retire to their offices. They tabulate and analyse their data, and write reports and proposals.

But where were the people in all of this? They were invaded, occupied, assaulted with questions, no explanations, no discussions. Everything filtered through the local elites, the interpreters, the urban university middle-class, the expatriates, and sometimes even the computer. The poor knew the team had 'parachuted' into their area, but the team most likely never even talked with the really poor and disadvantaged because the poor live up on the hillsides, down in the ravines, away from the roads, are away working, are sick, are invisible.

What was the purpose of this exercise? It certainly didn't involve the poor in their own development. It almost certainly didn't provide an in-depth understanding of their situation. It most certainly established an image. An image of powerful outsiders – outsiders who at best will come back and make things better for them, at worst come back and work with the elites to make their situation even worse.

The development literature is full of cases in which projects either failed or produced untoward results because of a lack of knowledge about the programme area. Roland Bunch (1982) tells of three such typical cases:

> In Afghanistan, a project failed to convince farmers to castrate their bulls even though the farmers knew it would make their animals easier to handle. The problem was that castration of younger animals would also inhibit growth of the hump on which the animals' yoke rested. Had project leaders been aware of the problem, they might have saved the project simply by introducing a different yoke.

> In Kenya production of pyrethrum actually dropped because of a major effort designed to boost production by organising village men into marketing co-ops. Project organisers simply had not realised that village women, who grew most of the crop, would cut production once their profits were diverted to the men's co-operatives.

> And in Bolivia, one project introduced a very productive variety of corn (maize) that, being too hard to grind, was best suited for making bootleg alcohol – a fact that escaped the attention of the project leaders, but not of the villagers.

Bunch goes on to suggest that probably no amount of professional information-gathering in Afghanistan would ever have made the connection between castration and the shape of an ox-yoke. Nor was it likely that any multi-disciplinary team of development specialists would have predicted that the corn varieties introduced into Bolivia would be used for making bootleg alcohol. Nevertheless, Afghan farmers could easily have told project leaders why they refused to castrate their animals, and Bolivian farmers knew soon after the first harvest of the new corn that a lot of it would be going into whisky.

The problem facing the rural poor form a complex network of social, political, economic, technical and ecological issues. No group of outsiders is going to be able to understand within a short period of time the real problems facing the poor, not even with increasingly sophisticated, complex and multi-disciplinary analyses. The real professionals and experts on the problems of the poor are the poor themselves. And the solutions must arise from an understanding by the poor of their own situations and of their own possibilities of improving these situations with or without outside assistance.

The six-month project

Listen to the Sri Lankan peasant cited at the beginning of this section. Value for money, it might be the best investment you could make for the success of your programme. Let four or five of your staff, experienced change agents, live in the programme area for a period of six months with the objective of learning, together with the people, as much about the area and its inhabitants as possible. Let them work in teams of two or three. Let them live among the people. Let them sit down once a week and discuss their findings with each other, and once a month with programme officers. No sign-boards, no buildings, no vehicles. Allocate just enough funds to pay salaries, living expenses and travel on public transport.

During this time together with the rural people, the change agents should carry out participatory action research, as described in Chapter 3, on the following questions as well as others that they develop in the course of their investigations:

1. What resources are available in the area? Who controls the use of these resources? How is this control distributed?
2. How do people make their living in the area? What are the various types of productive activities? What are the various forms of agricultural production for self-consumption and for commercial sale? What are the constraints on production?
3. Who are the poor and disadvantaged in the area? What do the poor themselves see as the causes of their poverty? What are the other causes of their poverty? What restraints are hindering their development?
4. Who are the advantaged in the area? Why are they advantaged? What is the degree of economic and social homogeneity? What internal divisions are there in the communities? What are these divisions based upon?
5. What dependency relationships exist between the poor and others? Is there exploitation of the poor? What forms does exploitation take? What is the degree of exploitation?
6. In what ways are the interests of the various socio-economic groups similar? In what ways are they opposed to each other? Which of these contradictions are mutually antagonistic and which are non-antagonistic?
7. What natural factors, such as water, soil conditions and erosion, are causes of poverty and hindrances to development? Have these conditions worsened during the past 20 years? If so, why? What is the potential for improvement?

8. What is the pattern of social conditions among the poor, e.g. disease, nutritional status, literacy, hygiene and sanitation? What are the causes of the unsatisfactory conditions? Which factors are primary causes of continued poverty?

9. What are the cultural and religious beliefs and practices of the people? Are these shared by everyone? Which of these benefit the poor? Which are detrimental? Why?

10. Which governmental services and programmes are operative in the area? Who are they available to and who is taking advantage of them? What other local and external organisations are active in the area? Who is benefiting, and how, from their programmes?

All of the above questions should be investigated with the people through discussions with individuals, families and small groups. Such discussions should be held with all socio-economic groups, but especially the poor. Discussions should also be held with officials, teachers and medical personnel as well as with other external agents such as bank officials and co-operative officials.

Through internal discussions, comparisons of findings, writing and revising notes, the change agents will gradually build up a comprehensive picture of the local situation. This broad picture will form the basis of their developing understanding of the condition of the poor in the programme area.

One final question then needs to be investigated. What is the response of the poor in the selected area to the presence of the change agents? Do they want the change agents to continue living and working with them? If the answers are favourable and the results of the six-month investigation are encouraging, then a long-term programme commitment can be made.

Baseline data surveys

Through the participatory action research process we have collected an enormous amount of reliable information – checked and re-checked with the people. Much of this information will be quantifiable, but most will be qualitative. For purposes of project evaluation and funding you may need some basic quantifiable data.

In order to make quantifiable evaluations of developmental progress, there is a need for broad-based, statistically reliable data. Quite often such data is required by funding agencies prior to making a commitment as well as subsequently for continued funding. The problem of course is not only how to collect reliable data, but also how to do this in a way that does not increase dependency thinking and which promotes self-reliant participatory development.

The data collected informally through dialogue can to some extent be used for this purpose. However, it may be necessary to carry out more formal and systematic surveys. These baseline data surveys should not be carried out during the early phases of the preparatory studies, but only after an adequate period of participatory action research. Mutual trust and understanding is essential for good results. One of the outcomes of the initial period of participatory action research should be an awakening interest among the poor to learn more about their own society. This interest can be utilised in carrying out any baseline data surveys.

Although we are primarily interested in improving the economic situation of the poor, it is often extremely difficult to collect reliable data relating to production and income. This is true not only because people are reluctant to provide such information, but also reliable measurements are very difficult to make. However, useful measurements can be made of those factors that either reflect the effects of poverty or contribute to continued poverty. In this respect such factors as health conditions, nutrition, births and deaths, basic education, potable water, sanitation and housing can be used as measurements of poverty and of progress.

The people, especially educated youths, should be used not only to collect such data, but also to prepare the surveys, to process the data and to analyse the results. This in itself is an important part of the educational process. The first step is to reach a broad understanding among the people as to why such a survey can be useful for them. Once there is a general consensus for the survey, then discussions can be held as to what should be measured and how, questions can be formulated, and the procedure for carrying out the survey decided upon. Finally, after the data is collected and processed, the people should also participate in the analysis, discuss conclusions and relate these to the improvement of their situation.

Marja-Liisa Swantz (1982) has described one attempt at using the participatory research approach in a study of low-income working women in Tanzania who were participating in a literacy programme. This example illustrates how the informant's own self-awareness can be strengthened.

The questionnaires used for the study were written in such a way that use was made of them also as a teaching device. The women exercised their newly learned skills by reading out loud the questions, one by one. The meaning of them was discussed with the women and those who were able wrote down their own answers. The process was slow, but contained a great potential for creating a greater awareness of the women's own life situation. For an illiterate woman to examine herself with the help of questions that she thus had a chance to pose to herself, meant a beginning of a new thinking process. It meant becoming conscious of things that the women had so far taken for granted. Questions were significant even when they concerned only her age, place of birth, family composition and her place in it, her income, her possibilities for advancement, her living conditions, transport, children's care, etc. They opened up new questions: The 'what' questions began to turn into questions of 'why', 'what for', 'what else' and 'what more'.

Preparatory studies, if they are to be useful and also promote the development process, must be participatory and be carried out over a substantial length of time – a minimum of six months. The initial period of the participatory action research process will normally create awareness among the poor leading to a process of conscientisation which generates action and development activities based on their own understanding of their needs, problems and potentials. This, rather than the traditional baseline data questionnaire, will provide a true basis for development.

Planning and Proposals

> Projects are not ends in themselves but a means to strengthen rural people's capacity to organise effectively.
>
> *First International FAO–FFHC/AD Consultation*

In recent years many government development agencies and most private agencies have considered rural development as an answer to the increasing poverty of rural populations and to the limited success that the modernisation models of development had in reaching and helping the rural poor. Rural development was to be attained through carefully planned projects: community development projects, IRDPs (integrated rural development projects), health projects and literacy projects. A new model for rural development projects based on statistically reliable base-data studies, detailed project plans and budgets, and elaborate project proposals became mandatory in order to obtain home office approval and funding. All of these studies, plans and proposals were compiled and developed by professionals sitting in offices far away from the rural poor's daily situation.

This present standard model of preparing project plans and proposals is coming under increasing criticism by experienced researchers and executives. Ronald Léger (1984), former Director of the International NGO Division, CIDA, Canada, maintains that rural development project failures seem to be related to the planning methods used by donor agencies and their local intermediaries. Among donors, the trend has been to use the classical blueprint approach to planning: a frame of reference for implementation based on rapid diagnosis through feasibility studies followed by a master plan usually more rigid than flexible.

This approach enabled the rapid initiation of many high-profile projects. Such projects were attractive to both donor agencies and recipient countries because they were supported by supposedly reliable cost-benefit analyses for quantified inputs and outputs. Léger has pointed out, however, that this master plan approach has three methodological implications which almost inevitably result in failure:

1. The project has a limited lifespan (most commonly three to five years) necessitating readily attainable quantitative objectives that do not always respect the rate of evolution of the development environment;
2. Final choices on types of intervention, technological models and activities involved in a project are made on the basis of available factual data that are static and make no allowance for socio-cultural variables; and

3. The implementation phase must follow a predetermined project design (master plan) based on assumptions concerning environmental behaviour that often prove to be incorrect.

Léger questions the basic assumptions of the classical approach to project planning and implementation and calls for a total rethinking of rural development strategies. Such a re-examination must be based on the realisation that rural development is a process in which rigid and conventional planning has serious limitations. Léger maintains that practical experience has, in fact, shown that success has often been the result of respecting a more natural rural development process in which the following six principles have been interwoven:

1. Rural development cannot be based on classical planning methods that assume a planning–implementation dichotomy;
2. Implementation must not be the application of a ready-made plan, since planning, execution and evaluation is a process of on-going interaction that permits flexible technological adaption and facilitates participation at all levels by the target groups;
3. The complexity of the environment requires an analysis and a detailed dynamic comprehension of the ecological, human, political, economic and institutional variables affected;
4. The complexity and slow pace of the environment's evolution requires that, from the outset, the intervention take place in a restricted geographical area over an extended time horizon of from 10 to 20 years (growth-generating and incremental-planning approaches);
5. The participation of target groups in the implementation and evaluation of activities must depend on their increased participation in the on-going design of the project (which is not the same as mere consultation after the options have already been decided); and
6. The comprehensive mobilisation of the population requires support from all the local structures (NGOs, private sectors, peasants' movements) in order to foster self-development and a better balance of resources and power both between the local people and government officials and among the different categories of the target groups (capacity-building approach).

These principles are in obvious agreement with the principles and methodologies of participatory action research and self-reliant participatory development. They are neither new nor revolutionary. However, if they are to be put into practice, donor agencies and recipient countries (in the case of bilateral programmes) will need to change their basic planning, funding and operational policies. Léger asserts that these policy changes will need to accommodate the following considerations:

1. A participatory action research effort in the selected area for at least a six-month period requires financing without specific project plans nor firm commitments.
2. Participatory planning, which is essentially incremental, requires financing of initially vague 'programmes' which are not conducive to economic and financial analysis and which necessitate a firm commitment for at least 10 years.

3. Participatory programmes do not have an initial clear-cut profile. Donors must therefore be willing to finance a process rather than a clearly defined project.
4. Participatory processes, which place paramount importance on the participation and organisation of the rural poor, require a special type of change agent and a redefinition of the dialogue process between the poor, agency officials and local government officials. Donor agencies and recipient country governments, in particular, must acknowledge and accept the political possibilities of resource transfer and control to organisations of the poor.

Unfortunately, very few international agencies have hitherto had the courage or conviction to alter their policies as a result of Léger's increasingly accepted conclusion that 'rural development is not compatible with classical planning approaches, which often lead to rigid intervention and leave little room for peasant initiatives and gradual adaption to change.'

We have earlier discussed development as a process occurring over time, its direction and speed determined by unpredictable interactions between many conflicting interests. It is therefore not surprising that a predetermined project design or master plan rigidly followed will usually not produce the expected results.

Accepting that a master plan is not only undesirable, but also counter-productive, what type of programme plan would be appropriate? The plan for a self-reliant participatory development programme should reflect the fact that we are dealing with a process. Therefore emphasis should be given to describing the general framework for this process. It is a question of the methodology being of more importance than the project activities. Inasmuch as it is the people who, over time, give priority to and implement various development activities, these activities cannot be pre-planned by others. Kamla Bhasin (1982) has clearly stated the implications of this process:

> If the people themselves are to participate in formulating 'projects', then organisation of the people will have to precede formulation of projects. We will have to start work not by formulating projects such as a health clinic, water system, etc. but by getting to know the people, establishing good rapport with them, analysing with them their situation and problems, and discussing what needs to be done and how. Our efforts should be to help people form their own organisations, and obtain the necessary knowledge and skill to initiate a process of development. Projects should be means towards people's development and strengthening of people's organisations and not ends in themselves.

It therefore becomes not only difficult, but also undesirable, to try to give specifics in such a programme plan. One can give a general time frame indicating a hoped for evolution of the programme, e.g. after one year small producer groups begin working together, after three years producer groups begin forming associations. But an attempt to set specific targets or goals, e.g.

20 producer groups within 18 months, would be self-defeating. One can also specify likely areas of activity to be taken up by different groups of people, such as market gardening or rice milling, but one cannot say that 15 rice mills will be purchased and in operation within 12 months. The area of operation can be specified as well as a general plan of expansion into surrounding areas, but it would be unwise to set up a plan specifying, for example, villages X, Y and Z this year expanding to villages A to H next year.

Such a vague programme plan does not, of course, appeal very much to project approval boards, home office programme coordinators or to funding agencies, especially government funding agencies with their bureaucratic rules and regulations for granting funds. It is not easy for those who must make their decisions far removed from the villages and the people to approve a plan which in essence merely states that we intend to work along these lines in district X for at least 10 years hoping to assist 12,000 families to improve their situation; and for this we need about a million dollars. It might be easier to accept a general plan based on principles and methodologies of work, than to approve a general 10-year budget. But this is what we must do, we must 'sell' a methodology rather than a list of pre-planned buildings, input purchases, teaching plans, pills and pumps.

Far more important than a programme plan, for the success of a development intervention, is the quality of the change agents and the methodology of self-reliant participatory development. No amount of blueprints and master plans will change this fact. Untimately, it is the people themselves who must produce results, and this requires a belief in the people's own capabilities comparable to that of President Julius Nyerere of Tanzania:

> At every stage of development people do know what their basic needs are. And just as they will produce their own food if they have land, so if they have sufficient freedom they can be relied upon to determine their own priorities of development and then to work for them.

Unfortunately, these sentiments are more easily expressed than implemented as President Nyerere must by now be painfully aware.

Budgeting and funding

> In people-based development budgeting becomes a very significant area: the whole question of how to get away from the bureaucratic need to spend. In fact the pace of disbursements should be determined by the beneficiaries. It is critical to begin to allow much more flexibilty and to experiment in this area, without being hit over the head by the controllers. (Hollnsteiner, 1978)

As established in the previous section, rigid project plans can be detrimental to the participatory development process. Traditionally, detailed project budgets have been prepared in conjunction with such project plans. In recent years there has been an increasingly active debate regarding the appropriateness of traditional budgeting procedures.

Dutch governmental and non-governmental development officials have concluded (SID, GRIS Notes, 1984) that on the question of project budgeting and funding, development assistance should be directed to those agencies and organisations which are able to promote processes of mobilisation, conscientisation and group formation. Conventional project financing is too limited in scope, of too short duration, and inhibits the flexibility of operation. A *process approach* is required.

The Dutch recognised that effective grassroots level development action requires donor agencies to relinquish some of their decision-making prerogatives to organisations of the poor. The choice of sectors to be involved in the programme, the type of actions to be undertaken, the speed of implementation of activities, the form of the people's organisation and similar decisions will be subject to the people's own priorities.

It was pointed out, however, that such a flexible approach often contradicts the conventional bureaucratic procedures because the bureaucratic process needs to allocate staff, equipment and funds according to a plan made long in advance. Rational allocation of resources requires long-term as well as annual decisions about exact amounts to be disbursed as well as specification of the purposes for which money will be disbursed. Financial accountability requires sophisticated controls, careful adherence to budgetary procedure, predictable cash-flows and so forth. Activities must not lead to further activities so as to avoid pre-emptive planning and loss of administrative control. Large capital-intensive projects are therefore preferred over long-term participatory programmes requiring relatively low levels of funding.

Moreover, agencies often expect projects to be easily replicable. In the case of participatory projects, no easy answer is possible, since spontaneity, conviction, commitment, identity and confidence cannot be duplicated in a pre-planned manner. For a similar reason the normal evaluation procedure according to general criteria of factors such as output and efficiency cannot be applied; instead, evaluations must be viewed as an on-going process of self-evaluation in which the main actors play the dominant role and are the subjects rather than merely the objects of the process.

All of this indicates an urgent need to revise policies and procedures in order to eliminate bureaucratic hindrances to financing a genuinely participatory development process. New policies and procedures must ensure flexibility as well as long-term commitment. Within the framework of an approved total budget for the project over its expected lifetime, flexible annual budgets can be prepared. These can contain detailed budgets for staffing, travel and other support activities. Detailed budgets can also be prepared for on-going project activities as well as new activities which have been identified and planned by the participant groups. Ample leeway must be provided for reserves for unspecified activities which are expected to arise as a result of the participatory process in the financial year.

Field administrators are often subject to considerable pressure from agency managers to keep down administrative expenses. These, unfortunately, are too often defined as salaries and travel expenses. However, participatory development requires a willingness to support people rather than things such as buildings, equipment, supplies and materials.

The American agency World Neighbors has been practicing self-reliant participatory approaches in its development assistance work in Latin America, Asia and Africa for many years. They assert that the so-called administrative expenses in a well-designed project can be as high as 80–90%. Within this salaries will tend to take up the lion's share – from about 40 to 65% of the total, even when salary levels remain modest and half the programme's work is done by volunteers. Transportation will often take another 35% of the budget although this will vary widely according to the local situation. Programmes that avoid give-aways and use truly appropriate technology seldom spend much money on agricultural inputs or equipment. Except for revolving loan funds, outlays for inputs and equipment should usually represent less than 10% of the total budget. Efficient programmes also tend to spend little on offices or buildings.

These percentages must, of course, be seen as general guidelines. What they do indicate is a need to turn conventional thinking about programme budgets upside down. Too much funding, especially for material inputs and equipment, can destroy an otherwise excellent programme. Over-zealous funding agencies must learn to respond to the real needs of the poor rather than to their own needs. Within limits, less expensive programmes in terms of expenditures per participant can be expected to create more self-sufficiency and more permanent results than more expensive ones.

The key to proper budgeting of self-reliant participatory programmes is flexibility. Within the general budgetary framework, field administrators should be authorised to over- or under-spend on individual budget items within previously agreed limits. Funders must not only be willing to accept such flexibility, but also be willing to fund personnel support rather than capital investments and material inputs. They must also be willing to commit themselves to longer funding periods than the typical three-year project framework.

Programme size and expansion

> Like a stream which takes the shape of the area and terrain through which it flows, new programmes will have to be flexible enough to respond to the special needs and character of the people and areas where they are being implemented. (Bhasin, 1982)

It has been emphasised many times now that self-reliant participatory development is a process, and should be seen more as a development programme rather than as a project. Questions of size and expansion must therefore be seen somewhat differently than when considering traditional projects. If we think of the growth of a crystal, then perhaps the process will be more easily understood. A crystal forms in a saturated solution when a few molecules attach themselves to a small foreign particle introduced into the solution. More and more molecules attach themselves to these molecules and the crystal begins to expand. It continues to grow in all directions until there are no more free-floating molecules available.

A self-reliant participatory development process evolves in the same manner: starting from the work of a few change agents, small groups of villagers come together and begin development activities. Others come and join these groups or establish groups of their own. Word spreads and individuals or groups come from other villages and then return to form new groups. The crystal grows by itself once the process gets started. Md. Anisur Rahman (1984a), on the basis of his extensive field research, describes this process:

> Such participatory processes get replicated spontaneously as has happened in most of the areas in the cases under review. There is no better stimulant to self-mobilisation of disadvantaged and oppressed people than the concrete demonstration of people like themselves standing up as human beings through self-mobilisation.

A rural woman in Zimbabwe interviewed by Partridge (1983) has described the same process in terms of her own experience:

> This area is changing a lot. There is much better communication between people in the area. People from far away even get together to discuss things, and so the ideas and the projects spread. When people from other villages saw us building the school here at Nyundo, they began to think they could also do that for their children. Then they came here to learn how it was done and get ideas. And as a result the people in the area are becoming one. And the children are beginning to behave differently because of this 'getting together'. It's taught them to respect each other and to respect other people.
>
> *Mrs Annah Dhambi*, chairperson of
> the Nyundo Womens Club, Mandoro, Zimbabwe

It is important to remember that the crystal began from one tiny speck. Two or three change agents starting in one village are the equivalent to the speck. Of course, within a fairly large area, several teams of change agents can be working simultaneously. It cannot be emphasised too much that it is necessary to begin with a very small intervention.

Roland Bunch (1982) provides a number of logical arguments for 'the importance of starting small'. He points out that large programmes tend to be inflexible because too much money has been invested in training, equipment and employees. Reputations are at stake. 'Large programmes run the risk of being poured in concrete before the wrinkles are worked out. They wind up either living with the wrinkles for a long time or spending a lot of extra time and money to smooth out hardened concrete.'

Small programmes, however, can evolve as time and experience expose better ways of working. Mistakes are less expensive and more easily corrected.

Less credibility is lost in the process. Small programmes also allow for and encourage more participation. The people and their leaders can provide feedback as well as participate in decision-making. Management is learned by doing, and the people gradually grow in sophistication as the programme grows in complexity.

In the words of Bunch, 'Large programmes necessarily involve large sums of money. Thus they run the constant danger of being powered by the "force of money" rather than the "force of conviction".' All the vehicles, equipment and offices attract people for the wrong reasons. Genuine feedback and honest opinions disappear because employees and the people wish to stay on good terms with the programme managers who disperse the funds. There is a tendency to speed things up by using more money. Allowances and incentives are paid to increase participation; salaries are inflated to attract employees not drawn to the programme for better reasons. Finally, large amounts of easily available money encourage corruption at all levels: 'It is not the agencies' money, but the people's enthusiasm that must be the driving force behind development.'

I once was chatting with a few staff members at a development project when a group of villagers came up and started discussing something with the project administrator. After the villagers left I asked, 'What was that about?' The administrator replied that they were villagers from across the river who wanted a loan to buy fertilizer. He then said, 'But I told them we couldn't help them because they're not part of our project.'

A genuinely self-reliant participatory programme need not be limited in size. As original groups become more and more self-reliant, change agents can turn their attention to working with groups from adjacent areas. Members of existing groups will often assist new groups to organise themselves and start their own activities. As the programme expands and gains strength, additional funding can be partly generated internally and partly acquired from established credit sources. This type of unlimited growth should be encouraged, and staff and funding should be made available to nurture it. After all, the primary aim of development assistance is to encourage self-sustained growth. It would indeed be foolish to stop support for a successful programme because we had originally only budgeted for a certain number of families in certain specified villages or because our time frame of, say, five years has expired. Questions of programme size and expansion must, like plans and budgets, be approached with openness and flexibility.

Programme Monitoring

Monitoring, in contrast to evaluation, denotes activities such as maintaining continual feedback from programme participants and carrying out simple surveys during the course of a programme, and have as their primary aim the improvement of the programme's effectiveness. The key to effective monitoring is participation. Participants should be encouraged to monitor their own activities as well as those of the programme and its staff. Monitoring is an integral part of the analysis–action–reflection process.

Reliable monitoring requires a considerable degree of openness and mutual trust. Without genuine trust, feedback will not be candid. Trust cannot be imposed or bought; it must be built up gradually by sympathetic project staff working closely with the people and sharing their problems and hardships. Without such an intimate partnership, poor people will be inclined to maintain a 'conspiracy of courtesy' in which people avoid criticism and unpleasantness. At worst, they may maintain their silence through fear of reprisal. In such cases, the participants may well know of waste, corruption, poor performance and misguided initiative long before programme administrators find out. Roland Bunch cites a case in which some 500 members of a 6,000-member cooperative in Latin America were so upset by an administrative decision that they considered withdrawing from the co-op en masse. Two weeks later, when this widely discussed problem was mentioned to the co-op's manager, he was completely taken aback. No one had said a word to him about the problem.

The first defence against such lapses of communication or abuses of position is regular contact between participants, change agents and programme managers. Everyone involved must be encouraged to discuss their own failures as well as those of others in an atmosphere promoting improvement rather than punishment. Positive use of criticism and self-criticism are a central element in such contact. Workshops as well as informal discussions are instruments in this process. Although additional information and viewpoints can be gathered from other organisations and individuals working in the area, ultimately:

Good feedback will best be achieved when the villagers find out that they can openly criticise the programme without giving rise to bad feelings or repercussions, and that their suggestions will be acted upon. Programmes that put a high value on the villagers' opinions, take criticism well and make decisions accordingly, will receive the best feedback from the villagers. (Bunch, 1982)

7. Working With People

If you put trust in people they start becoming responsible for their thought and action. When the people feel that they have the freedom to think, act and relate to each other, they take on a lot of responsibility.

Vasant Palshikar, Indian activist

One of the major causes of poverty is the economic and mental dependence of the poor on others who are more wealthy and more powerful. The powerful are able to play the poor off against each other. The poor family feels isolated and impotent.

Poor people know they are poor, sick, etc., but often they do not want to confront the situation. Many of them think the problems they face are their individual problems and they can do nothing to change the situation. By getting the people to look at their problems collectively we help them see the commonality of their problems and to understand the structures which are oppressing them.

Khushi Kabir, Nijera Kori worker, Bangladesh

Through the methodology of participatory action research the poor can gain an understanding of their situation and the causes of their poverty. This understanding can lead to an awakening process, or conscientisation. This new-found consciousness can bring the poor together in order to improve their situation. The poor family is like a twig; alone, it is easily broken. But if the individual twigs are gathered into a bundle, they cannot be broken.

It is difficult for the poor to break away from the vicious circle of dependence and poverty individually. It is only through collective effort and organisation that they can reduce dependence and initiate a course of participatory, self-reliant development. Thus participation implies mobilisation, conscientisation and organisation – in that order.

(Wignaraja, 1984b)

The most important instrument in the self-reliant participatory development process is the small group of poor men and/or women who have a common interest in working together to individually and collectively improve their lives. In every part of the world there are examples of small groups of people, sometimes allied in larger associations, who have been able to change their lives for the better through their group action. This is what the development process is all about. The importance of group formation for rural development was underlined in the Declaration of Principles and Programme of Action of the World Conference on Agrarian Reform and Rural Development. *The Peasant's Charter* states:

> Encourage people's organisations providing various economic, social and cultural services to develop self-reliance at the community level and assist them in such ways as meeting legal and financial requirements, training leaders and other initial needs exercising care that their independence is not compromised.

This chapter is about working with groups of poor people. This should be the major activity of change agents. Their success will depend on their understanding of group dynamics and their aptitude for working with people. Their success will be proved when the people say, 'We have done it ourselves!'

> We shall organise, and it shall be our organisation, not yours. But let us not name the baby before it kicks.
>
> *Indian peasant* (quoted by Rahman, 1981)

The Dialogical Method

> Kalu was a bonded laborer. He had borrowed Rs.650/- six years back. In return, against a minimum wage of Rs.3/- per day, he was paid a daily wage of only one rupee. He paid Rs.4380/- over 6 years as principal plus interest on this loan! The quantum, the method, the form of exploitation; who the exploiter was; the process of gradual weakening – were all 'discovered' during discussions at the group meeting.
>
> *Notes from a Shibir* (in PIDA, 1984 by Harsh Sethi)

The objective of group work is to awaken in each member of the group a better understanding of themselves and of the realities of their situation. We want the group to learn to critically analyse: Where are we? Where do we want to go? What must we do to get there? What is keeping us back? What can we do to overcome these obstacles? By learning to answer these questions, the group can proceed to planning and implementing activities to improve their lives. This has apparently been well understood by the peasant leaders of the Bhoomi Sena movement who have stated it as follows:

> An outsider who comes with ready-made solutions and advice is worse than useless. He must first understand from us what our questions are, and help us to articulate the questions better, and then help us to find solutions.

Many experts probably feel uncomfortable with such a theory. By using participatory rhetoric and approaches, such experts hope for the people's active support for their projects; but it is clear that the projects are their own rather than the people's. The principal tool used to promote such a process of conscientisation is the dialogical method: talking *with* people, and not *to* them. A dialogue is a conversation in which there is an open and frank interchange and discussion of ideas. In a dialogue all parties are free to ask questions and provide answers and insights. A dialogue implies equality between the participants.

Discussion should begin with the real experiences of the group. The theme chosen should relate to the work the people are doing or the life they are leading. Discussion can begin by each participant in turn telling the group about an aspect of the theme in terms of his or her own experience and feelings. Some participants will talk freely while others will at first find it very difficult to say more than a few sentences. But nobody should be passed over; each one should be encouraged to speak, and the group should wait patiently. Only if the silent waiting of the group is seen to disturb a very shy participant should he or she be passed over.

In the course of these first rounds of discussion, the participants will begin to sense the difference, begin to be attentive and to respect the other participants. During these preliminary narrations common elements will begin to stand out. The discussion can continue by identifying these common elements and the group picking one out as the starting point. Invariably, patience on the part of the change agent will pay rich dividends. By giving each participant time to lose his or her shyness and fear of speaking, the change agent can show that he or she is genuine about participation.

The change agent's role is to ask questions in order to carry the discussion and analysis forward, to draw people to talk and to think, and to provide information which may not come out of the group. A great deal of patience is required as some participants may narrate things which the change agent does not think are directly relevant to what is being discussed. One must remember that these details might be relevant to the person who is narrating them and they should not be dismissed out of hand.

Kamla Bhasin (1980b) warns change agents 'not to try to predetermine the results of their dialogue with the people'. This is an easy trap to fall into, and it cannot be emphasised enough that it is the people who should decide what they want to learn. Bhasin suggests that 'for change agents it should be enough to facilitate free and open discussion and provide a systematic method of analysis.'

The group has to be encouraged to see the underlying causes of what they are investigating. They should learn to identify and understand the inter-relationships existing within the village as well as with factors outside the village. In addition they must come to understand the method of analysis which is being used so that they can analyse other relationships on their own. Through case studies based on the group's own experiences, one can discuss almost any economic, political or social issue. The best way of involving people in learning is to begin with specific situations about which they know something so that they can contribute to the discussion. Group work can begin by defining the reality in which the group lives. Questions like the following may help in directing discussions towards this under- standing:

- What is your village? What defines it? What is a village?
- Why do people live here? How do people make their living?
- How did the village come into existence? How was land distributed? How is land distributed today? What changes have taken place? Why?
- What is grown on the land? Why? What do the inputs cost? Where are they bought? Where is credit available? What does it cost?
- What are the yields? To whom are they sold? When are they sold? For how much? How much is stored for later use/sale?
- What else is produced in the village? By whom? Who gets the profits?
- Who is sick? What is wrong with them? Why are they sick? What do they do when they are sick? Why?
- Who goes to school? Why do they go to school? Why don't others go to school? What do they learn? How do they use what they learn?

The participants should begin to look at their own village historically and analytically. They will begin to reflect upon the village as a system and a structure. In response to the probing question, they begin to think, to make connections, to understand some concepts. Through this type of dialogue, fundamental questions like the relationship of man to nature, the origin and history of their society, the distribution of the means of production, can be raised in a manner such that they are live and relevant questions. In the beginning most of the questions will come from the change agent and it is on these questions that the participants will reflect. Ideally, the questions should come increasingly from the participants themselves. The change agent must encourage this.

In these first discussions of the village, its structure, and how it functions as a system the change agent plays a very active role, but it must be played within the framework established by the questions and answers – flowing along with the answers given by the group at each step. A lecture by the change agent entitled 'the village and its structure' would be quite differently organised. It would be more comprehensive, more academic and probably would impress the group as very learned. But the group would not have learned very much from it – they would either forget what was said or merely parrot the ideas presented in the lecture.

By being involved in a dialogue instead of passively listening to a lecture, the group builds up an analytical understanding of their own village based on their own observations. It is unlikely that they will forget what was discussed. Their understanding will be based on awareness rather than an acceptance of someone else's explanations. They have started developing the skills needed to handle analysis on their own. They will gradually become confident of their own powers of thinking and their ability to speak out. They will not allow other people to lecture them as though they were children. They will not feel inferior to people posing as their superiors.

This method, however, requires that the change agent is honest and open; otherwise this dialogical method becomes a subtle technique used to bring others to accept one's own predetermined conclusions. This would undermine the entire process. The change agent must have a natural and complete respect for others, a willingness to explore together in interaction. Change agents accept the experiences of others and build, on the basis of these experiences, an understanding of truth together with the others.

The great advantage of the participatory method is not only that the group has a better understanding of their reality, but that any action decided upon will be based on considerations of this understanding of reality, the perceptions of the people themselves, their immediate needs and problems rather than on preconceived theories and dogma. When actions are decided upon by the participants out of their own understanding of their situation, then there is a genuine unity of theory and action which can lead to a further round of reflection and action starting a self-sustaining process.

Kamla Bhasin (1980a) has summarised the role of the change agent in the dialogical process:

> The task of the change agent is to help people reach their own conclusions and not necessarily always the conclusions of the change agent. By working and struggling together the consciousness of the change agents and the people should change and reach higher levels. A change agent helps in starting a process of thinking, reflection and action.

Unfortunately, the dialogical method which is at the core of self-reliant partipatory development is difficult to grasp from a written explanation such as this. It needs to be experienced to be properly understood. Likewise, it is difficult to learn through a training course. It can be learned through watching experienced practitioners working with people's groups, and polished and improved through one's own experience.

What is an Interest Group?

This might sound like a question with an obvious answer, but in reality there is a good deal of confusion in many people's minds as this relates to development work. In the context of self-reliant participatory development we are referring to any group of any size composed of men and/or women who have come together to pursue a common interest related to individual or group improvement in the spheres of economic, political and/or social development. Only in very special circumstances will such groups be based on community-wide membership.

The crucial factor in group membership is that each member perceives some direct or indirect benefit to himself/herself or to his/her family. The concept of 'for the common good' is relevant only when the individual member sees himself/herself as part of that communality. The group may have formed to pursue one specific interest, such as group support in the case of death in a member's family (social), the building of a school (social), the purchase of digging hoes (economic/individual) or an ox-plough (economic/group), or the registration of land rights (political). Most likely the group will have a series of goals all aimed at improving the standard and quality of life of the group's members.

One special type of interest group which needs closer analysis is the producer group or investment group. Many observers automatically assume that such groups are involved solely in collective production or investment. This is not so. In the context of self-reliant participatory development it would be more appropriate to speak of a group of producers or investors. Although each member of the group may be pursuing individual production or investment activities, membership in the group can still provide benefits, such as collective purchase of agricultural inputs at wholesale prices, investment loans from group funds, access to external credit and marketing assistance. Such group support is the classic objective of independent cooperative societies which in Europe have become major factors in national economic and political spheres.

Most rural producer/investor groups will operate along these lines of collective assistance to the individual producer. However, some groups will also perceive advantages to be gained through collective ownership or production. A group might purchase an ox-plough or insecticide sprayer for use by the members in turn. A group might begin collective brick-making. A group of women might gain access to one parcel of land and decide to farm it collectively, or they might re-parcel it to individual members. In practice, few rural economic activities are easily amenable to collective ownership/management, but this in no way lessens the advantages of group support to individual enterprise.

How Groups Are Formed

One of the most critical elements in group process work is the formation of the group itself. The process starts when a number of individuals are motivated to form a group and agree to undertake concerted or collective activity which will further their interests. Here individual interest is enmeshed with group interest. Agreement on the formation of a group is a big leap forward. Formation of a group thus signifies a change from a state of resignation to a state of awakening. A process of self-awareness has already begun.

(Hossain, 1982)

Throughout the Third World countless interest groups are continually being established – either spontaneously or through the intervention of governments and private agencies. Most Third World governments take an active role in the formation of cooperative societies, women's groups and village development councils. Churches and development agencies, both local and international, are continually exhorting people to form groups.

However, the vast majority of these groups fail to improve the living conditions of their members. They either disintegrate, become passive recipients of external assistance, or deteriorate into mere social meeting points. The reasons for these failures usually lie in the failure of the organisers, as well as the members, to analyse the factors that precondition group success. The following sections attempt such an analysis. This analysis must be repeated by change agents with every group with which they are working. Ultimately, however, each group must make their own decisions relating to each of the factors.

Motivation

The first principle of group formation is that the poor must be motivated to come together to work for their own common good. This motivation must not be imposed from outside. If it is, the group will fail. Many agencies organise people into groups in order to carry out activities which the agency has decided are for the good of the people. This will not lead to a viable people's organisation.

Antoine A. Fayossewo (1978), FAO–FFHC/AD Programme Officer in West Africa, has correctly drawn attention to the critical difference between motivational work intended as a means of making people do something, as contrasted with creating awareness and conviction. The former is 'doomed sooner or later to fail' while the latter can lead to promising advances 'in the areas of nonformal education, participatory research and projects dealing with production, consumption and distribution'.

The poor must see that coming together to work in small groups is not only to their own advantage, but also leads to increased solidarity and strengthens the poor as a group. They quickly become aware of these benefits once they have broken the barriers of mistrust and mental dependency. They then become motivated to work together for mutual advancement.

Voluntary membership

Voluntary membership is the second key principle of group formation. No one should be forced to join a group against their own wishes. Membership will not be in the interest of either the group or the individual unless there is individual motivation to join the group. Members of groups must have the right to resign their membership at any time. Of course, there will be peer pressure on individuals to join groups, but this must be conceived by the individual as a positive pressure.

On the other hand, groups must have the right to accept or reject new members as they wish. A group that is forced to accept unwanted members will seldom develop the necessary trust and cohesiveness needed to succeed.

Common interest

The third principle of group formation is that the members must share a common interest. This will normally be a result of the motivation of the individual members for coming together to form a group. Groups composed of members with dissimilar occupations, such as poor farmers and poor fishermen, will often find themselves pulling in different directions unless there is some other over-riding problem which needs to be solved before they can pursue their interests as farmers and fishermen. Normally, producers and traders will have opposing interests. Groups composed of both would probably be dominated by the traders at the expense of the producers.

The poor must discover and decide upon these questions of common interest and working together. Even men and women in the same families will often have highly divergent interests and needs. Although the decision rests with the groups themselves, change agents should ensure that these questions are debated.

Case Study 2 – The importance of common interest

Kwo-Lonyo Women's Group and Nyakagai Fishing and Farming Group are both located in Nyakagai Parish in northwestern Uganda. Kwo-Lonyo (Life is Wealth) Group is composed of 16 mostly middle-aged and married women who depend almost entirely on petty commodity marketing, predominantly fish and farm produce. These women have many things in common, including type of business, life-style and associated problems. On the other hand, the Nyakagai Group consists of 19 men who differ in many ways: some are poor fishermen, some farmers and some traders. Some members are opinion leaders and locally elected officials.

Kwo-Lonyo emerged from real common interest and with a purpose, while the Nyakagai Group emerged with a lot of dependency thinking and without class and occupational differences being considered to be a potential area of conflict. Kwo-Lonyo's clear objectives are carrying out collective ventures, assisting each other in trade and other issues, and learning handicraft skills from each other. Nyakagai has instead objectives geared towards both fishing and farming. These objectives are not being pursued because some members have hidden motives and do not really trust each other. The only binding objective was the opportunity to buy, from an aid agency, subsidised fishnets which the group could then re-sell on the open market at considerable personal profit.

After two years Kwo-Lonyo has built up a group fund of Uganda shillings 85,000 in member deposits and Shs 170,000 in net worth. This net worth was built up mostly from interest on loans to individual members to finance their petty trade. The group was lending out over Shs 200,000 per month. The financial position of Nyakagai, however, is difficult to establish because the treasurer has his own method of keeping the books, which he doesn't share with others.

The open book-keeping procedures followed by Kwo-Lonyo, coupled with the counting of actual cash at group meetings, have created trust among the members. As for Nyakagai, which was formed earlier, the accounts are not entirely open and often do not correspond with the actual cash on hand.

Neither group has yet paid out a dividend, but some members of Nyakagai are insisting that a dividend be calculated so that they can get their share and quit the group. Most of the members have lost trust in the group. The leadership is resistant to change and is dominated by the richer and more influential members. Only the leaders can call the group to a meeting. Some of the members want to leave in order to form a more effective group; others who are less serious want to get out because no quick gains have been realised.

The major advantage of the Kwo-Lonyo Group which makes it grow ever stronger than its male counterpart is the close personal relationship based on trust and common interest. This has made it possibe for the women to assist each other even on personal matters. They rotate the leadership every year. In the Nyakagai Group the men mistrust each other because of the class differences and their historical experiences. Many of the members operate from more than one place; they are used to the dishonest methods of the official cooperatives; and it is impossible to replace the leaders all of whom are opinion leaders in the area.

In conclusion, these two groups illustrate that a group is more likely to survive and prosper if it has emerged out of common interest, has a uniform composition, clear objectives and no destructive hidden agendas, and a leadership which is flexible and feels itself equal to the other members,

Compiled by *Ongiertho J. Emmanuel*, change agent, Jonam, Uganda

---

Composition

If you have big and small fish together in a pond, the big fish will not let the small get any feed. If you want the small fish to develop, you have to take out the big fish from the pond.

Indian farmer (quoted by Bhasin, 1979)

The composition of a group is an important factor in determining the success or failure of the group in promoting development activities for its members. Success will be largely dependent on the group's ability to function as a unit. Each member must be willing to subordinate personal interests to those of the group as a whole. Individual ambitions must not be pursued at the expense of collective gain.

Experience has shown that even groups apparently as similar as landless agricultural labourers, and marginal and small farmers have in reality divergent interests which make cooperation difficult during the early phases of organising for group action. Hossain (1982) reports that mixed groups of marginal and landless peasants in Bangladesh decided through experience to form separate homogeneous groups, landless and marginal, Rahman (1985a), also working in Bangladesh, recorded the following statement from a landless leader:

> This village had earlier a joint organisation of landless and small farmers in which the leadership was dominated by small farmers. The result was that the interests of the landless were neglected, and there were also cases of misappropriation of funds controlled by the small farmers. As a consequence the organisation broke up, and the landless formed their own separate organisation.

Rahman discovered, however, that these same landless peasants were now willing to consider opening membership to those among the small farmers who were really poor as long as the management of the organisation remained in the hands of the landless.

Normally, groups will be most effective when they have a large degree of homogeneity, especially in terms of socio-economic status, although other locally determined cultural factors such as caste, age and religion may also play a role in determining group cohesion. No given rules can be established. Here again it must be the groups themselves who determine the composition of their membership. The change agent's role is to ensure that the question is thoroughly debated within the group.

Case Study No. 3 – Nok Cibo Acaye Group

The name Nok Cibo Acaye means 'Being few, we are despised'. This is because most of the members and the initiators of the group are people from Zaire who fled the civil war in the early 1960s. The group has 11 members of whom eight are men and three are women. There are two elderly couples and six young men; the wife of one man is also a member. The young men are poor fishermen. The young wife earns income from the sale of cooked food and from brewing local beer. The elderly couples are poor peasants. Only four of the members are native to the locality; the others are immigrants.

One of the group's objectives is to raise capital through regular monthly savings deposits from the members and by lending this money to members at interest. These loans are to enable members to carry out viable economic activities. The interest earned from the loans is invested in group ventures.

Each member is supposed to deposit Shs 300 every month, but over time the deposits have become irregular and the total amount saved is only half of what it should be. In the past two years 70 loans have been issued out of which only eight have defaulted. However, these defaults have all occurred recently. This resulted when most of the young members began to lose interest in the group.

The group has invested in a plank boat worth Shs 31,000. It is rented out to fishermen on a daily basis. The average income is Shs 500 per day. The boat presents a management problem for the group. The supervisor claims some fish as a reward for his work, but some members feel he should volunteer his work as is being done by a member of a neighbouring group. Records of earnings is another problem as witnesses always raise doubts about what is recorded at meetings. These situations have lessened the trust that earlier existed among the members.

Despite the accounts book being open to all members, book-keeping presents a problem as the treasurer, who is illiterate, continually questions the book-keeper and a majority of the members still fail to understand the balance sheets. This too has become an area of mistrust.

The mistrust arising from the membership composition and the management problems often pull the group towards collapse. The Zairean members are not sure how long they will stay in the area; two of the original members have already left. The differing age structure causes problems as the youth want to reap immediate material benefits. The youth lack respect for the older members, but are unable to openly challenge what they see as wrong decisions. This results in planning and management problems. However, the older members show more interest in group activities as indicated by their greater savings efforts and prompt repayment of loans.

Most likely this group will dissolve and one or more new ones emerge according to interests, age groups and possibly national origins. This is happening already as some of the younger members are applying to join groups of their own origins.

Compiled by *Sebi Ali Ubanjagiu*, change agent, Jonam, Uganda

---

Size

Membership of a group is an important part of the self-development of the poor. If the exercise is to have a positive effect, then each member must have the opportunity of expressing himself/herself in discussions, of experiencing that his or her thoughts and opinions are important and are listened to, of learning to share responsibility and to take responsibility, of trusting and being trusted. The poor often adopt strategies of keeping quiet, staying in the background, of protecting themselves by remaining passive. Their participation in a group should increase their self-confidence and assertiveness.

The size of the group, especially during the early phases of group awakening, must be small enough so that each member can directly participate in the discussions and the decision-making. Large groups will be dominated by those who already have some degree of self-confidence. On the other hand, the group must not be so small that it is ineffective. A certain minimum 'mass' is required for effective group action and mutual support.

There is no universal answer to the question of group size. The FAO *Small Farmers Development Manual* emphasises the importance of group size especially in relation to decision-making and the sharing of responsibilities and benefits. Based on several years' experience in Nepal, it maintains that 15 to 20 members is an optimum size. Experience elsewhere indicates that groups of less than 10 are unviable, and that groups of more than 25 quickly become unparticipatory. In any case, each group must be given the opportunity to discover this for itself. The change agent can encourage reflection on this matter by posing appropriate questions to the group.

As we shall see later, large numbers of poor people sharing the same interests and concerns can organise themselves in small groups which can then eventually join together to form an association to increase their effectiveness.

Autonomy

The next important principle of group formation is that the group must be autonomous: it must have total sovereignty in making decisions regarding the composition of the membership, the size of the group, objectives and bye-laws, leadership, finances and activities. This is perhaps the most difficult principle to put into practice.

Change agents, through their experience of working with other groups, will have strong opinions about group size, composition and other questions of group organisation. However, these opinions must not be imposed on the group. Not only does each group have the right to make these decisions itself, but the exercise is also a valuable learning experience for them. Making these decisions is often one of the first steps in the development of feelings of self-worth and independence.

In many countries of the Third World, groups are forced to register as official primary cooperative societies if they are to obtain official recognition and credit. In most cases this means a loss of their autonomy, as questions relating to size and membership, bye-laws, dividends and loans must first be approved by the cooperative officers, often by the commissioner in the far-away capital city. Experience has shown that these official cooperatives seldom serve the real interests of the members and are easily manipulated by the elite and outsiders.

Objectives and bye-laws

Successful groups are almost always those which have taken the time to discuss and decide upon their objectives and the rules and regulations, or bye-laws, by which the group will operate. Change agents should assist groups to identify those objectives which will contribute to the unity of the group and which are achievable in the foreseeable future. New groups in their initial enthusiasm tend to make long lists of unrealistic objectives.

It is difficult, however, for new groups to establish bye-laws which anticipate all the problems the group may encounter. It is therefore important that they agree on procedures for changing the bye-laws as needed. The bye-laws should establish guidelines for membership, leadership and decision-making, meetings, membership fees and savings deposits, loans to members, payment of dividends and benefits.

Many new groups establish elaborate systems of fines for lateness, absence from meetings, disrespect and even drunkenness at meetings. These fines usually prove to be counter-productive as they create dissension and disunity because they are a negative form of motivation. In addition, they don't work because they are difficult to collect. It is, however, also difficult to convince people in advance of these problems. Change agents should assist groups to analyse these problems when they arise. Ultimately, groups must have a procedure for expelling members when necessary.

Groups often fail to anticipate the need for rules relating to the departure of a member from the group, either voluntarily or not. Obviously, such departing members are entitled to the return of their savings deposits. But what about fees and a share of the profits or net worth? Such problems do not have fixed solutions and depend a lot on how the group is earning its profits. However, change agents must encourage groups to discuss these problems before they arise otherwise arguments easily develop.

Leadership and decision-making

> What is people's power? Is it the power of our leaders? What if they deviate? We want to keep our power in our own hands, and keep it alive so that no one can ever fool us.
>
> *Member,* Bhoomi Sena Movement, India (quoted by Wignaraja, 1981)

Two of the most important questions relating to the formation and operation of small producer groups are the questions of leadership and decision-making. Unless a group can find satisfactory answers for these questions, it will fail. Western forms of organisational leadership, in which the united membership elects by majority vote a steering committee with officers (chairman, vice-chairman, secretary and treasurer), are now widespread throughout most of the Third World. National voluntary organisations, especially those with international affiliations, all have these forms as well as a constitution and bye-laws. Even remote village organisations have elected officers.

However, such organisations are usually dominated by the rural or urban elites who fill all the official positions. Such offices have become positions of prestige and power – power all too often abused. Poor people know all too well how these positions have been monopolised by the elite and used to channel benefits to themselves and their nearest family and supporters. Petty corruption in traditionally structured organisations is, unfortunately, rampant.

One of the primary purposes of the participatory approach is the development of the self-confidence and abilities of each participant. This cannot be done if a few dominate the leadership. Each small group must decide how it is going to organise itself, whether to have specific leaders and officers as in the traditional model, or whether to rotate leadership among the membership. The role of the change agent is to ensure that all aspects of the leadership question are discussed by the group. It can be suggested, and rather strongly, that leadership roles be rotated frequently during the first year so that all members can gain experience. If groups insist on having a permanent chairperson they can be encouraged to have a different discussion leader for each meeting.

Observation has shown that those groups which know of the traditional model, but have little experience with it, may choose to elect leaders because of the prestige implied to their organisation by this model. Others with greater experience of the abuses arising from the traditional model often choose not to have elected leaders.

Many traditional societies have no mechanisms for changing leadership if the leaders prove to be incompetent or corrupt. It becomes too embarrassing, too provocative, to change. These organisations generally become impotent as the members become passive and disillusioned. Their confidence in organisations becomes even weaker, and the participatory process dissolves. No leaders at all would have been more suitable.

> We have realised the need to unite and solve problems together. We have learnt the importance of participation in decision-making and problem-solving. We have now a sense of responsibility and discipline. There has been a change in our outlook. We now value meetings and we rush to meetings.
>
> *Filipino farmer* (quoted by Rahman, 1983b)

Decision-making in most organisations is carried out by majority vote after open debate – the majority rules. Those who are on the losing side are expected to follow loyally the majority – the loyal opposition. This means, however, that one segment of members will always be in disagreement with the decision.

Small groups of poor people must live their lives in very close proximity to each other. They cannot afford the luxury of the 'polite' factional dissensions that majority decision-making produces. They need to stay united if they are to attain their objectives. The need for harmony in their daily relationships will often cause them to vote along with those few who take strong standpoints on particular issues.

Decision-making by consensus, i.e. continuing discussions until a decision is found that is acceptable to all group members, will normally better preserve harmony and unity within the group. This type of decision-making also better promotes participation by everyone as it is expected that each member voice his opinion. Decisions cannot be reached until everyone has agreed that they can accept the solution proposed.

Consensus decision-making takes considerably longer than majority voting, but the greater strength and unity achieved make consensus more viable in the long run. For the poor, with their all too few options, this becomes all-important. Most small groups will use a consensus approach. Change agents must learn not only to be patient with the approach, but also to encourage it. The process of reaching a consensus is an important part of the conscientisation process.

Sometimes when it proves impossible to reach a consensus, and often for very good reasons, the group may decide that a particular decision does not need to apply to all members. Those members who wish to can remain on the side-lines and join again when they are in a better position to follow-up. Poor people are sensitive to differences in capacities and abilities: it is not uncommon for groups to set lower membership fees for the poorest members of their groups.

Meetings

> Previously we were individualistic, now we have a spirit of solidarity. We now meet anywhere, anytime. We have become talkative.
>
> *Filipino farmer* (quoted by Rahman, 1983b)

The group meeting is the key event in the participatory approach and in the life of the group. The frequency of group meetings must be decided by the group. Initially, the presence of the change agent will be essential for the process of conscientisation, and the change agent will need to assist in the scheduling of meetings. This should not be done in an authoritarian manner: 'I will be coming on Thursday evening, and I want you all to meet at Pedro's house at 7 o'clock.' A suggestive approach should be taken: 'I need to plan my visits to the other village groups, can you please tell me when you will be meeting next week,' or 'I will be coming this way next Thursday – if you would like me to meet with you, please let me know when and where.' After a while, the presence of the change agent will become less of a necessity, and it is desirable for the groups to meet increasingly on their own.

Groups will normally meet about once every two weeks. Once groups have been functioning for some time, their meetings will probably become more irregular and more spontaneous – when the need arises. If a group is meeting less than once a month, then something is seriously wrong. Because of their work situations, most members will only be able to meet in the evenings although this will be dependent upon the locality, the primary occupations of the members (fishermen will often meet during the day when they are resting), the season of the year, etc. Women and migrant labourers will have more difficulty in scheduling their meetings. If members are spread out over a large area meetings can be held in conjunction with market days or festivals.

Groups can meet anywhere convenient for the members, usually at someone's home or a favourite outdoor place of assembly. Schools, churches or temples, community halls can be used although in many cases the poor will not yet have access to these places. Let the members decide; they will normally choose a place where they all feel comfortable and can be themselves. Meetings at the change agent's house or the project office, if there still is one, should be discouraged. It is important that each group establishes an independent identity.

A meeting at someone's home normally ensures the necessary degree of informality desirable for participatory processes. Seating should be informal, preferably in a circle so that everyone is facing each other. Try to discourage the tendency to seat officers and visitors on chairs in front of the rest of the group. The change agent should join in the circle as an equal member of the group. Visitors should be prompted in advance to play the same role. It is essential that the group develops a feeling of its own importance: that it is not inferior or lower than others. When a group of poor people openly, but politely, ask visitors why they have come and what do they want, you can be fairly sure that they have developed healthy feelings of their own worth.

In the previous section decision-making by consensus was discussed. Each member's participation is not only essential for his or her own development, but also for building a genuine unity of purpose. The change agent should, especially in the early stages, try to bring everyone into the discussions. But even more important is helping the group to understand this need, and to establish appropriate practices which ensure participation of everyone at all times.

No one should be permitted to dominate the meetings. Groups must be assisted in establishing strong sanctions against such individuals. This can best be done through the practice of criticism and self-criticism by all of the members. The change agent can here be an example in terms both of staying as much in the background as possible and in openly discussing personal shortcomings. Tensions within the group must be brought to the surface: if left to smoulder they will eventually destroy the group.

The most difficult task for the change agent is staying in the background, learning the delicate art of only intervening with a question or recounting his or her experience when the group has temporarily lost its dynamism or is stymied by a problem outside its field of knowledge. It takes a patient, gentle hand to allow the group to develop from within, finding its own direction and speed. It also takes a very enlightened organisation to give sufficient trust to the change agents to carry on according to their own judgments.

Group meetings are the most important fora for the development of group consciousness. But as Oakley and Marsden (1984) discovered during their analysis of participatory programmes, such group meetings do not normally follow conventional rules and practices, nor do the groups develop in accordance with conventional group dynamics theory.

Women's groups

Yes, I've changed. I can move about anywhere, with no fear of anything. I feel like a new person, free to do what I feel like doing. I feel new because I'm doing something I never thought I could do: I'm going to school. Now my husband can understand my coming to school, which could have been a problem in the past. I can act without consulting my husband. Long back, men believed it was wrong for women to go to work. But through this 'working together', gathering together and discussing things, many men have changed. Men can look at the poultry project and the dress-making project and see something practical and progressive which they never thought we could do.

Mrs. Bless Magandanga, mother of seven
children, Zimbabwe (quoted by Partridge, 1983)

As discussed in Chapter 3, women are a particularly oppressed group within the Third World. In that same chapter the crucial importance of the participation of women in development was discussed. Similar observations led the World Conference on Agricultural Reform and Rural Development to single out the role of women's groups in development and to challenge all development agencies to promote collective action and organisation by rural women to facilitate their participation in the full range of public services and to enhance their opportunities to participate in economic, political and social activities on an equal footing with men.

In a previous section we considered the advantages of groups having a relatively homogeneous membership. Although this was primarily related to the questions of occupational and socio-economic status, these same considerations apply in nearly all societies to women as a separate interest group.

> Just imagine how it hurts to suffer working on land which doesn't belong to me, and all the money I get from growing things is taken by my husband.
> *Woman in Zimbabwe* (quoted in *Ideas and Action*, No. 158, FAO, 1984)

As pointed out by Oakley and Marsden (1984) women in rural areas face a layer of structural and cultural constraints which restrict and bias their participation. Joint organisations of poor men and women will usually be dominated by the men who are either unwilling or unable to appreciate 'the female-specific nature of many of the problems that women face, or of the different networks in which they interact, which produce a very different, but seldom appreciated, set of needs and interests.' The result will be a failure to give priority to these needs and interests.

Not only are women's interests and needs different from the men's, but their freedom to participate on an equal footing with men is often seriously hampered by social and cultural traditions. Rahman (1985a) asked members of a poor women's organisation in a village in Bangladesh whether they would consider merging their group with that of their men-folk. The reply was that in a joint organisation many women members would not even be able to speak at meetings because women are not supposed to speak in the presence of their *bhashurs* (elder brothers or husband). Although this represents a very specific prohibition, women in most societies have been conditioned from childhood to remain passive in the presence of men.

Nijera Kori, an NGO in Bangladesh which originally only worked with women and now also works with poor rural men, continues to organise separate groups of women and men at the village level because they believe that in mixed groups the special interests and issues of women are not adequately dealt with, nor are women able to assert themselves and develop their leadership potential.

This approach is sometimes criticised by those who maintain that it not only isolates women, but also weakens the organisation of the rural poor by fragmenting the poor in separate groups. Nijera Kori attacks this problem by encouraging the formation of joint committees to plan together work on common issues. They maintain that encouraging women to organise separately in large numbers, and giving them opportunities to develop their understanding, consciousness and leadership, strengthens rather than weakens the organisation of the poor.

General opinion seems to favour separate women's groups, but these should be encouraged to collaborate with organisations of poor men to promote common interests. Normally, the women themselves should decide whether to form separate groups, but it is important to ensure that their decision is as free as possible from pressure from their men.

Case Study No. 4 – Can Ocuka Women's Group
Translated literally, Can Ocuka means 'poverty has forced me'. This name reflects not only the gender of its members (women), but also the constraints of the area in which they live. There are 16 members; the average age is 40; all but one is married although four are either divorced or widowed. The group has been together for three years.

Their home area along the Nile in northern Uganda has poor soils and irregular rainfall coming in two short seasons. As a result of these conditions fishing is the main occupation of the men, and fish processing and marketing that of the women.

The group started as a savings group; originally each member saved Shs 100 per month which has now risen to Shs 500. Average savings are now Shs 20,000 per member. Very early on the group established an internal loan fund for members. Each member is now borrowing Shs 10,000 every two months at 25% interest (Shs 2,000). The loans are used by the members to buy fish for resale or to buy supplies for preparing foodstuffs or local beer for selling at the fishing landings. The group assets now total Shs 750,000.

Apart from its loan programme, the group has embarked on joint investments. It has financed the construction of a fishing boat which is rented out bringing the group a daily income. It has bought a cow and its calf and three oxen and an ox-plough for use on members' fields as well as for hiring out. It has borrowed money to buy a donkey which is being used to carry water, firewood and sand for building purposes. It is saving to buy a donkey cart. Realising that women suffer most from deforestation, it has set up its own seedling nursery. It has also started bulk purchasing of household equipment for sale to members at cost price.

It has distributed dividends to members at the end of the past two years. The size of the dividend is based on each member's savings deposits. These dividends have been as high as Shs 9,500 for the pioneer members of the group.

Book-keeping has been a problem because almost all of the members are illiterate. The group secretary also keeps the group's accounts, but the money is held by the treasurer who is highly trusted by the group and who remembers the monthly transactions in her head. Trust is a binding force within the group.

The Can Ocuka Group has solved the problems of male resistance to their right to attend meetings and to property ownership. Other women are responding to the innovations pioneered by Can Ocuka, and they are becoming a challenge to the men in the area to do likewise.

Compiled by *Catherine Awor*, change agent, Jonam, Uganda

Group Activities

Inevitably at some time during the process of participation some kind of economic activity will be undertaken by the group. Either such activities are used as the means to creating assets and greater economic strength in order to allow the group more effectively to participate in development, or such activities are used as the means to stimulate group involvement, solidarity and the development of the capacity of the group to take action. Whatever the ultimate purpose of the activities, they do play a central role in the process of participation. (Oakley and Marsden, 1984)

The need 'to do something' is central to the existence of the group. A group will lose all reason to exist unless it directs its attentions within a reasonable time to some type of collective social or economic activity, or to collective assistance to individual members. Unless members realise a tangible personal benefit within a reasonable time, they will leave the group or become inactive. Groups consisting of the poor must eventually improve the economic situation of their members otherwise they cannot be sustained. Normally, economic activities will be the first priority of the poor.

However, timing is extremely important. Initiating a collective activity too early can be just as disastrous as waiting too long. There must be a minimum of group cohesion and mutual trust as well as a collective consciousness able to address the realities with which the group is struggling. Unless the members have an understanding of the situation and the causes of their poverty, they will risk demoralising failure if they pursue ambitious activities too soon.

It is absolutely essential that the group chooses which activities it will pursue.

Members must set their own priorities. This choice must be based on their own analysis of their reality. They must identify their problems, analyse causes and investigate possible solutions, and choose their own course of action.

If their analysis has been correct and if they do not expect that the agency supporting the change agents is going to supply them with their needs, then most groups will usually decide first to establish a group fund through some form of collective saving or from the profits of group labour. No matter how small the individual contributions are to such a fund, they should be encouraged. The group fund becomes the starting point for many types of activities and its value in promoting self-reliance and participation must not be underestimated. Rather than keeping these funds under a mattress where they are idle and may be stolen, many groups set up an internal loan fund for members. The interest from these loans helps the group fund to grow more rapidly.

In the early phases of group development it is important that the activities chosen encourage participation and strengthen the group. Even poor people are sophisticated enough to realise that these apparently secondary goals are fundamental in determining the long-term success of the group. This aspect of the choice of activities should be discussed openly as part of the preparatory process to action. Participation and group strength are therefore primary goals of initial activities.

Oakley and Marsden (1984) have formulated, on the basis of extensive studies of participatory organisations, a set of principles which can be useful in selecting and implementing group activities so that these are consciously related to the strengthening of the process of participation:

(a) *involvement*: the group as a whole must be involved in the basic aspects of project formulation, decision-making and implementation, and the whole operational base of the project must be organised with this principle in mind;

(b) *minimise dependence*: every effort must be made to minimise the dependence of the activity, either in material or human terms, on assistance from outside, otherwise group autonomy will never be achieved;

(c) *sustainability*: the activity must be able to be sustained in the context of locally available resources. It must represent an initiative which can be taken up by the group itself and further developed. In other words, it must not be beyond the capabilities of the group;

(d) *next step*: similarly the activity must represent, technologically, the next step forward for the group, and not be a technological advance which is beyond the natural development of the group;

(e) *effective as opposed to efficient*: it may be necessary in the short term to forego our slavish adherence to the economic principle of efficiency, and undertake economic activities which are an effective use of resources and can bring about some economic advance, although this may not represent the most efficient use of those resources.

Although recognising that the above principles cannot be used as a universally applicable model, Oakley and Marsden emphasise that group activities, if they are to develop the group's ability to participate as a collective unit over time, cannot be undertaken in a purely mechanical way. Each group should not only consider questions of practicality and viability when choosing their activities, but should also reflect upon how the activity can best serve to strengthen self-reliance and participation.

Women

> Women need to earn money because most of the expenses at home have to be met by them. When a man gets money, he spends it on beer or girl friends.
> *Woman in Zimbabwe* (quoted in *Ideas and Action*, No. 158, FAO, 1984)

Poor women will usually give priority to income-generating activities, either new activities or improvements in the productivity and profit-earning capacity of existing activities. Poor women have tremendous demands on their time, and they will be interested in labour-saving innovations. Concerns such as health, nutrition and sanitation can be related to reducing expenditures and improving productivity. Unfortunately, there are still too many programmes for women's groups which promote traditional 'middle-class' activities. Fayossewo (1978) insists that, 'It cannot be said too often that the little patchwork of activities made up of sewing classes, needlecraft, weighing babies and the like can no longer be considered the fundamental elements of a programme to motivate rural women.'

One of the most successful organisations working with women's groups is the Self-Employed Women's Association (SEWA) in India. Maitrayee Mukhopadhyay reports that over the past decade SEWA has become an effective trade union involving women in the unorganised sector: vendors, collectors, dealers, garment workers. SEWA bargains for and represents its members in matters relating to trades and occupations. It has established a women's bank to provide credit and savings facilities, lack of capital being the primary constraint on all women's trade groups. The women's bank also helps with procurement of materials, tools and equipment, and provides training and technical assistance on problems of production, marketing and management.

In addition to economic issues, women's groups may give priority to social issues directly affecting their own specifically female concerns such as desertion, wife beating, and other forms of sexual harassment. Some Nijera Kori groups in Bangladesh have protested against obscene cabaret-type dances which have become part of some village entertainment and which, the women feel, excite men to be sexually aggressive.

The Self-Employed Women's Association has also developed social security and welfare benefit schemes for its members which include maternity, health, widowhood, and death benefit schemes as well as childcare facilities and literacy programmes. SEWA has also had to contend with the existing Indian labour laws in order to gain recognition for self-employed women. Although SEWA has several thousand members, every member belongs to a small group of 20 to 30 women. Leaders are elected up to a board of representatives.

Working with women's groups can be very rewarding. They often have a greater degree of solidarity than men. They are used to listening to others and they are used to cooperating to get things done. Once mobilised, they often demonstrate impressive degrees of courage and persistence.

The role of the change agent

> If an outsider tries to initiate a project on a participatory basis, he or she has to acknowledge that it is not his or her project. He or she is only a companion trying to help establish a grassroots group; he or she must avoid developing a paternalistic relationship towards the people.
>
> *Heinz Moser* (quoted by Rahman, 1981)

It is absolutely essential for the change agent to ensure that the group makes its own decisions as to what it wants to do, when it wants to do it, and how it will do it. The change agent can contribute to these decisions by entering into a genuine dialogue with the group, making suggestions, asking questions, drawing ideas and reflections out of the participants, directing attention to those suggestions which seem to have greater potential for realisation, posing problems and difficulties.

A second important role is that of ensuring that the group makes its decisions on the basis of a thorough analysis of the problems, possible alternatives, probable complications, and available resources. A skilful probing with questions will generate active discussion on the part of every member, and avoid impulsive decisions on the part of the group as a whole. The change agent's questioning and critical suggestions may lead to a reconsideration of former decisions.

However, the decisions must be taken by the participants themselves. Making decisions, even wrong ones, from the very beginning of the group's life is essential for establishing a continuing self-reliant development process. By taking decisions themselves, the participants will discover in themselves reserves of creativity and insight which will encourage them to act, and stimulate them to confront new problems.

In the early stages of group development change agents are often the only link to the outside world. The change agent has access to both theoretical and practical knowledge which can be useful for the group. The change agent knows the institutions and programmes that the group can approach for additional information, training and knowledge. The change agent can point the group in the direction of outside financing and other resources which may be available to them.

The change agent should, of course, willingly share his or her technical knowledge and skills with the group, but with regards to bringing in external assistance the change agent should refrain from taking the primary role. It is an essential part of the group's learning experience to approach these external agencies as much as possible on its own or, if necessary, accompanied by the change agent. The change agent must ensure that the group receives adequate training in the technical and management skills (purchasing, banking, book-keeping, marketing) necessary for implementing successfully their chosen activity.

Income-generating activities

When assisting groups to initiate income-generating activities, change agents and their agencies have a tendency to think primarily in terms of group-owned and managed activities. In reality such activities are difficult for a group to manage especially if they require daily supervision such as a poultry project, pig-rearing or a village shop. In practice, either the supervision breaks down, or someone is tempted to steal, or a few members take on all the responsibility and often resent having to share the profits with others. How many women's groups have been encouraged to start group-managed poultry projects, and how many have been successful?

However, there are certain income-generating activities that can be successfully carried out by groups. A group of 10 young men in southern Uganda have successfully established a brick-making group. After three years the group has assets of over Shs 500,000 and each member is earning about Shs 20,000 per month from the project. This has been successful because the work requires cooperation, and each member is paid according to the work he does. Another group, 12 Muslim women in northern Uganda, sent one of the members to Kampala to invest the group funds in bags of imported, used clothing. The group sold about half the items on the open market and the rest at discount prices to members. They made about 200% profit. Another group of better-off peasant farmers had access to a hired tractor and invested their savings in timber trading. Each member has benefited through dividends based on each member's savings deposits.

It is difficult for change agents and their agencies to assist individual investors. Income-generating activities are best promoted within the framework of a small group of like-minded investors/producers. But how does an individual producer benefit from group membership if the group as a whole is not managing the income-generating activity?

One way is for the group to pool its funds, send a member to the nearest major market centre, and buy inputs such as hoes, fertilisers, insecticides and acaricides at wholesale prices on behalf of the members. Another way is to hire transport and sell its production as a group closer to the final market at higher prices. One trading license in one person's name (or the group's) may suffice for the entire group. Purchasing group assets to be shared by individual members is another way, such as a sprayer, plough, ox-cart and eventually a storage building or a pick-up truck. Of course, group assets require management rules, but these can be worked out and supervised by the group.

Another important way in which an individual producer can benefit from the group is by borrowing investment capital from the group fund. Of course, these credit funds operate best when the members have an opportunity of making a profit on a regular basis, such as trading, selling fish, eggs, beer or charcoal. Obviously, it is much more difficult for crop farmers who must wait until harvest time, but it is still feasible.

Another advantage of promoting individually operated income-generating activities through small groups is the need for moral and psychological support for the individual producer. It is difficult to struggle alone. The support and encouragement of friends and colleagues is of great importance. Standing up to the exploitation of a middleman who is cheating on weights, quality judgements or prices can only be done by a group or groups working together. New skills and new knowledge can be shared within a group, and the group can more easily call upon the services of extension workers and development workers. Groups can also more easily gain official recognition, if this is considered important or useful. The intangible benefits of greater self-confidence, awareness and determination can best be developed in the group context.

Therefore, one of the first questions that a group must ask itself is whether it is going to initiate a group investment activity or individual member investments, or both. This will depend on an analysis of the types of investments proposed and whether they are best managed by the group as a whole or by individual members.

Identifying investment opportunities

Without a doubt the most difficult task for change agents is helping groups to identify viable investment opportunities within the context of a poor and isolated environment. If this was an easy task, then poverty would not be the problem that it is. Poor people and poor countries have little capital and limited markets. This means that everyone ends up producing the same labour-intensive goods for the same cash-strapped market. The resulting profit margins are extremely low. This means that groups must often try to find new or better products or services.

There are two major routes to greater profits and hence greater income. Either *increase the productivity* of what you are now doing, or *diversify your production* into new areas of production, commerce or service. Increasing productivity is usually the easiest (assuming that markets are not saturated), and involves increasing your production without increasing unit costs, or maintaining your present production at less cost. To do this requires either new and more efficient/effective skills (e.g. mulching), techniques (e.g. ox-ploughing), inputs (e.g. hybrid seeds), assets (e.g. storage facilities) or a combination of several of these. The problem, of course, is learning about these new and better ways of doing things (the capital required must be obtained either through collective savings or credit).

This is where the extension services and aid technicians are supposed to play a part. Change agents can play an important role in linking groups to such sources. The good technician will help the group to analyse its present forms of production, suggest and analyse possible improvements, help the group experiment with these, and finally help them locate new sources of inputs, if necessary.

Increasing productivity should be the first thing that groups and individuals investigate as they are already familiar with the production and marketing of these products. It is much harder to find new and marketable products to produce or to trade in, or new services to offer. If it were easy, there would be no need for development workers. There are several paths to follow in trying to identify these new products, trading items or services.

The first area of investigation must be available markets – both local and external markets (the nearest town, big cities and even export markets). What products and services are in short supply and why? What products and services, which might have a market demand, are completely unavailable or unknown? There must be a market or else your work is wasted – as has happened to the women's groups and groups of the disabled which have been formed to produce more, and often inferior, handicrafts. Several groups in Uganda have bought an ox-cart and oxen and are now earning good money hauling sand and coffee husks. They identified a good service demand – for inexpensive short-haul transport of heavy commodities.

The main problem with market investigation is that it requires a lot of hard work and information. The lack of information regarding markets is probably the main reason why many poor people remain poor. Information must be gathered by one's own efforts and analysis assisted by friends, relatives, change agents and their agencies. Agencies that can help provide rural producers with market information are providing an invaluable service.

Another area to investigate is that of existing markets. Are there any products or services that the group, or individuals in the group, can make or do better or more cheaply? If so, they can gain an entry into the existing market. This may, unfortunately, displace other producers, but this is how nations develop. A group of blacksmiths and carpenters in northwestern Uganda are now producing tools which are much cheaper and just as good as or better than imported tools – unfortunately, Ugandans still need to be convinced that this is possible! A women's group in southern Uganda is producing vaseline based on kerosene and other locally available raw materials – in this case displacing an imported product. Take a look at all of the items in your shops that are produced elsewhere – surely many of these items can also be produced locally.

The next area of investigation is that of skills. What skills do the members of the group have? Can others learn them? Can they be combined to produce a product or a service that can be marketed? What skills do friends and relatives have that they might teach us? What skills are marketable? Where can we learn these skills? A women's group in Sri Lanka began a local bread bakery on the basis of one of the members convincing her uncle from a neighbouring town to come and show them how to build the oven and how to mix and bake the bread. Teaching new skills or linking rural people to appropriate instructors should, of course, be a major area of activity of change agents and their agencies.

The final area of investigation is a resource inventory of all possible available resources in the area. This would include land, soil types, clays, stone, sand, timber, reeds, herbal plants and grasses. Are any of these not being exploited? Could those already being used be exploited more efficiently or for different products? Who owns the rights to these resources? Can some type of arrangement be made for their utilisation? A group of women in northern Uganda 'discovered' a source of potters' clay – no pottery was being made in their area. Some of the group travelled with a change agent several hundred kilometres to learn pottery-making from a professional potter.

In summary, investment opportunities can be identified through market investigations including local and external markets, products and services in short supply, cheaper or better products or services; a skill inventory (both old and new skills); and a resource inventory.

Case Study No. 5 – Jocan Penindo Women's Group

The name of this group translates as 'a poor person doesn't sleep'. This group in northwestern Uganda consists of 20 women of which 15 are middle-aged and five elderly. All are illiterate except for three who are moderately good at reading and writing. None of the women had previously belonged to any type of group. Although they were individually running some small-scale economic activities, there was not much profit-earning nor savings kept for emergencies and additional investments. All the women have the support of their husbands for being group members. At the time of writing the group has been operating for two years.

The group set the following objectives: to promote unity and co-operation; to raise capital through savings so that members can get loans for individual economic activities; to encourage group investment, especially in essential commodities for resale; and to give members moral and financial support in times of family emergencies.

Each woman contributed a Shs 200 membership fee and committed themselves to a fixed monthly deposit of Shs 100. After six months and during a local food shortage, the group invested Shs 24,000 in the purchase and transport of six bags of cassava from Kampala. This was sold for a Shs 36,000 profit although labour was not charged for marketing.

Encouraged by the results of this first venture, the group invested in saucepans and wash basins. Some of these were distributed free to group members and the remainder sold to cover the costs of the venture. This was a novel way of distributing dividends to the members.

At this point the group established a credit fund for members. Any member could borrow Shs 2,000 for investment purposes for two months at 25% interest. The loans proved very productive and were promptly repaid, the interest being added to the group fund. Now, at any one time, about Shs 60,000 is on loan to members.

A third commercial venture was launched, again with household equipment – metal serving trays and bowls. Most of these were bought by members. A profit of 40% was made on the trays and 13% on the bowls.

The group has now acquired a donkey on credit which is being used for hauling water and firewood. By hiring out the donkey for transport jobs they hope to repay the external loan.

After two years the group is making good progress in achieving their goals. The group fund has now reached Shs 110,000 of which Shs 78,000 is in members' saving deposits.

Because of their low levels of formal education, members are still struggling to learn better book-keeping skills with the help of external change agents. But the group is a good example of how extremely poor women in a remote rural area can slowly begin to mobilise their savings, identify investment opportunities and invest their meagre resources for their own benefit.

Compiled by *Evie Anek*, change agent, Jonam, Uganda

Viability analysis

Once a list of potential income-generating activities has been produced, these should each be analysed in terms of what negative factors might reduce production or limit marketing. This is called a feasibility study. These factors might be a shortage of labour at certain key periods of the production cycle; lack of storage facilities; poor roads; or lack of transport. Each of these negative factors should be analysed to determine whether they can in any way be overcome or compensated for. Activities which involve insurmountable negative factors can then be dropped from the list of possible investment opportunities.

The final step in choosing an income-generating activity is a complete viability analysis, or profitability analysis, of each of the potential activities in order to choose the most profitable or the one that provides the best balance between profit and risk. Viability analyses involve costing of all of the factors of production and marketing, and comparing the costs against expected sales. A cash flow analysis is also necessary, especially if capital is being borrowed on credit.

Space does not permit a thorough discussion of viability analysis, but useful training manuals can be obtained from O.E.F. International which specialises in helping women to improve their standard of living through income-generating activities. Its address is 1815 H. Street N.W., Washington DC 20006, USA.

Planning group activities

It is not the function of change agents to plan the implementation of social and economic activities for the group. It is, however, their duty to assist the group to master the planning process. This can be done through a simple checklist of planning questions such as: Why? What? Which? How? With what? This checklist can be used even by illiterate groups by devising appropriate symbols for the questions and using pictorial presentations in the discussions.

1. *Why?* Why have we come together to do this activity? What are the problems we want to solve and why are we having these problems? The identification

of problems and the analysis of the causes is the first step in the planning process. Example: We have come together to find out why we are getting low prices for our vegetables. We have identified three reasons: (1) we have no way of storing or preserving the vegetables so that we must sell them when the market is glutted; (2) we must sell them to the middleman who sets the price and cheats us on the weighing and grading; (3) the insects and blight lower the quality.

2. *What?* What are we trying to accomplish? What will indicate that we have reached our goal? This discussion should lead to an agreement on objectives or expected accomplishments as well as an agreed upon way of measuring success or failure. Example: We are going to reduce the number of cases of diarrhoea among the children to 30 in the rainy season and five in the dry season. Within six months we will eliminate any deaths from diarrhoea.

3. *Which?* Which obstacles might we encounter in trying to carry out this project? What precautions can we take to avoid these problems? What alternatives do we have if they nonetheless arise? These discussions are a useful exercise in contingency planning as well as helping groups to thoroughly think through the project before they try to implement it. It may well happen that they decide to abandon or modify the project at this stage. Example: Roofing sheets may not be available for the school building. Experiment with cement and sisal fibre sheets as an alternative.

4. *With what?* With what resources is it possible to carry out the planned activities? Do we need land? Water? Labour? Machines? Capital? Materials and supplies? Special skills? Time? What alternatives are available? Can we substitute one type of resource for another? Is the project technically feasible? These discussions should provide the group with a list of all the inputs necessary as well as alternative solutions. Example: The irrigation channel will take 12 feet of land along its entire course. We will need training by the surveyor to lay down the course; digging tools, labour and several weeks time to dig the channel; cement, sand, water and timber to build gateways; money to purchase cement and timber.

5. *How many?* Once the group has the list of required inputs, it can begin to plan how many or how much of each resource is needed. Example: Ten plots of hillside land, each 0.2 acres; 25 coffee seedlings for each plot; 50 kgs fertilizer per plot.

6. *How much?* How much is each item on our list of purchased inputs and services going to cost? How much will each member be able to provide? How much can we lend each member from the group savings fund? How much credit can we get from the bank, and at what terms? How much can we expect to earn from the activity? Is the project economically viable? These discussions should lead to a detailed income and expenditure budget, and more importantly a decision whether to proceed or not. Example: Two hand sprayers will each cost $40. Fungicides will cost $8 per acre, insecticides $10 per acre, transport $20. Eight members can each pay $10, the other 12 can only pay $5. Each member can borrow $3 from the group fund repayable at harvest time at 10%. The group can borrow $60 from the Rural Bank at

15%. Members will pay $0.25 per hour for using the sprayer; non-members $0.50. Net income $50 per member.

7. *How?* How are we going to achieve our objectives? What are the activities or actions needed to be carried out in order to progress towards our goal? How are we going to market what we produce? Example: (1) build up group savings fund; (2) arrange for extension worker to give training in the choice and use of fertilizers; (3) purchase fertilizers; (4) hire a lorry.

8. *Who?* Who is going to be responsible for each action or activity and who is going to assist? These discussions should produce a list covering who is going to do what, and how much time and effort will be expected of them. Consideration will have to be given to differences in skill, availability, etc. Example: Pedro will arrange for the training in disease prevention. Jose and Jairo will purchase vaccines. Rosemary and Carmen will arrange the visit of the veterinary doctor.

9. *When?* When is each activity going to take place? When is the earliest that an activity can begin? When must it be completed? Which activities must be completed before others can start? What delays could arise? What changes can be made if such a delay happens? These discussions should produce a time plan which is realistic and which allows for unexpected circumstances. Example: Reserving of tractor hire must be done in July; cattle to be grazed on land from July to September; plowing to begin on the 1st September at Biki's, followed by Tani's, then Bala's. If rain falls during the week, then the high ground at Baba's can be plowed first.

10. *Where?* The final question in the planning process is where are the activities going to take place, where are the various inputs going to be purchased, where can assistance be gotten. Example: the bakery can be located behind the market. Training in baking can be done at Star Bakery in Paranthan. Fire-bricks can be bought at Kochikada; flour from the co-operative.

Some questions overlap others and are best answered in conjunction with these. Once all of the questions have been discussed, the entire plan has to be reviewed as a whole in order to check that there are no contradictions or omissions. During the implementation the plan should be regularly reviewed and revised. Finally, when the entire activity has been completed, the plan should be reviewed again so that the lessons learned can be followed in preparing the group's next plan.

Financing and external assistance

The provision of inputs and credit to group activities will be discussed in a later chapter, but it is appropriate here to ask whether outside assistance will create permanent dependence on the agency or others with regards to ideas, technology, materials, financing or management skills? This question must be considered by agencies intending to provide financing or other external assistance to participatory groups. If the answer is unsatisfactory, then it would be a disservice to provide assistance and the group should be told so. It is then up to the group to decide what their next step is.

Common Causes of Failure

> In one village organisation of the poor we saw a horrifying absolute dependence on external deliveries. The leaders stated that their organisation existed only to get external credit and would collapse without this. They wanted more credit until their fund would grow to a million Takas; they could not dream of ever doing without the NGO workers who were always correct in guiding them and had never said anything with which they could disagree. (Rahman, 1985a)

In spite of the straightforwardness of these village leaders, their's is a rather pathetic example of how one type of dependency (on the moneylender) is replaced by another (on the NGO). Although the latter is undoubtedly much less oppressive, it is nonetheless inhibiting real development.

Group failures are not uncommon even with the most intelligent use of the self-reliant participatory methods. These are only total failures if nothing is learned from them. This section will examine some of the reasons for group failures. Hopefully, similar mistakes can be avoided in the future.

Too little preparation

De Silva (1983) and his colleagues have observed in their studies of organisations promoting participatory development in South Asia that many change agents did not involve themselves deeply with the groups in the village investigations, and that they instead mechanically formed groups of the landless in the villages. They then encouraged these groups to start collective projects without real involvement on the part of the groups. No spontaneous interest was generated among the landless in those villages and, consequently, most projects failed.

Getting groups to start collective activities before they have reached a sufficient stage of group consciousness is a frequent cause of failure. There must be a minimum of group cohesion and determination if collective activities are to be successful. Failure of activities leads quickly to group failure unless the conscientisation process is restarted and new actions started after a period of genuine reflection–analysis by the group.

Too little confidence

All too often the major organisational and management work of credit unions and co-operative groups is taken care of by the change agents or project managers rather than by the people themselves. Apparently, this happens because of over-enthusiasm on the part of the change agents to run everything and to run it well. Underlying all of this may well be a real or imagined fear of being strongly criticised by their supervisors if things go wrong as well as an underlying lack of confidence in the people.

The expected result, of not giving the people the opportunity to run their own groups and organisations themselves, is that the outside change agents need to stay on in the same villages for years on end. Without the change agents these programmes would stop. Apparently, for these change agents and their agencies, the projects and their successful implementation are more important than the building of strong self-reliant organisations of the poor. The irony of such a situation is that such agencies end up being obstacles in the way of self-reliant efforts towards development.

If an activity is genuinely too complex for the people themselves to manage, then it should never have been started in the first place. Every time that we do something for the poor we perpetuate their dependency, their passivity and their lack of self-confidence. The Golden Rule should be 'Don't do anything for the people that they can do for themselves'. Even such a seemingly harmless activity as purchasing and hauling cement for a group, although quicker and easier, creates a dependency and postpones the day when the group must eventually solve the problem of cement purchasing on their own.

Not enough immediate benefits

I have seen many well-meaning attempts to promote participation fail and have encountered many disillusioned idealists because there was a failure to realise that for people whose energies are devoted wholly to survival, participation, unless it involves immediate and tangible pay-offs, is simply a luxury they cannot afford.

Martin Scurrah (in Cohen, 1980)

This is essentially a failure to really let the poor choose their own priorities. Too often we signal to the poor our own priorities and they, for various reasons ranging from fear of losing our support to too much respect, take our priorities as their own. Our priorities are often directed towards health, sanitation, childcare or ecology rather than finding enough money to buy seed and fertilizer for the next planting season which begins two months from now! Of course, the long-term objectives, especially ecology, are of crucial importance, but the poor must have a foundation to stand on before they can invest in their long-term future. Their first priority is their immediate needs.

However, some groups in their hurry to build up the size of their group funds put all of their profits into the fund without dispersing any of these earnings to group members in the form of shares or dividends. This is alright as long as everyone in the group genuinely agrees with this policy. But some members may need the money now, and don't dare speak up. If the policy continues, these people will leave the group.

Non-constructive participation

The above failures can be characterised as errors of omission: there was a failure to provide enough opportunities for genuine participation. On the other hand, there are situations in which participation in groups is not always constructive. Often a strong individual will assume leadership of a group and everyone else will assume passive roles rather than learning to participate. In many cases such leaders abuse their positions even to the point of dishonesty.

Either through lack of experience or because of cultural inhibitions, groups are unable to correct or remove these leaders. This in turn reinforces their passivity and convinces them that organisations are a waste of time and money.

Lack of experience in making decisions as a group often causes disagreements. Factions may develop and, if serious enough, can lead to the disintegration of the group. Even well-made decisions can lead to failure, causing disappointment and mutual casting of blame. Quite often, too little is known about handling money. Financial losses because of insufficient planning, poor decisions, graft or nepotism will also cause division and mutual recrimination.

The end result of these and similar negative learning processes is that the poor become even more distrustful of their neighbours; their scepticism with regards to the value of joining organisations increases; and their lack of confidence in their own abilities to solve problems collectively is reinforced. Such negative experiences with participation teach manipulation, deceit, exploitation, individualism, hopelessness and dishonesty. They are destructive rather than constructive. They do not produce development; they prevent it.

Participation is therefore not a panacea for all the ills of development projects. Participation is a difficult process which can easily become divisive and destructive. It is not enough to assume that it will automatically lead to unity and progress. Change agents must therefore be constantly alert for danger signals and assist groups to learn to identify and correct these dangers before they lead to irreparable damage.

In addition to the more subtle causes of group failure described above, experience in many countries by many organisations indicates that the following are the most common causes of group failures:

1. Group membership is non-voluntary. Groups have not had autonomy over the choice of members. Membership is too diverse, i.e. non-homogeneous. Better-off members dominate and control the group.
2. Groups are too large, thus making it difficult or impossible to hold open and deep discussions. Participation becomes uneven with some active and many passive.
3. Projects are imposed on groups either directly or by suggestion. Group priorities are not respected, planning is done by outsiders, and the projects do not respond to the needs of the group members.
4. Group leaders have been nominated or appointed by outsiders rather than chosen by the group. Leaders are not rotated regularly, and groups become dependent on a few individuals.
5. Book-keeping is controlled by one person. The books are not regularly open to the members. Actual cash on hand is not presented at every meeting for control.
6. Lack of unity and cohesion. Lack of regular meetings, poor attendance, no group savings fund, no group credit programme, irregular loan repayments.

    Although there is no one way to promote successful participatory groups and certainly no simple 'inoculation' against group failures, groups are less likely to fail if they are helped to become aware of these common causes.

Case Study No. 6 – Can Deg Ming Men's Group

The name of the group means 'poverty does not need stupidity' which is rather ironic considering the problems that the group has had. The group came together two and a half years ago on the initiative of a few members who learned of similar groups in a nearby parish which were being assisted by change agents. Four months later they had their first contact with the change agents.

The group which lives along the Nile in northern Uganda consists of 11 men. All of them do small-scale farming and fishing although the chairman, a very dynamic man, also did some carpentry. In the beginning the group started as a real example to others. As they had little savings, they earned money for their group fund from group digging for wages and by burning charcoal to sell in the nearby town. Eventually, each member also paid in a Shs 2,000-share over a one-year period. Through these efforts the group managed to accumulate Shs 78,000.

The group was assisted by the change agents to set up rules and regulations as well as simple book-keeping procedures. They were linked to a source for purchasing reasonably priced fishing nets and twine. They were also linked to some fisheries technicians who showed them how to make modern fish traps. They also built a smoking kiln for processing fish.

It was at this point that things began to go wrong. The three elected office bearers had a fair amount of education and on this basis totally dominated the others who lacked self-confidence. The leaders took all of the decisions. The fishing gear which belonged to the group was monopolised by the chairman. Loans were issued, but the office bearers issued loans to themselves and to their favourites in the group without consultation with the members. These loans were never repaid. Although simple book-keeping was taught to the group, the office bearers kept the books to themselves for fear that the members would detect their malpractices. Although group rules were being broken, the leaders failed to call regular meetings so as to avoid confronting the problems. When some of the dissatisfied members took the problem of unpaid loans to the village council, the chairman, who had the largest loan outstanding, disappeared from the area. The group has collapsed.

The main reason for the collapse was the lack of true conscientisation among the ordinary members which resulted in a lack of collective decision-making and domination by a small clique of better-educated leaders who used the group efforts to their own advantage. This has taught us the importance of going slow in the beginning and spending more time to help all of the members of a group to become conscientised.

Compiled by *Jesta Akello Okori*, change agent, Jonam, Uganda

Summing up

> We have learnt how to have dignity and self-respect and confidence in our own abilities.
>
> *Filipino farmer* (quoted by Rahman, 1983b)

This chapter has dealt rather lengthily with various aspects of working with groups of poor workers and producers. The approach has been derived from the successes and failures of groups and movements rather than from theoretical considerations.

In closing this chapter, it might be worthwhile to review the key factors which appear to lead to group success:

1. Group membership must be voluntary and must be decided by the members themselves. Groups should be homogeneous, i.e. the members should have a common interest and belong to the same socio-economic class, especially during the early stages of group experience.

2. Groups should remain small so that all members can participate equally in open and intensive discussion. The gradually increasing conscientisation of each and every member is vital to the success of the group as a unit.

3. Decision-making should be by collective deliberation. Group leaders function primarily as discussion leaders, and should be elected by the group rather than nominated or appointed by outsiders. Leader functions should rotate frequently between all members.

4. Unity and cohesion can be built up through regular meetings, collective savings and credit funds, projects, etc.

5. Groups should choose their own collective activities and set the priorities for undertaking these activities. All questions relating to the planning and implementation of activities should be decided by the group itself. External agents can provide advice and ensure thorough consideration of potential problems through discussion, but the groups must retain complete autonomy over decision-making.

6. Group activities should initially be directed primarily to income-generating and cost-saving activities or to reducing the social and political constraints inhibiting their economic development. Groups will normally expand their activities into non-economic concerns after they have made initial improvements in their economic situation.

Successful small groups of producers will generate interest among other neighbouring poor producers. These are easily encouraged to establish and develop their own autonomous groups. As these groups discover that they can make further improvements through co-operation, they will normally establish their own association of poor producers. These associations are a primary goal of development.

8. External Relationships: Inside Looking Out

Once a group of poor people have gone through their own process of conscientisation and have begun to organise themselves to take action to improve their own lives, they cannot avoid interation with outsiders. These outsiders are a varied lot and include, among others, traders, middlemen, moneylenders, religious leaders, community leaders and elders, politicians, government extension workers and officers, development workers and their agencies and, for women also, the men in their community.

In the best of situations these interactions can be neutral or, better still, positive. But given the contradictions in poor rural societies and in many Third World countries, these interactions can easily take a negative turn against the formation and progress of organisations of the rural poor. Negative influences can take the form of either direct or indirect undermining and repression in order to destroy the group or through subtle co-optation with the aim of redirecting the group's own efforts.

Co-optation in this context means the taking over of a group by an outsider or outsiders for the purpose of redirecting the priorities and activities of the group for the benefit of the outsiders. These outsiders might be local elites, politicians, government officers or even change agents and their agencies.

This chapter attempts to look at some of the problems of negative interactions and co-optation. First, however, let us look at the special problem of co-optation of rural groups by change agents and development agencies. On the surface this might appear as a benign (harmless) form of co-optation, but in reality it can destroy the sustainable development of the group. One way this occurs is through the redirection of the group's priorities to those of the change agent or the agency, e.g. specific political agitation, activities or investments that promote the image of the change agent or agency but sidetrack the group from its own genuine priorities. Groups are often forced to participate in surveys and mobilisations often for the benefit of far-away home offices and funders and which divert the group's time and energies away from more immediate concerns.

More damaging to the process of self-reliant development is the well-meaning dumping of grants, subsidised inputs, credits or appropriate technology gadgets on promising groups, so that the change agent or agency can take credit for helping the group to progress and develop. Change agents and development agencies who truly believe in the self-reliant participatory process must constantly guard against such malpractices which ultimately defeat their own objectives.

Local Elites and the Power Structure

The rural rich have been sucking the blood of the poor. These tigers who are used to the blood of the people manage to get into all of the committees of projects and organisations in the garb of sheep. But as soon as they get a chance, they start sucking the blood again, this time through the development organisation.

Indian farmer (quoted by Bhasin, 1979)

Casual visitors to villages in the Third World are usually quite unaware of the often brutal power structures that control the lives of the poor. The villages seem so peaceful and the people so friendly. Here are some examples noted by Bhasin (1979) of the reality that lies behind the facade:

The peasants in a village had formed a credit union group on the advice of a development worker. They were motivated to join hands to free themselves from perennial indebtedness to the village moneylender who charged very high rates of interest. Many of them had lost their land because they could not repay the debts. As the credit union started growing, the moneylender threatened the leaders with dire consequences and called the worker a communist. Is organising a credit union then a matter of politics or not?

Some change agents had encouraged some farmers to start a pig-selling group to increase their bargaining power. The group obviously led to a substantial decrease in the profits of the middlemen. The leader of the club was badly beaten-up and given a warning that if he continued his activities, he would be further punished.

With tears in her eyes, but anger in her voice, one of the para-medics showed us the grave of their co-worker, Nizam, who was murdered in broad daylight. Nizam's work in the village had threatened the fraudulent practices of a good many people, including illegal possession of government lands, smuggling and selling health centre drugs. Among those involved in the illegal activities was the only qualified physician in the area. In collaboration with local officials, the physician hired thugs to have Nizam murdered. Nizam lost his life and now an almost incredible struggle for simple justice seems to be availing nothing.

Under the surface the reality is not very pleasant at all. Rural communities are quite different from the romantic picture of happy, unsophisticated people living in harmony with nature and each other. In fact villagers are subject to intense pressures from within and outside the community. Power and socio-economic benefit are jealously protected, and all attempts to alter existing relationships will be vigorously resisted by those who stand to lose their relative advantages.

Every community has its power structure. Some people or groups will have more social, economic or political power than others. Often the powerful dominate all three of these spheres, but not necessarily. Sometimes religious leaders have immense social and political power. Sometimes an old and respected family will maintain its social power while having lost its economic and political powers. Normally, those who have economic power will also wield political power, and may even dominate socially. In some few communities, organised groups of relatively poor people may be able to control political power. The actual structure in each community will be dependent upon many different factors including land distribution, control of capital and traditions. But one aspect of the power structure remains constant, and that is that those with power will seek to maintain it against all threats.

Those who control land, labour and capital will not look kindly upon those who try to alter the distribution of these factors of production. Only in those cases in which a particular factor is not scarce will it be possible to redistribute without struggle. If, for example, credit is easily available at modest rates, then moneylenders will not be in a position to resist further broadening of credit programmes. Improvements in productivity can, however, be achieved without altering the control of land, labour and capital by, for example, investing in fertilizers or high-yield seed varieties, but as soon as someone's economic advantage is threatened there will be a reaction, often a very violent one.

The Nijera Kori organisation in Bangladesh has for several years been helping poor people to mobilise and fight for specific demands. This struggle has given the poor self-confidence and a feeling for the strength of unity, and they have learnt to shed their fears and to speak up in front of officials and landlords. But they have consistently experienced backlashes by vested interests. When groups openly protest against corrupt officials, or demand higher wages, those against whom these protests are directed may organise violence against them. There have been several cases of group members and Nijera Kori workers being beaten up and implicated in false criminal cases.

This experience is not unique. Throughout the Third World, groups of poor people who unite to improve their own lot are resisted, often violently, by those who stand to lose as a result of the gains made by the poor. The fact that the promotion of a genuinely self-reliant development process will normally lead to resistance from local elites and the existing power structures means that change agents must reflect upon their true responsibility to the poor.

Although the primary role of the change agent is to help poor people understand their situation and help them organise themselves to improve it, a secondary role involves relations with the local elites and the power-holders. This is not an easy role to define, but essentially involves helping the poor to avoid unnecessary or potentially damaging conflicts which they cannot win, as well as trying to reduce the level of conflict by maintaining good relations with the elite and with government officials.

Development programmes which offer only services in the form of technical advice and supplies are welcomed by the village elites. But trouble flares up as soon as change agents help the poor to organise effectively into pressure groups such as credit unions, co-operatives and peasant organisations. Activities which aim at increasing the power of the poorer people, and those people who participate in such activities, are declared to be subversive, anti-social or political.

Maintaining good relations with local elites and power-brokers involves public relations activities on the part of the change agents, and a mild strategy of 'something for everyone'. Change agents should use some of their time to maintain cordial relations with the elite, being careful, however, not to compromise their relations with the poor. It is important to avoid falling into the trap of thinking that the elites represent the 'enemy' although in some cases this will be painfully true. It is more constructive to think of them as people with relatively greater advantages than the poor, and therefore less in need of our attention. The skilled change agent tries to have friendly personal relations throughout the community.

The relatively better-off often have needs in common with the poor. They will be particularly concerned with education, health and communications. These needs and interests should be investigated and identified using the same methods as with groups of the poor. Interest groups can be formed around specific activities which concern the well-to-do such as expanding a school building, establishing a clinic, repairing a road. These activity groups can be led and controlled by the elite so long as the benefits of the activity are potentially available to the entire community even though initial beneifts may be skewed in favour of the well-to-do, for instance they can afford to send their children to school.

Community-wide social projects allow local elites to demonstrate their social power while at the same time benefiting all. Although the elites may benefit more from the activity than the poor, the poor are not worse-off than before. The problem for the change agents and the agency is to find the right balance between community-wide social projects and income-enhancing or empowering activities for the poor. For the poor, the latter must be given first priority followed by social projects benefiting the poor. Social projects primarily benefiting the more well-to-do have a low priority, and economic activities an even lower one. These are principally to maintain good relations.

Direct confrontations between the poor and the local power-holders should be avoided as far as possible. But, inevitably, there will be conflict and confrontation – often in very subtle forms. Such conflicts do not benefit the poor, unless they are able to win them.

Case Study No. 7 – Getting out in front
Some change agents from an international agency moved into a fishing village on the southern coast of Sri Lanka and began working with a group of about 30 very poor fishing families. These families lived together in a tightly packed village in a lowland area away from the well-to-do in the community.

The primary source of income for these families was fishing, but they owned no boats and worked as crew on the boats owned by the well-to-do. According to long tradition in this area, crewmen were paid a given percentage of the catch. However, it did not take very long for the change agents and the fishermen to realise that the boat-owners had not been giving these poor fishermen their rightful share of the catch.

The change agents had been working in the village for only two months when the poor fishermen, encouraged by the change agents, decided to organise themselves into a fishermen's association and they soon confronted the rich boat-owners with demands for their rightful share of the catch.

At a crucial confrontation on the beach one day, the boat-owners, who had with them some fairly professional looking thugs, demanded to know who had put the fishermen up to all this agitation. The fishermen, who were physically the underdogs and who had no alternative income, meekly replied that it was the change agents who had put them up to it.

Within a few days the police arrived inquiring about the activities of the change agents, and two weeks later the government agent visited the local office of the agency and told them to remove the change agents from that village. The association collapsed, and the fishermen lost all confidence in their ability to change their situation. Within just a few months, the change agents had become rudely aware of the realities and dangers of participatory development.

Over-enthusiasm on the part of the poor as well as the change agents has been the downfall of many an initiative to organise the poor for their own advancement. In this case, there had not been a thorough analysis of the situation; there had been no long-term effort to build up resources, develop alternatives and internal strength before attempting to alter power structures. These poor fishermen believed that their power came from the international agency rather than from within themselves, and the agency failed them, not because the agency lacked power, but because of too much haste and not enough patient analysis and gradual development of internal strengths.

The author was the field director of this agency at the time

Government Officials

> Government officials are like dogs. They go after those who throw pieces of bread at them. They bark at and bite those who cannot feed them.
>
> *Indian tribal peasant* (quoted by Bhasin, 1979)

Such opinions are not always apparent to visiting aid administrators who, together with government officials, are given warm and friendly receptions during their brief and ceremonial visits to villages. These reception committees are usually headed by the village elites who have learned to profit from their good relations with government officials. The poor, however, have usually adopted one of two strategies for dealing with such visits. They either melt into the background, try to remain invisible, passive and unseen, or they assume a role of submissive ingratiation in an attempt to curry favour and advantage. They will seldom express their true feelings for fear of possible negative consequences. To submit minimises risk.

A group of change agents working with Kamla Bhasin (1976) discussed these questions and summarised their discussions in the following way:

> Village people often have a bad opinion of government servants. Some of the peasants whom the group met said that the officers came as masters to push and order them around. They seldom had the time to sit down to talk to them, to live with them. They came in their awe-inspiring uniforms and were always afraid of dirtying them in the dirt and dust of village problems. All they were interested in was good reports from their bosses and not good relations with the poorer people. Each visit of an official could mean a loss of at least two chickens, which had to be cooked to 'entertain' the officials and earn the village a 'good' name.

Governmental development programmes and projects are supervised, and in many cases executed, by government officers working at divisional, district, provincial and ministerial levels. As MacDonald (1981) has indicated, these are part of a system which is hierarchical and downward flowing as a communications process while, on the other hand, peoples' participation implies decision-making at the grassroots level and horizontal and upward-flowing communication. With tongue in cheek, he concludes,'There is, obviously, an area of possible tension here.'

It is unproductive to dismiss government officials as being bureaucratic. The first step in improving relations between the people and officials is to analyse the working situation of government employees in order to understand some of the causes of the often disinterested and negative attitudes towards the poor.

Government service is by its very nature rigidly structured. Planning and decision-making is done at higher levels, and orders are passed down to field-level officers who are given little or no authority to make modifications reflecting local conditions. For purposes of control and for justification of budgetary grants considerable emphasis is given to report-writing. It is only natural therefore that field officers give as much or more importance to report-writing as to actual work in the field. In any case, limited travel allowances restrict fieldwork in most Third World countries. Promotion all too often comes as a result of 'fitting in' and writing good reports.

Field officers are sector oriented. They have technical training in their field, but little or no training in those social skills necessary to work with the people. Through fear or actual experience, lower level government officials often do not feel free to criticise policies which they consider wrong or programmes which are not effective. Sincerity is sometimes punished while promotions are given for unquestioned support of superiors. There is generally little scope for free and open discussions in government service. It is therefore not very surprising that government programmes are executed mechanically, and results are quite different from the expectations of the planners.

The need for better relations

> Participation should not only emphasise 'effective struggle' but also constructive conflict resolution.
>
> *D. D. Solomon* (in Cohen, 1980)

No country can progress if the people are in basic conflict with their government, and have basically negative attitudes towards its representatives. Ultimately, mutual trust and respect must replace fear and suspicion. The development process needs to be driven by positive impulses.

Extended conflict can eventually destroy participatory movements. Thomas Baumgartner (in Cohen, 1980) has observed that 'conflictive encounters will in general lead to hierarchical and authoritarian organisational structures. Behaviours formed during this period make it afterwards very difficult to realise internal participation'. Participatory development is not synonymous with revolution, and violent revolutions are never genuinely participatory. As Mustafa El Sayed (in Cohen, 1980) has pointed out, 'participation implies acceptance of certain rules of social interaction viewed as legitimate, at least temporarily.'

Small groups are especially vulnerable to external intervention. Individuals and groups who have an interest in preventing participatory development will use their power and influence to create difficulties between the groups and government officials or politicians. It is therefore in the interest of such small groups to avoid open conflict with government officials, and to do what they can to develop cordial relations and mutual understanding.

> Because we are a group now and we stick to each other, we have suddenly become more powerful. The moneylenders are afraid to exploit us now. The government officials speak to us; they even speak nicely. We are also no more afraid to enter the bank or the office of the co-operative society.
>
> *Peasant group in Nepal* (quoted by Bhasin, 1979)

The basic contradiction in the relationship between officials and the poor is the unequal balance of power between them. The poor feel weak and disadvantaged when confronting officialdom. This can be changed by increasing their self-confidence through group participation.

In reporting on the progress of a FAO-sponsored participatory programme in Nepal, Bhasin (1979) has observed that the small farmers and landless peasants no longer sit passively at the outskirts of meetings, but participate actively and confidently. They are no longer afraid, as they used to be, to air their views before government officers.

An important step towards improving relations is the realisation that many government officials, even at the lowest levels of the hierarchy, are genuinely sympathetic to the needs and aspirations of the poor. These officials should be identified and encouraged. Seminars and workshops can be sponsored so that sincere officials at various levels of the bureaucracy can come together to discuss participatory development and to find ways and means of making government programmes more responsive to the needs and aspirations of the people they are expected to serve.

Unless a government is actively trying to suppress their activities, groups should make a sincere effort to keep government officials – extension workers, teachers, health personnel, police, administrators – informed of their activities and the purposes of their meetings. They can occasionally invite officials to their meetings, as well as allow them to share the limelight during important events and celebrations. When possible and convenient, group members can make a point of paying courtesy calls at the homes or working places of officials.

There are, of course, dangers involved in having too intimate relationships with officials. Rahman (1984a) feels that not many governments, unfortunately, have the necessary enlightened view to encourage poor people to independently challenge the power of the privileged, and even those governments which are inclined towards grassroots organisations prefer close government involvement in them.

Although there are strong official impulses to co-opt and control people's organisations, the picture is not completely discouraging. In many countries, there is genuine support for participatory organisations at the highest levels of government. This support often, however, becomes dissipated at the local level, usually because of the pressure put on local officials by the local elites and power-brokers. It is important in such circumstances to have good relations with higher-level officials who can intervene on behalf of the people and the organisation.

No people's organisation is going to achieve development on its own. Ultimately, a partnership of the people with their government must be forged. Self-reliant participatory development must work towards this goal. Peter Quennell, an evaluation officer with UNDP, has expressed this clearly in the following:

Totally autonomous grassroots developments, proceeding regardless of the wider context, are something of a myth. No serious development practitioner would today dispute that the bottom-up approach is the only one that remains viable: all recent evidence points in this direction. But also, it is true that such developments cannot simply, on their own account, provide the roads, the transport, communications, or the water and fuel essential to their own success; or for that matter, the credit, agricultural inputs, marketing, or the basic education and health services. These can for the most part only be made available through government programmes. Grassroots developments may point to the needs, but they cannot hope to meet them all on their own.

What is needed is a genuine partnership between the people, working for their own development through their own autonomous organisations, and a government structure which is truly responsive to the needs and priorities of its people as expressed through the people's own organisations.

Official interest organisations

Official organisational structures, i.e. co-operatives and rural unions, were among the first structural imports into the rural areas of the Third World. These organisations have without doubt benefited middle-class farmers and other local elites who, through their active participation, have managed to channel benefits to themselves. However, the rural poor have not been able to participate in any meaningful way and have therefore not benefited correspondingly. The FAO Rural Organisations Action Programme study, in 1979, confirmed this and also identified how such organisations can lead to the further impoverishment of the rural poor. This failure is not a reflection on the co-operative institution *per se*, but more on the bureaucratic constraints which limit the successful functioning of such institutions.

Agricultural co-operatives, multi-purpose co-operatives and other forms of co-operatives, as well as rural savings and credit unions, are found today throughout the Third World. In all but a few cases these have been organised under the auspices of central governments, and are today still tightly controlled and regulated by these governments. Nearly every district has its co-operative officers in charge of organising and supervising local co-operative branches.

Official co-operatives in the Third World are top-down organisations. At the national level they are usually controlled by government bureaucrats answerable to politicians or the ruling military. At the local level, their boards of directors are more often than not controlled by local officials, politicians and elites. Practically no poor farmers, fishermen or the like are board members. Very few of the really poor producers are members – unless this is dictated by government policy.

Co-operative operations are tightly regulated by bureaucratic regulations and routines. Many local co-operatives cannot, for example, sell-off unneeded or run-down assets, borrow money or change their bye-laws without the permission of the national commissioner of co-operatives. Marketing functions are often totally integrated into government marketing board systems. Because they are not controlled by their membership, these institutions are susceptible to numerous forms of corruption, nepotism and favouritism.

Official co-operatives and similar institutions run on these lines are not people's organisations, and can only be termed interest organisations because they serve the interests of those who control them. These institutions not only do not serve the interests of the poor, they quite often work directly against them.

As genuinely participatory groups join together into their own interest organisations or producer associations, these will become subject to various pressures to merge into the official co-operatives. Poor people know that this is not in their own interests, and will normally do what they can to avoid being co-opted in this way. Change agents should encourage them to continue their resistance. If necessary, development agencies should assist interest organisations in obtaining top-level legal assistance to fight this battle.

Change agents and government officials

The change agent can easily become a focus of official suspicion and, if not careful, his or her actions can seriously jeopardise the already insecure situation of the poor. Imagine the reaction of an official if he learns indirectly that a young, educated outsider is meeting secretly with small groups of very poor peasants. The meetings take place under the cover of darkness in the hut of a well-known troublemaker. This outsider furthermore avoids the village leaders and government officials. And worst of all, the outsider tells the poor that they are being exploited, and that they should organise to disrupt the peace and order of the village.

It is a foolish agency with irresponsible change agents that does not take the time and effort to meet with all local government officials prior to starting their work among the poor in a new area. Assuming that the central government has approved the programme, the next step is to explain the programme to the local officials, and gain their initial support. Subsequently, representatives of the agency should meet regularly with key local and national officials to report on progress and discuss and clear up any misunderstandings before they develop into what can easily become serious problems.

Change agents working directly with small groups can provide a vital link between the groups and local officials. Being representatives of a nationally recognised agency, the change agents can give legitimacy to groups before they have acquired strength and acceptance on their own. Change agents should do their utmost to maintain cordial personal relations with all government employees in the area, and make a special effort to keep key government officials informed of their activities.

Change agents should discuss with their groups the question of relations with local officials, and encourage the groups to maintain positive relations. Change agents may initially need to accompany group members on visits to government offices until they have developed their own self-confidence. It is important that their contacts with officials be based on a foundation of dignity and self-respect.

Combining with Other Groups

> If you're going to the top of the mountain, don't go naked and don't go alone.
>
> *Puerto Rican organiser*, South Bronx, New York
> (quoted by Janice Periman in SID, *GRIS Notes*, 1982)

Small groups with 15 to 20 members can do a great deal to build up the self-confidence of their members, and through their small-scale collective efforts such as group savings funds, collective purchases of inputs and collective investments can assist members to improve their economic security. But small groups are very vulnerable and lack the strength to make significant impact in such areas as health, education, legal rights, systematic exploitation, marketing or transportation.

Small groups federated with other like-minded groups can form interest organisations or associations which can provide greater protection of the interests of their members than can be achieved by the individual, isolated groups. Through larger associations poor people can gain bargaining strength especially with regards to marketing of produce and the purchasing of inputs and raw materials. Collective purchasing and marketing in bulk allows them to move higher up the commercial chain in order to realise greater savings and sale prices. They can better carry the financial burden of larger capital investments such as tractors or lorries. Loan funds based on collective savings can become larger and more secure.

Self-reliant participatory development through the collective effort of small groups has a natural multiplier effect. Progress in one village provides a stimulus to the poor in neighbouring villages to take collective initiatives of their own towards self-reliance. Ideas and experiences are shared, and alliances forged between producers in surrounding villages.

Once an interest organisation has been formed by the alliance of several small groups in one area this multiplication of participatory groups becomes even more vigorous. A local interest organisation in one area becomes a model for a similar organisation in a neighbouring region. Ultimately, these regional associations may federate into national associations of small farmers, fishermen, artisans, etc. Such interest organisations can only continue to represent their members' interests as long as the membership retains complete control of the decision-making processes.

> We know that the struggle is big, and we must join our brothers and sisters all over, and someone has to give the big leadership. But who will lead has to be discussed. What are your interests in helping us, and what are the terms of the deal?
>
> *Indian peasant* (quoted by Wignaraja, 1981)

Interest organisations of the poor should not be 'set up'; they should grow as a tree grows – from the roots upwards. Groups will naturally begin interacting with neighbouring groups having similar interests. These interactions will normally lead to informal co-operation. When the groups see the advantages of more formal forms of collective effort, they will take the necessary steps to form their own associations. It is at this stage that the advice and assistance of sensitive change agents can be useful.

Time and natural evolution are the keys to the successful formation of strong independent organisations. Small groups must be allowed to develop their own initiatives, to gain experience in working together and in managing their own collective interests. They need to learn through their own experiments the practical application of group dynamics, collective decision-making, financial management, etc. All of this takes time and considerable trial and error. Pushing small groups into forming larger associations before these skills are firmly embedded in the broad mass of the membership will only lead to disaster.

Setting up a formal organisation before people are ready for it almost inevitably results in a hierarchically-structured organisation with rank and file members sitting back and letting the educated, better-off leaders take the initiative and make decisions. In such cases, the membership's involvement will remain minimal and uninspired, and the organisation will eventually fail to serve the real interests of its members.

Those groups thinking of joining together into a larger association should be strongly encouraged to maintain the individual small groups as the primary focus of their collective activities. The larger organisation then becomes a federation of member groups rather than a single organisation with individual membership. Such a federation provides opportunities for broader participation as well as better control by the membership.

Although it is considerably more difficult to maintain collective leadership in a larger association, many grassroots organisations have nonetheless chosen this path. Usually each small group sends one or two of its members to represent their interests in the association. These representatives form the collective leadership. Normally representatives are rotated, often as frequently as every six months, so as to avoid vested interest in retaining leadership. This is a cumbersome way of running an association, but at the early stages of organisational development it is a wise course of action. This type of organisation becomes unwieldy if the membership begins to exceed several hundred members associated with 10 or more member groups. Larger associations require different forms of representative leadership, and can emerge over time as experience is accumulated.

Large organisations tend to become rigid in their decision-making and remote from their membership. Leadership becomes entrenched and absorbed. with maintaining its position and enhancing its own benefits. Factionalism often develops and the strength gained by larger numbers can disintegrate from within. These dangers can be minimised again through openness and alertness on the part of the mass of members.

One of the obvious dangers of coming together in an assocation is that this larger unity will attract considerably more attention than the non-united small groups. Officials, politicians and other influential persons will, for various reasons, try to win favour with or control of this potentially powerful entity. Political parties will become interested, and perhaps even try to infiltrate or take over the organisation. The best protection against these threats is continued organisational openness and non-permanent collective leadership.

The question of formal recognition or legalisation of people's organisations is one which can only be approached in relation to the specific legal and political situations in each country. While the organisation is new, this is usually not a critical problem, but as it becomes increasingly effective this question must be faced. It is basically a problem of finding a middle way between legality and maintaining independence. Ultimately, the resolution depends on the attitudes of the power centres towards independent organisations and the relations between these power centres and the specific organisation.

It is at this point that associations of poor producers will need legal advice and assistance. There may be other similar organisations that have already been through the process of gaining official recognition and can provide such advice and assistance. There may be advocacy groups or individual legal advisors who are able and willing to assist. Helping an association to gain legitimacy is an important role for development agencies.

The FAO *Peasants' Charter* (1981) stresses the need for the development of farmers' associations, co-operatives and other forms of voluntary autonomous democratic organisations of primary producers and rural workers:

> To provide the basis for effective participation by the people, governments should consider action to encourage the establishment of self-reliant local, regional and national federations of peasant and worker associations and rural co-operatives, with positive government support and due regard to their autonomy.

In spite of this and similar and equally impressive pronouncements on the importance of the emergence of independent, autonomous people's organisations in the Third World, experience has shown that most Third World governments still prefer to have full control over associations, co-operatives, and the like. New organisations are sometimes suppressed, or more subtly co-opted: they are absorbed into the government apparatus by the appointment of government officials to the controlling bodies of the organisation.

There are none the less many examples of people's organisations emerging throughout the Third World. Some have remained essentially local, others have attempted to ally themselves at national levels with similar groups. Their success has been determined by local factors. Some are still serving their member's interests, others have been co-opted or, as in the case of the independent peasants' federations in Chile, dissolved by repressive regimes. The ultimate creation of autonomous independent producers' associations and people's organisations at regional and national levels is of crucial importance to the progress and development of the poor.

Case Study No. 8 – Paroketo Fishermen's Association

The Paroketo Fishermen's Association (PFA) is an association of small groups of fishermen in northwestern Uganda. It was formed four years ago and is a registered limited liability company dealing in the provision of fishing and farming materials and services to its members who live in Paroketo Parish. There are now 18 member groups; each group has 15 to 20 members. Each member group is entitled to a maximum of three shares in the company. Each share is valued at Shs 10,000.

The original objective of the founding members was to mobilise the fishermen to collect funds in order to purchase nets, twine and hooks in bulk. Later the assocation's policy was re-directed to include general grassroots development activities. Thus the association started to enlarge its membership to include small savings and investment groups. Originally, membership was for the male fishermen, but now also includes women.

The objectives of the PFA are: (1) to purchase in bulk fishing and farming implements, and sell these at reasonable prices to its members; (2) to unite the people of the parish to develop a common strategy in planning and implementing socio-economic development activities, and in particular prevent over-fishing in the river; (3) to act as a base for providing essential services such as clean water and medical care to the community; (4) to purchase and market members' fish and produce at higher sales prices; (5) to provide training in organisational and managerial skills to the member groups; and (6) to provide credit and other financial services to members.

The association's day-to-day operations are carried out by a team of seven directors elected annually from among members. The directors are controlled by the executive committee which consists of one representative elected by each member group. They normally meet once a month with the directors to discuss policy matters, review financial reports, and raise any issues from the member groups. They are expected to report their discusssions back to their member groups.

The association has recently established a credit scheme for members for short-term productive investments. This scheme is implemented by a specially elected loan committee consisting of five members drawn from different member groups and headed by the PFA treasurer. This committee disburses and monitors the loans and ensures collection. Loans totalling Shs 450,000 have been given to nine groups and 11 individuals.

The major achievement of PFA so far is the establishment of a shop for selling fishing gear and farm implements, and links to importers to bring and sell these items to the members and to the public. Members receive discounts. The association has also managed to educate and mobilise the people on the importance of group action. Many new groups are now emerging and joining under the PFA's umbrella. Progress is being made in implementing development plans in the parish: shallow-well construction has begun in one of the most productive areas of the parish; people and materials are being mobilised to construct a parish health unit. In addition to the loan scheme, the PFA is planning to become a purchasing agent for its members' produce. For this purpose they have purchased a used pick-up truck.

The association still has problems. Being initially formed by a core of founder members in a top-down process, the PFA is still in the process of changing to a true association of member groups. There still exists a gap between the directors and the groups. Too many groups still look at the directors as the 'owners' of PFA rather than merely a steering committee. Funding is still a constraint as group shares do not greatly contribute to the capital formation. The association is presently focusing most of its attention on commercial activities rather than implementing productive development ventures. These problems will hopefully be resolved as the member groups become organisationally stronger and less dependent on the directors.

Compiled by *Odaga Jatex*, change agent, Jonam, Uganda

Dilemmas of Participatory Development

Janice Perlman, an American sociologist with long experience in working with participatory groups in the United States, has identified three sets of dilemmas which make grassroots groups internally fragile. If groups are not to fail, then they, with help from their change agents, must find an equilibrium point between the horns of these dilemmas:

Ideology vs. Pragmatism
• If groups begin with a political ideology defined by the change agents (usually middle-class) they often cannot grow in membership among the sectors of low-income people since they do not start from where 'their heads are at'.
• On the other hand, if the group is simply pragmatic, people develop the 'what have you done for me lately' mentality and are reluctant to continue participating once the 'me' that benefits goes beyond themselves or their families.

Action vs. Reflection
• If action is stressed exclusively, people feel left out of the learning, decision-making, understanding. They are used as 'troops' in direct action or as 'unpaid hands' in self-help. They are excluded from the democratic process of participation even within their own group.
• If consciousness-raising is stressed exclusively, however, people tend to lose

interest since no concrete results are visible. Being time-consuming and cumbersome, the democratic decision-making process can lead to drop-outs among those with key survival needs to be dealt with.

Localism vs. Coalition-building

- If groups remain local and isolated, they are ultimately too weak to significantly effect change. Once the small-scale modifications (sprayer, well, etc.) are dealt with the group has nowhere to go in affecting major issues such as marketing or minimum wages. They are still in dependency situations – isolated – re-inventing the wheel.
- Much greater effectiveness can result from sharing of experience, networking, making alliances and coalitions to join forces with other local efforts. This is the way bargaining strength can be built, resources exchanged and power can begin to shift. The danger, however, is in skimming off the best local leadership into the larger organisational network and the dissolution of the local bases of strength. There is also the risk of losing the flexibility, relevance and energy of locally-based innovations, and becoming impotent.

A fourth dilemma applies to change agents and their agencies rather than to organisations of the poor:

- If change agents devote considerable time and effort to the process of conscientisation and allow groups to develop at their own speed and according to their own priorities, then their supervisors and funders may become impatient at the lack of visible and measurable results.
- If change agents minimise the time spent on conscientisation efforts and push groups into development activities with visible results in order to please funders, then the groups' long-term sustainability and self-reliance, will be jeopardised.

A fine sense of balance is needed to manoeuvre successfully through these dilemmas. Through frequent reflection and self-criticism, change agents can to a large extent manage to avoid moving too far towards any of these extremes. Likewise they can help the groups to become aware of the dangers and take appropriate corrective steps.

Although there is almost a total lack of statistical material on which to base any conclusions, it is perhaps not unreasonable to assume that more participatory groups fail than succeed in their attempts to establish viable organisations. This does not necessarily mean that the approach is wrong, but rather indicates a greater need for constant reflection as well as increased experience-sharing among change agents and groups.

9. Savings, Credit and Inputs: Essential Components

> We discovered after quite some time that what they were teaching us about self-reliance and working together was far more important than the money which we were expecting from them.
>
> *Mr Evaristo Matsvaire*, village change agent
> Zimbabwe (quoted by Seawell, 1984)

'Everything costs money.' 'The poor are poor because they have no money.' 'You can't save if you don't have anything to save.' These exclamations sum up the dilemma that poor people face within a money-economy. In order to improve their situation, the poor must invest money in new activities, and improvements in the productivity of their present activities, as well as cover the costs of operating these activities. Their dilemma is by definition that they have little or no reserves to invest; most of what little they have must go to keeping themselves alive.

Development has been achieved throughout the course of history through investing savings and credit – as well as some stolen resources from wars and colonial conquests. As the poor are not likely to benefit from slavery, imperialism and exploitation, we shall have to keep to the legitimate forms of savings and credit.

Self-reliant participatory development processes should start on the basis of local resources, knowledge and technology. However, they won't progress very quickly unless more advanced knowledge and external resources are gradually absorbed. Change agents and their supporting agencies can be helpful in this regard, but producer groups must be able to stand on their own efforts and have full control over the process. Groups can borrow in order to expand their production, but they must maintain the capacity to repay their loans while at the same time meet their consumption needs and continue building up their savings. External assistance must not exceed the capacity to absorb it or self-reliance is destroyed.

Bunch (1982) has described a visit he made to an agricultural project in South America six years after his agency had closed down the programme. Expensive equipment had been installed and a co-operative established. The visit was to see how the work had continued – but it hadn't. The equipment had broken down and never been repaired. The co-operative building was empty. Yet people pleaded with him 'But if your agency would just come help us again, we could do so much!'

Every development worker has seen numerous similar examples of massive quantities of inputs either unused, rotting or rusting away. In most cases these inputs were provided as some form of 'give-away' – the people who received them did not invest their own resources in obtaining them. Give-aways are not only ineffective, they are detrimental. They instill people with attitudes of dependency, subservience and the idea that they are incapable of doing things for themselves. Give-aways in any significant quantity will destroy self-reliant development processes.

Development agencies can provide supplementary capital for the poor in the form of credit – either free, with low interest or with commercial interest – or as donations including matching grants. But, ultimately, the poor must rely on their own savings supplemented by locally obtained credit.

Although the dilemma for the poor is to find the money to improve their situation, the dilemma of the development agency is how to provide the money to the poor without destroying the self-reliant development process i.e. without creating new dependency relationships. The dilemma for the rich development agencies of the industrialised nations is even greater because they believe that their donors expect them to do as much as possible to directly help the poor. It must therefore always be remembered that the primary goal is self-sustaining development. This chapter will discuss these alternative sources of investment capital for the poor and how these sources affect the self-reliant participatory development process.

Factors of Production

Before looking at sources of capital, it might be worthwhile to quickly review all of the factors which may be needed whenever anything is produced. Capital obviously is important, but land and labour are equally important. Capital-poor rural groups can initially use their labour with or without their own land to produce small amounts of surplus capital which they can invest in, slowly improving their production.

Depending on what is being produced, other factors might be needed such as tools and machinery, raw materials and inputs, or buildings. These can be obtained by combining once again capital, labour and land. Capital may also be needed to obtain or develop specialised skilled labour. Every production process also requires energy which can be in many forms – human, animal, wood, petrol or diesel, electricity. The more advanced forms will again need capital.

Finally, every production process needs some amount of management skill as well as the willingness to risk investing the factors of production; this is called entrepreneurship. Capital can purchase management skills, but entrepreneurship must be found within the individual investors.

The Positive Spiral of Economic Development

In order to increase production or improve productivity some amount of capital must be invested in the factors of production necessary to achieve the desired increases and improvements. This capital must come from savings or from credit which is someone else's savings. Savings is and must always be in this equation – even free grants represent someone's savings either voluntarily through donations or involuntarily through taxation. There must be savings somewhere in the system; and if a local system is to become sustainable, it must eventually generate its own internal savings which can be plowed back into new investment.

The relationship between savings, capital, investment and production can be shown diagrammatically. This diagram might well be called the positive spiral of economic development (see Figure 9.1) as opposed to the vicious circles of poverty. It cannot be stressed too strongly that savings is always one of the keys for breaking every vicious circle of poverty.

Figure 9.1
A Positive Spiral of Development

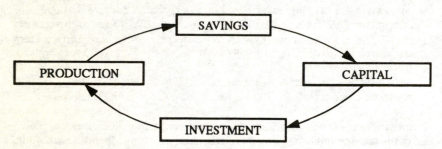

Savings can, however, be supplemented by credit, and some of the future production must go to repay the credit, and usually with interest. If the value of the production does not exceed the costs of achieving the production, then there will be no profit and hence no savings, and this particular development will grind to a halt. Hopefully, production will be profitable enough so that some of it can also be consumed by the investor – a dividend for having done well.

There are three additional external inputs that can be added to the circle (see Figure 9.2). Land and labour together can be inserted directly into the production process by poor people initially lacking capital. Technical assistance in the form of new ideas and innovations is important for new investment. In the industrialised world this is called research and development. I hesitate to add the third external input which is capital grants. The hesitation is based on the extreme unreliability of such an input, especially for poor people, and because of the acute danger that it will create a new dependency which ultimately breaks the circle again.

Savings and Group Funds

The reduction of dependence on the moneylenders and landlords purely

Figure 9.2
External Inputs and a Positive Spiral of Development

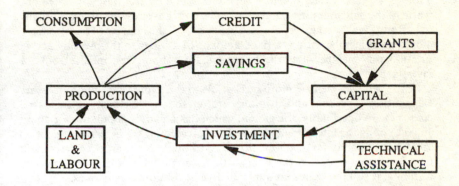

with external assistance from banks, government, NGOs, would lead, however, to a new dependency relationship which, while it may apparently hasten the process of development, would not create either collective self-reliance or individual self-confidence. An attitude of independence has to be fostered from the beginning and, even at the risk of a somewhat slower progress, the group should be encouraged to (a) utilise fully its own resources, particularly labour, (b) innovate less capital-intensive methods, and (c) generate regular internal savings.

(Haque, Mehta, Rahman and Wignaraja, 1977)

The basis for all genuine development is savings, i.e. the setting aside of resources for investment in productive activities rather than using these resources for immediate consumption. It is no coincidence that Japan and Germany, the economic power-houses of the late 20th century, have domestic savings rates of 20% and 14% respectively.

Savings are also the basis for all social insurance, i.e. setting aside resources to cover the costs of future calamities such as sickness, death, unemployment or old age. Savings also provide the basis for future purchases of expensive consumption items and social amenities such as housing, motorcars, water and sanitation.

Saving is not widely practiced in Europe and the U.S. today. Inflation, easy credit, tax deductions for interest payments and state social security programmes have made it less profitable or less necessary to save. But in every viable economic system there must be savings. A system based only on consumption and credit is a house of cards.

The poor do not share the luxury of not having to save. Although they are often seriously affected by inflation in basic consumer goods prices, they do not have access to credit or social security programmes, and certainly cannot take advantage of tax laws. Ironically, those who most need to save have the least capacity to do so. But save they must; the first step towards development is the habit of regular saving.

Except for the totally destitute, the poor can and do save and have always done so, especially the women. Women in Asia have traditionally taken one fistful of the daily rice ration and set it aside, either as a reserve or to eventually sell. Rotational savings groups are widespread throughout Africa; once a month each member brings a fixed amount of savings to the meeting and in rotation one member uses the collection for school fees, medical bills or investment.

Unlike women, men are more susceptible to the temptations of unnecessary expenditure. Smoking and drinking are on the rise in most Third World countries. In one county of Uganda, which has an adult population of about 10,000, change agents estimated that the equivalent of US$3,500 was spent on an average Sunday for alcoholic drinks. Although this is an effective way of transferring money from the men to the women, who do the brewing and distilling, it still represents an unproductive utilisation of resources.

Pierre Pradervand (1990) reports that in 1987 Thomas Sankara, then president of Burkina Faso, told him that his country spent more on imports of tobacco and cola nuts than the total value of its exports. In a striking example of on-the-spot awareness-building, Pradervand tells how he asked one village man, who chewed 50CFA/F (US$.16) worth of cola nuts a day, to come forward. He then drew 18,000CFA/F (US$59) from his wallet, gave the man a box of matches, and asked him 'Will you please set fire to these bank notes?' The man looked at Pradervand with astonishment and refused. The astonishment deepened as Pradervand told the village that the 18,000CFA/F equalled the cost of his yearly consumption of cola nuts.

The first step in the process of saving is motivation. Without having gone through a process of conscientisation in which they analyse the causes of their poverty and the steps they can take to alleviate it, the poor will lack the commitment to start regular saving. But once they become motivated, they will find ways to begin saving. The pride of self-respect and self-reliance glows in the faces of poor farmers who stand up and tell visitors how they have stopped smoking, drinking or gambling, and are now proud contributors to their savings fund from which they are going to buy a sprayer, or plough, or ox-cart.

For those of us who are astronomically rich in comparison, the small amounts saved appear pathetic. The point is not the size, but the process. This process, which is so essential at the start, consists of regular saving no matter how small the amount, even a few pennies every week is an acceptable beginning. The objective is as much to build self-respect as it is to accumulate a tiny start capital. It is from this self-respect, this basic feeling of 'we can do it ourselves', that the development process must begin.

Development agencies should not provide any capital in any form until the people have developed their self-respect through mobilising those resources of their own that they can. Although extremely short, these first steps are essential if the poor are not to stumble later on.

Poor people are often constantly in debt. To survive they take loans at exorbitant interest rates whenever they experience food shortages, sickness, births, marriages or deaths. Unlike production loans, which hopefully lead to future income, these consumption loans are what ensure their survival, on the one hand, and their continued exploitation by the money-lenders, on the other.

The way out of this dilemma is through group saving. Groups should organise their own savings fund into which each member should be expected to deposit a fixed amount every month. These funds can then be used for group investments or lent with interest to individual members to invest in their own productive activities. With continued collective saving and the profits earned from investments and interest payments, the group fund will grow. Within a short period of time the group will be able to give members consumption loans – for medicines, marriages, funerals, etc. – either with or without interest payments.

The psychological importance of collective savings should not be underestimated. The 'public' weekly or monthly payment into the group savings fund provides an enormous stimulus to the individual members to make their savings efforts. The fact that the total savings grow weekly by an amount many times larger than the individual contribution provides a strong incentive to continue the process.

The poor are exceedingly suspicious and are very reluctant to entrust their meagre savings to others. The mere fact that they collectively overcome their mutual reluctance and pool their savings is a huge first step in developing solidarity and unity of purpose. The collective savings fund becomes the visible evidence of their determination to work together for their common benefit.

Case Study No. 9 – Nga Konyi Mixed Group

The name of this group, which is located on a remote stretch of the Nile in northern Uganda, translates as 'Who can help you?' Nga Konyi is a mixed group of 10 men and women whose ages range from 18 to 45 years. The group started a year ago as a rotational savings group in which each member brings a fixed amount to each meeting and one member in rotation takes all the money collected for consumption or investment purposes. Through discussions with the change agents, the members realised that with rotational savings they were not accumulating any capital so they changed to a savings group.

At first the group decided on a fixed monthly deposit of Shs 200 from each member, but recently it has allowed each member to deposit as much as he or she wants. The group also decided that eventual dividends will be paid out in proportion to each member's total savings.

The group set the following objectives: (1) to build up a group fund for group investments and for individual investments through loans to members; (2) to buy an oil pressing machine to produce simsim (sesame seed) oil for sale; and (3) to build a village first aid post.

They also raise funds through group digging for wages. When they dig for members the fee is reduced as a sign of trust and mutual support. The money earned is divided equally between those who participate and this is deposited in their individual savings accounts. They have started issuing investment loans to members at 25% interest per month. Over 50 loans have been issued with no defaults. The loans are being used for fishmongering and for trading in farm produce like sugar cane and bananas.

The group has invested in a fish-smoking kiln, a goat and a 200-metre fishing net which members made themselves. The net is used by members who share the profit with the group. The women in the group have made a fishing trap which they use themselves; it is very unusual for women in this area to fish. The women also participated in making the kiln as well as in the group digging. Financially the group is progressing. The group fund now totals about Shs 90,000 of which half is individual savings deposits and half earnings on their investments and loans.

The group meets twice a month. The chairperson is a man, but the vice is a woman. However, at each meeting a different member leads the discussion. Each member is given the chance to talk before decisions are reached. The women talk bravely without fearing the men, which is also unusual in this area.

Compiled by *Cwinya-ai Santunino*, change agent, Jonam, Uganda

---

Revolving group loan funds

An important aspect of establishing viable economic processes is financing. One alternative system for providing credit to the poor is the use of revolving loan funds. These allow organised groups of low-income people to make loans, set interest rates, etc. according to social as well as economic goals. (Lassen, 1980)

Learning to manage group resources, especially money, is an essential prerequisite for beginning external borrowing on a collective basis. Setting up and running a revolving group loan fund is the best training for managing larger undertakings. Groups must have total autonomy over their own group funds. They must decide on the size and frequency of members' savings deposits, and whether these are to be interest-earning or not. They must decide for what purposes the fund is to be used, and establish rules to regulate to whom loans are to be made and for what purposes. They must set the terms of repayment and interest rates. Autonomy over their own financial affairs contributes immensely to their self-confidence.

When given the opportunity, groups of poor producers can show surprisingly good results from the management of their own group loan funds. Seventy-five small groups in southern Uganda increased their aggregate member loan funds in one year from US$1,800 to US$12,800 (1US$ = UShs 600 – 1989). This represented a real growth of over 250% after inflation which was quite high. Most of the loans were given for one-month periods which means that over US$85,000 was made available during the year as credit to the over 1,000 men and women belonging to these groups. Everything relating to these loan funds was decided by each group individually.

Probably the most difficult decisions for the group to make relating to the management of their group fund are those relating to the security of the funds. Who is to keep the accounts? Where is the money to be kept? The key to security is openness. Accounts should be reviewed regularly and be available at all times. Many groups choose several members to keep the accounts jointly, and rotate members frequently. If funds are kept in cash, they should be controlled at every meeting and the accounts book presented. Often it is impractical or legally impossible for small groups to open bank or postal savings accounts in the group's name. Many groups have found that the safest way of keeping funds is to lend them out to members.

Change agents should do what they can to encourage groups to begin saving and to establish their own group fund. This can be done by helping the group to analyse the costs of borrowing from the moneylenders, having them consider the security as well as the savings they can achieve through accumulating and using funds collectively, and encouraging them to evaluate possible investment schemes as well as revolving group loan funds.

Informal training in simple book-keeping and money management is essential if the group is to avoid the, all too frequent, disaster of mismanagement and fraud. All that is needed to get started is a cash book with separate savings accounts for each member, and if they set up a revolving loan fund, a loan account for each member. The net worth of the group can be calculated simply by subtracting liabilities (deposits, etc.) from assets (cash, loans outstanding, etc.). Although this is not double-entry book-keeping, it is adequate for most groups in the early stages of their development. Group funds provide an ideal entry point to the difficult field of teaching functional literacy and numeracy.

Banking is frequently a frightening experience for those who have not previously had encounters with bank officials, savings books, signatures and bank balances. This is a field of adventure in which the change agents can make introductions, provide training and encouragement – not by doing the banking for groups, but by 'walking through' the process with them. As with everything else, change agents should guide and encourage, but never take responsibility.

Case Study No. 10 – Setting up a group loan fund
The Lok-tek (literally 'talking is difficult') Group in northern Uganda was badly affected by the recent civil war in which members lost money, animals and material assets. The aim of the group, which is now one-year-old, is to replace this lost wealth and then improve the welfare of members. The group consists of eight men and eleven women.

Monthly member savings deposits started at Shs 10, later increased to Shs50, and are now Shs100. For some time these small funds were idle, so the group decided to set up an internal credit scheme for members.

At the meeting to launch the scheme, the agenda was (1) delinquent members; (2) monthly deposits; and (3) giving loans. The names of those members behind in their deposits were read; some came along with their arrears, others apologised as they had some problems. Fines were collected from those who came late or had been absent earlier. The monthly deposits were collected.

At this point a courageous lady rose and said, 'Mr. Chairman, you are really taking too much time on these side issues. Today we came for giving out loans which are even overdue now. Give us these loans and we go away to do our work.' The chairman replied, 'We are following the agenda as read and the loan item was put last because it might take long as it is the main item.' Another member said, 'Mr. Chairman, let me talk. The other two agenda items are not side issues; they are the cornerstones. The loans you will get are from the group funds, so collecting outstanding deposits will increase the group's ability to give loans to more members. If the group fund is now Shs5,000, five people can each be given Shs1,000. But if more money is collected and the fund reaches Shs7,500, then seven members can be served. Therefore we are not lost, but following a right procedure.'

Moving to the final agenda item, the treasurer gave the financial position: funds brought forward were Shs6,680 and today's deposits are Shs1,660. Seven people have clean records. The chairman then said, 'We are now aware of our financial strength. Members should now contribute their ideas about how these loans should be issued. Feel free and tell us your mind without fear.' The debate started:

'Divide the group into two and serve one group now and the other one next month.'

'Get the total funds and check the number of members who can be served with the available funds.'

'More deposits to be made and the loans to be given later.'

'The loan to be given without regard to each member's deposits with the group.'

'I joined the group later, but I have made all the deposits from that time to date. Can I be considered for a loan?'

'Ten members should get loans of Shs800 each and the balance remain with the treasurer. This is to be done in order of each member joining the group; the oldest first.'

'An interest rate of 5% monthly is fair because there is still no profitable activity to be done.'

'10% monthly is appropriate for ease of calculation.'

'20% monthly is good because one month is too long and hence a lot of profit will be realised.'

After much discussion the group felt 10% per month was fair with a loan sum of Shs1,000 and repayment in one month. Eight members received loans. Selection was by nomination and then approval by the entire group.

The loans were mainly used for commercial activities, and those who got loans moved up and down buying and selling vegetables, fish and charcoal. Profits were 100% per week and all loans were repaid with interest at the next meeting at which time each member narrated how they used the loans, their benefits and the problems they had. Benefits ranged from household utensils to chickens; cash savings ranged from Shs1,000 to Shs3,000. The loan recipients were indeed happy.

In the second round, 11 members were served successfully. A third round has been given to 15 members. In conclusion, I say that credit can be an engine of growth and development because individual capacity to save and invest increases. Group loan funds have a special quality because members view them as their own funds so there is almost no defaulting. With time our people will replace what they lost in the war and then become even better off.

Compiled by *Can Francis*, change agent, Gulu, Uganda

External Credit

Although the development process must be based on some degree of internal saving, the poor will at some point in time lack sufficient internal capital to carry out more ambitious development activities within a time frame which corresponds to their aspirations and increasing capabilities. It is at this point that they must seek external credit.

It is essential, however, that external credit is not provided before they are ready for it. Their first activities should be funded by their own savings through their group fund. After having gained self-confidence and experience in managing their own collective funds, the poor can seek out sources of institutionalised external credit.

In many nations of the Third World, credit institutions and banks are state-owned or state-controlled. Theoretically, all citizens have an equal right to obtain credit from these institutions assuming they can fulfill the formal requirements of creditworthiness. In practice the poor are either disqualified or subject to discrimination. Many live in locations too remote from banks and credit offices, and the officials of these institutions do not generally come to the people. Others are intimidated by the officiousness and the formalities, or are not willing to confront the disdain all too frequently shown to them by credit officials. Even where there is no prejudice against the poor, officials do not find it profitable in terms of time and money to process and manage the small loans needed by the poor.

But when credit is available and the officials are willing to assist, the poor are most likely legally disqualified. Where there have previously been credit programmes for the poor, the poor are often defaulters and automatically disqualified for new loans. The poor generally lack the required collateral, usually land titles or other saleable assets, to secure the loan. Acceptable guarantors are unwilling to back the poor. Most credit institutions have no instruments which make it possible to grant loans to unincorporated or unregistered groups.

The poor have a right to public credit facitilites – perhaps some day it will even be recognised that they should be given privileged access to public credit inasmuch as the better-off will always be able to obtain commercial credit. But for most of the poor, this is a right that they have been unable to take up. Except for a few enlightened institutions and officials, this right will apparently continue to be denied to the poor until they themselves, from a position of collective strength, are able to persuade the bankers of their creditworthiness and the justice of their requests.

Making credit available to the poor

The FAO-supported Small Farmers Development Programme in Nepal and the Grameen Bank in Bangladesh, now supported by the International Fund for Agricultural Development (IFAD) and others, have convincingly demonstrated that credit programmes can be successfully operated for groups of small farmers.

The single most important conclusion that can be drawn from the FAO and IFAD programmes is the significance of the organised small group for reaching the poor with institutionalised credit. These programmes persuasively demonstrate that small groups not only make credit more effective in terms of numbers, but that they also provide greater protection against default. Hopefully, more credit institutions, including commercial banks and credit societies, will direct their lending activities to groups rather than individuals, and adopt less stringent guarantees of loan security than land and fixed assets, as well as waive requirements of some form of official group registration.

IFAD maintains that the most important safeguard against default available to a development finance institution is its capacity to make a second loan. IFAD experience indicates that if the eligibility of a group or even a whole association to receive loans is linked to repayments of the earlier loans, there will be group pressure on the borrower to repay the loan. In general, the rate of recovery in small farmer credit programmes financed by IFAD has been very satisfactory and has often been higher than that for agricultural loans to large and medium-scale farmers. IFAD's experience seems to suggest that the traditional concept of land as security can be replaced by group guarantees; assets or materials purchased with loans; or liens on crops or other goods produced by linking credit with marketing services. Unfortunately, banks and other formalised credit institutions have not shown much willingness to accept collateral other than land titles, and are certainly reluctant to put their trust in the effectiveness of group discipline.

A second conclusion to be drawn is the importance of regular and close contact with the groups by functionaries working in the field. This unfortunately suggests that commercial banks and credit societies will be reluctant to direct resources into this work. Perhaps change agents can compensate for this through their own work with the groups during the period of initial contact with the institution.

These two programmes have established that loans channelled through organised small groups of the landless and small farmers effectively eliminate the twin problems of insufficient collateral and high rates of default. In addition, they have shown that it is possible, if there is enough determination, to take the credit facilities to the poor.

Change agents can assist small groups in making their first approaches to credit institutions for loans. Assuming that good relations have previously been established with bank officials, an introduction of the group to bank officials by representatives of the agency can help establish the group's credentials. The group will need training in how to prepare their application for a loan as well as learning the various regulations and procedures. Here again it is a matter of 'walking' the group through the process rather than doing it for them.

More important perhaps is persuasion at all levels, if necessary even in the top echelons of the Ministry of Finance, to change regulations or policies so as to make credit available to independent groups, whether officially registered or not, on a basis of 'soft' collateral. The examples of the FAO and IFAD programmes can be used effectively, and perhaps the representatives of these UN organisations would be willing to assist in these lobbying activities. Going one step further, the establishment of similar UN-sponsored programmes should essentially solve this problem.

In order to quickly break through the collateral problem, it is often tempting to establish a credit programme in co-operation with a bank, in which the development agency 'guarantees' the loans given by the bank to the poor by depositing with the bank an amount equal to the loan capital. This was tried in Sri Lanka by an international agency which wanted to make large amounts of credit available to the poor while not making them directly dependent on the agency. The administration of this programme was exceptionally difficult and cumbersome, and in the end proved to be a failure. Such guarantees take the pressure off everyone except the agency's fieldworkers. The bank has no incentive to do the necessary legwork to collect the loans, and the borrowers have no incentive to pay them. Additionally, at least in Sir Lanka and most probably everywhere in the Third World, the banks proved too inefficient and bureaucratic to administer these loan programmes effectively. Development agencies can lobby on behalf of the poor, but the loan must be a commercial transaction between the bank and the borrower.

One of the ultimate goals of a development agency should be to help integrate each and every small group into the existing institutional credit facilities where possible; this should be done under conditions which strengthen collective activities and are practical and financially feasible for the poor.

When should a development agency itself provide credit to the poor? Should an agency provide credit when there are existing public and commercial credit institutions operating in the area? Does it make sense for an agency to meet the credit needs of the poor with donor funds while public credit institutions continue to serve the rich?

Ultimately, the poor must gain access to public and commercial credit. The dilemma for the development agency is whether to provide credit in the short term, hoping that the recipients will eventually gain access to the institutional system, while being aware of the danger that this credit takes the pressure off both the poor and the system to change the conditions of access. Withholding credit in the hope of forcing access means that the poor may wait indefinitely for the credit they need to fuel their development activities.

In many cases the choice will be to provide credit, and continue to work for eventual access by the poor to institutional credit. Often there will be no alternative because the institutions just do not reach into the areas where the poor are living. The goal, however, should be clear: to integrate the poor into formal credit systems.

In addition to providing external credit when no alternative sources are available, agencies should use their credit programmes to demonstrate that the poor are creditworthy. These programmes provide an excellent opportunity to help the poor to develop the necessary confidence and abilities to handle credit provided by external credit institutions. An important part of any credit programme should be education on rights to public credit and how the public and commercial systems work. The ultimate objective is to withdraw from providing credit to individual groups as early as possible, and help these groups negotiate new credit from existing institutions.

This book is not intended as a credit manual for setting up an agency-operated group credit programme. There are already several books and manuals on this topic; one of the most useful is *A Manual of Credit & Savings for the Poor of Developing Countries*, Oxfam, 1987. The more important principles of good credit programmes are:

1. Credit should be given primarily to organised groups of people who share a common interest. These groups should undergo a process of conscientisation which has given them a commitment to work together for the collective good of all the members.
2. Groups should have built up their own collective savings funds and be willing to invest these funds in their own development activities.
3. Loans should be given to groups and to individuals through their group for viable productive activities to be carried out collectively or by the individual members.
4. Groups are collectively responsible for the repayment of loans with interest. Interest should be set higher than inflation and sufficient to cover operating costs. This must be done otherwise the loan fund will lose its value and the profitability of investments will be overestimated. Groups can charge members additional interest.
5. Change agents should work primarily with organising groups, helping them through the conscientisation process, and assisting them to formulate projects and apply for credit. Loan officers should process applications and follow-up loans, otherwise change agents will be compromised.

6. Guidelines for eligibility, repayment schedules, defaults and provisions for emergency rescheduling must be established. Experience shows that monthly repayments of principal and interest provide the best results even if they are set on a sliding scale. Frequent contact between the group and its credit officer is important. Forms, agreements, etc. must be printed in the local language.
7. Groups which have successfully repaid a loan are eligible for a new loan. Groups should be assisted in applying for loans from existing public and commercial credit institutions.

Operating loan funds for the poor is a tricky business. It is a delicate balancing act involving, on the one hand, maintaining a business-like and viable loan fund without becoming an oppressive loan collector and, on the other hand, trying to fuel the development process for the poor without establishing new dependency relations which in the long run destroy the process.

Donations and Matching Grants

A project which relies on large amounts of capital and external inputs is an example which cannot serve as a model. It cannot be supported on a large scale due to the scarcity of resources. The project would then degenerate into a selective approach, with all its disparity-accentuating characteristics.
(Haque, Mehta, Rahman and Wignaraja, 1977)

Anyone who has travelled extensively in the Third World has seen their share of abandoned schools, clinics, training centres and factories which were built with foreign aid. Donated water pumps, windmills, tractors and other expensive equipment stand rusting and unused. Why? Yes, there are shortages of foreign exchange to buy spare parts, fuel and raw materials. Yes, there are not enough trained mechanics. Yes, there are no operating funds. But why?

Why is the lorry with the lovely signboard 'By the Grace of God' still rolling along even though it's a disaster on wheels? Why are the temples newly painted and decorated for the festival? Why is the old water mill still grinding grain? Why is the Sunday school in the little mud chapel packed with children?

Is it just a question of bad planning or is there something more basic behind these disparities? Is it just a question of inappropriate technologies, or too much, too soon? Or does it have something to do with the problems inherent in 'giving things to people' and 'doing things for people'? Except in times of widespread disaster, are there any good reasons for giving things free to people except to make ourselves feel good? What role do pride and self-respect play in using things wisely and investing in development?

Our ultimate goal is self-sustaining, self-reliant development. If this is so, then it makes no sense at all to maintain poor people in an artificial world created by an aid agency rather than helping them to prosper in the real world of real prices, real bottlenecks, etc. Self-sustaining, self-reliant development will never be achieved through giving people donations. In every development activity there must be a mighty portion of self-reliance. People invest their energies and their resources in things they believe in, things that mean something to them, things that they have chosen and control themselves.

The best indication of the viability of a project is the amount of labour, materials and money that people are willing to provide from their own resources. If people know that they need to contribute little or nothing to the cost of a school, then they really 'need' that school even though they know that teachers don't stay and there are no books. But ask them to put in 75% of the cost, and perhaps they suddenly find other things they would rather do with their time and money. If a community builds a school entirely on its own, then you can be pretty sure that it somehow is going to find teachers and pay them.

Matching grants can be useful tools of development, especially for community projects. A matching grant is based on the total 'cost' of a project including unskilled and skilled labour, locally collected or donated materials, and all purchases of materials and services. A 'pure' matching grant is 50% of the total 'cost' from each partner, but many donors are willing to give as much as 80% which is then matched by only 20%. The higher the donor share, the less critical becomes the judgement of the other partner and the greater the dependency created.

The poor are professional bargainers. They know their customer. If they think that you really want that school, then they're going to bargain their share as low as possible. Once you get into the business of giving matching grants, then you had better have a clear policy. It's no good saying that, 'Well, this village is much poorer than that one. They'll only have to put up 10% instead of 25%.' In no time at all there won't be a village within miles that is able to put up more than 10%! It's better to err on the side of self-sustaining development: set a fixed, high rate for the people's share – a minimum of 50% is recommended.

Matching grants should only be given to communities or to large poor people's organisations. Preferably the latter, as the poor will usually end up providing most of the labour component in any case. It is a good idea always to require a cash component, even from the poorest communities, as this will guarantee commitment. It is better to leave the unskilled labour component out of the cost calculations – it is the material resources component which provides a real measure of the community's commitment.

A clear agreement, preferably written, should be drawn up stating each partner's commitment to the project. The entire project should be planned and implemented by the people. They should plan the work schedules, purchase the materials, hire the skilled artisans and supervise the work. After all, it's their school or road. If they can't organise the implementation, then they are not going to manage the maintenance either.

The PRODERO project in Honduras provides an illustration of how a donation/matching grant can be used by an existing, well-organised peoples' organisation to further their own development. After hurricane Fifi, the government decided to distribute to small farmers throughout the country fertiliser and other farm inputs that had been supplied as international assistance. In most of the country these supplies were distributed free, but in the PRODERO project region the goods were turned over to organised groups of peasants whose members agreed to meet two conditions: they would all participate in a one-week course emphasising soil conservation and enrichment; and they would sell the goods to their members, with payment after harvest time. In this way a one-time disaster donation enabled these groups to establish their own revolving funds to provide credit to their members in the future.

Introducing New Technologies

> We were learning ourselves, however slowly. You came with your science that you developed with your money and power, and its dazzling light blinded us. Can you throw the light not on our face but on the road so that we can see it better and walk ourselves, holding your hand occasionally?
>
> *Indian peasant* (quoted by Wignaraja, 1981)

I once was witness to an interesting exercise in the attempt to transfer technology from the drafting boards of the North to the poor of the South. The young energetic expert on solar technology arrived with his beautiful drawings of solar stills, solar cookers and solar driers. He was in a desperate hurry and had our staff running around seven days a week at his beck and call.

We arranged for a number of small plots of land in our project areas to be used for his experiments and in no time at all an interesting assortment of mud, brick, wood and glass gadgets had sprouted out of the sand and dust. Our young expert was certainly not afraid to dirty his hands. He hired some local masons and carpenters, and a few of the poor people in the project as labourers, and together they produced these monuments to appropriate technology.

A few of our staff and some of the project people were instructed where to fill the water, how to place the vegetables for drying. The last step was to put up a wire fence around the gadgets to keep out the cows and the children – and unintentionally the poor people themselves because they still respect the European expert's fences. Afterwards our 'appropriate solar technology' consultant flew back to his office.

He came back six months later – he had a nice grant from his government – to see how his contributions to improving the lives of the poor were working and to see how these really good ideas were spreading through the projects. And they really were 'appropriate' – some of them cost next to nothing, even for desperately poor, dry-zone farmers. But some of the gadgets had been ill-used, some removed altogether, because people wanted the plot for something else, and none of them were in daily use.

Needless to say, our young man was furious. Furious with our staff for not having followed up his project, and furious with the poor people who couldn't see the usefulness of things right before their own eyes. As a footnote to the story, it might be worth mentioning that the cost of his project, including his salary and air travel, was equivalent to the cost of 50 low-cost houses for the poor. They really were clever gadgets. He really was enthusiastic, and he was very much against importing expensive technology. Think of all the firewood they could have saved. What went wrong?

During the early development decades emphasis was put on modernisation and industrialisation. The poor nations desperately needed to increase their productivity, and the best way of doing this was to introduce modern machinery and technologies. At the national level, huge modern factories were built and equipped – paper and plywood industries, canneries, flour mills, fertiliser and cement plants, ice plants and packing plants. In the rural areas ambitious irrigation projects using huge diesel pumps would provide water for the fields to be tilled by tractors. Modern machinery together with new high-yield varieties, fertilisers and pesticides would revolutionise agriculture.

The results are to be seen throughout the Third World: empty factories, rusting machinery, abandoned tractors, unused irrigation channels. Fuel and spare parts became too expensive and drained national treasuries of foreign exchange. Managers and mechanics were too inexperienced and were in very short supply. Factories required unavailable raw materials. Transportation systems broke down. Markets were small – there were not enough wage earners to buy the manufactured goods which often were more expensive than imported goods.

Even where modernisation was successful in terms of increasing productivity, the poor in many cases did not benefit. Textile mills replaced hand looms; grain mills replaced hand mills, machinery replaced farm labourers. The poor lost their employment and were displaced from the land as they lacked the money, knowledge and organisational power to turn modernisation to their own advantage.

Although some national elites and international agencies are still willing to use millions of aid funds on the continued transfer of complex modern technologies, during the last decade there has been increasingly severe criticism of the direct transfer of modern technology as a way of solving development problems. There is now a fairly broad consensus on the need to adapt technology to individual local circumstances. What appeared to be needed were technologies that were less capital-intensive; more labour-intensive; used forms of energy other than imported petroleum products; could be produced locally to avoid the need to import spare parts; and had a simpler technology that local people could manage and repair themselves.

Out of this analysis arose the appropriate technology movement. This movement began in the early 1970s although the Intermediate Technology Development Group, which is perhaps the leading agency in the movement, was established in England in 1965 by Dr E. F. Schumacher, the spiritual father of appropriate technology. Dr Schumacher's book, *Small is Beautiful*, captured the spirit of its time and crystallised the work that had been going on into a movement which now encompasses well over 1,000 appropriate technology groups throughout the world. Dennis Frost, former chief executive of the

Intermediate Technology Development Group, describes this period:

> Appropriate technology was at that time still a radical concept. It was then largely unrecognised by the conventional wisdom of aid agencies, and hotly disputed by some who claimed that appropriate technology was merely a new form of colonialism, designed to keep poor people poor by denying them the benefit of modern technology and fobbing them off with cheap, second-rate products and processes.

The movement has had considerable success in developing and introducing appropriate and intermediate technologies in the Third World. Its aim has been to design technologies that can be manufactured by small workshops in the developing countries. These technologies would create local employment, provide local maintenance, repair and spare parts facilities, and make available to small producers cheap and reliable machinery designed to meet local needs and conditions. By the mid-1980s the sight of locally-made wind pumps, water tanks, roofing sheets, threshers and shellers had become common in Africa, Asia and Latin America.

But what about the man we met earlier in this section? The flipside of the appropriate technology coin is unfortunately tarnished with numerous examples of failures. Dennis Frost and ITDG recognise this problem. Frost states that one of the criticisms of the appropriate technology movement has been that some of its enthusiastic supporters have sought to develop do-it-yourself technologies without reference to the need for good engineering design and sound construction, or without regard to what people want and can afford to use. The results are often masterpieces of invention, frequently made from scrap or spare parts which cannot be obtained in quantity and that have little bearing on the needs of the community as a whole.

The observant traveller now sees rusted and abandoned wind pumps of assorted sizes and designs, broken hand pumps, crumbled mud stoves, dilapidated solar equipment of all descriptions. Although some of these technologies are badly designed, too expensive or inappropriate, there is no question that many of them do work and are appropriate and some are in fact used successfully by poor groups. But why aren't there more successes? Why isn't there a greater spread of these technologies? If we are to understand why many so-called appropriate or intermediate technologies fail to gain acceptance and widespread use among the poor, then we should try to analyse the context within which these technologies are often introduced.

Gianotten and deWit (1983) have pointed out two tendencies. At one extreme are those who see appropriate technology as an expression of their rejection of Western society. According to this view, the Third World has to be saved from highly 'technicalised' society and it is therefore necessary to promote appropriate, in the sense of unsophisticated, technology. Samir Amin calls this trend 'hippy technology' and sees it as a sentimental, conservative and paternalistic political option. The other extreme is the promotion of appropriate technology as a new commodity, controlled and imposed by the multinational corporations and falsely presented as being a 'technology of liberation' such as solar panels and solar heaters.

A third tendency, and far more common, could be designated as off-the-shelf or out-of-the-workshop technologies. These are the well-designed, cheap, appropriate gadgets designed and tested by qualified and dedicated mechanics and engineers, usually European. The designs for these technologies are ordered from the magazines and books by hardworking, well-intentioned voluntary agency field officers, also European. Missing from the development of this technology are the poor people for whom it is intended. Appropriate technology, no matter how good it is, is all too often external to the self-reliant participatory development process. It falls into the trap of 'providing things for' and 'doing things for' people. The poor are not involved; it is not their technology.

Haque and his colleagues maintain that a technological revolution has to be achieved internally because of its social implications. The people must not be alienated by the transplantation of elitist technology not rooted in their lives. Technological development has to be based on local resources, and on people's own initiative and perceived needs.

Technology, of any kind, will only be successful if it becomes an integral part of the lives of those who are to use it. They must want it. They must see that it fulfils a need in their lives. It must be something that they themselves choose because they understand it and can control it. They will not invest their time and money in it unless they believe in it. The poor cannot afford the luxury of gadgets that can be thrown away when something goes wrong. They can't go to the local store to buy a part that's manufactured far away. It has to be their technology, and they must be so familiar with it that they can make it work and keep it going at a cost that is within their reach.

Appropriate technology will be most successful when it develops from the real needs of the people as defined by themselves. It will be successful when it is developed or adapted by the people to meet these needs. Of course, they cannot develop technologies completely on their own until they have technological experience. The role of technological change agents should be to help them to acquire this experience by working with them rather than bringing new technologies to them.

Participatory technological development

Poor people have little experience with machines. Their lives are 'organic', based on simple tools and human or animal energy. The basis for technological development intended to solve rural problems must be the actual conditions of the poor and they must participate as an integral part of the development team if the new technologies are to be truly assimilated into their lives.

According to Haque and his colleagues (1977) a related factor in alienating people is the use of technology beyond the comprehension of the people at a particular stage, therefore requiring technicians and experts who are quite distinct from the masses. They advocate that technicalisation at the local level should be built up with emphasis on the people understanding, acquiring and even improving on the technology which then becomes their own. The role of the specialist is to prepare the people to internalise knowledge and not just to set up and run the machine for them. The tasks undertaken by the group therefore should progress from technically simple to complex, as the people become ready for them.

Obviously, poor rural people cannot be expected to develop, on their own, new technologies significantly improving their productivity. How then can technology be developed and introduced in such a way as to avoid the problems of outright transfer of foreign technology? Participatory technological development is a strategy to stimulate technological development and adaptation among the poor. Jake Galvez Tan (1985) defines it as a systematic approach of evolving or adapting technology among the people of a community based on participatory processes. According to Galvez Tan the possession of appropriate technologies is not enough to uplift the conditions of the poor, nor can these guarantee their liberation from relationships of dependency, oppression and control. Each technology and its development has to undergo a process of evolution through the active participation and experimentation of the people who would use it.

Without people's participation in the development, evolution and delivery, as well as in the decision-making relating to this process, attempts to introduce appropriate technologies will fail or the benefits will not accrue to the intended beneficiaries. Without participation, even appropriate technology can become another form of imperialism that may increase dependency, exploitation and monopoly by a few.

Participatory technological development deliberately aims to raise the level of critical consciousness of the people leading to a lessened dependency on outside forces represented by the technicians and their respective institutions. Jake Galvez Tan has identified four areas of activity in which the people can directly and creatively take part in technological development: (1) safeguarding indigenous technologies and improving them; (2) making the existing 'appropriate' technology genuinely appropriate through modifications in design, scale, materials, etc; (3) testing technologies which are claimed appropriate elsewhere, in order for the community to gauge their usefulness; and (4) participating in technical discussions intended to broaden and increase the people's critical consciousness of technological issues of local and national concern such as energy sources and high-yielding varieties of seeds.

The participatory technological development approach consists of six major steps to be implemented by the poor:

1. *Identifying and analysing problems* and setting priorities for which problems to tackle first are basic to the participatory approach and should be quite familiar by now.
2. *Eliciting possible solutions* from the people's own experience and/or suggesting new technologies as possible solutions; setting priorities for experimenting. This is perhaps the most crucial step because it involves the initial selection of an appropriate technology. The people must first discuss the possible technological solutions with which they are familiar. After

exhausting all of these ideas the change agent can introduce to the discussion other types of technologies which may be beyond the experience and knowledge of the people.

The change agent should not try to 'sell' these ideas, but merely inform the group that they exist and explain that they may or may not be appropriate solutions. In other words, the change agent broadens the range of options open to the people. The people are still left to decide what must be done, given the options available. The change agent waits for the people to ask for more information regarding the new technologies which of course is then provided. The change agent must try to ensure that there is genuine interest in the new idea and that it has been adequately compared with the other suggested solutions.

3. *Planning and preparation of experiments* to test possible solutions chosen by the people. After all the available information has been carefully considered, the people must select one technology which they deem potentially best and most appropriate to their situation. Then, together with the change agent, they must plan in detail how they will test out the new technology. Informal groupings can be formed and assigned tasks and responsibilities for conducting the experiments.

4. *Carrying out experiments* – the experimentation phase. It is important that everyone understand what is happening and why. The people should be encouraged to make realistic and practical innovations along the way. All results should be recorded, systematised and combined for better understanding. These must be thoroughly discussed and carefully analysed by the people in a series of discussions leading into an evaluation session.

5. *Evaluating the experiments.* The criteria for the evaluation may vary from one technology to another and is dependent on the problem being solved. The choice of criteria must be discussed and decided upon by the people involved. Most technologies are evaluated from the economic point of view: investment and operating costs, efficiencies, maintenance and spare parts, operating lifetime, etc. Possible adverse social effects should also be considered.

6. *Implementing successful experiments* or investigating possible alternative solutions. This step begins after the experiments have been successful and the people have decided to make use of a particular technology, and consists of careful planning by the people for the use of the new technology. Regular discussions should be held to ensure that the further development of the technology is benefiting as many individuals as possible and is not being monopolised by a few.

As with all participatory development approaches, the above process assumes that the change agent, attempting to assist a group of people solve a problem through the introduction of a new technology, has already integrated himself or herself into the community. It assumes that the change agent has thoroughly studied the problem together with the people. External technicians who are brought in to help with specific problems and do not have the time or opportunity to become integrated must, at the very least, work closely with the resident change agents. The poor must be encouraged to think, analyse and be critical of whatever ideas are presented to them and accept criticism of their own ideas. This process of developing critical thinking is the main objective of the participatory technological development approach.

The six steps described above constitute the analysis and action components of the approach. The reflection component is equally important. The change agent must encourage reflection through group discussions about the actions taken. This develops the ability of the poor to conceptualise and theorise. It focuses on the rationale behind the activities and how their particular attitudes, lifestyle, beliefs, fears and apprehensions have been enhanced or inhibited, reinforced or negated. It should give them a clearer understanding of the forces working in the environment and within themselves.

The people should become aware of what is worthwhile and should be reinforced, and what is detrimental and should be avoided. This is the time when they should be made more conscious of the process used to provoke them to experiment and the rationale for each of the six steps. They should finally reach an understanding of which technologies are appropriate for their situation and which are not. They should furthermore begin to understand the historical and economic perspectives which are the reasons behind the continuous attempts by various outsiders to introduce inappropriate technologies.

Finally, it is important to help the people to realise that they have the power within themselves to solve their own problems, that the experiences they have gone through and the processes which they have learned are tools in solving any problem that may confront them. Developing attitudes and values of self-confidence and less dependency on outside forces is the primary goal.

Participatory technological development is based on the principles of self-reliant participatory development. It is a natural part of the process of helping the poor to gain greater control over their lives. To be successful, technological development must be seen as a form of human development and as part of a process of social transformation.

To conclude, investment inputs and new technologies are needed to push forward the process of development. Investment capital can be generated internally through savings or externally in the form of credits or grants. Basing development solely on internal saving is a slow process and, for some, their margin of survival is so small that development seems impossible.

Rahman (1984b) has stressed the negative effect of using credit as the 'entry point' for the formation of grassroots organisations. If access to credit becomes the chief motivating factor for the organisation of small groups, this will impede the development of collective awareness among the poor of the need to organise for more important reasons. Unless the poor organise in order to achieve their rights to a fair share of resources and to solve problems through co-operation and saving, access to credit alone will not lead to progress.

Development can be likened to a motorcar. Investment is the engine of development. Savings is the fuel that keeps the engine of investment going. Credit can be likened to a super-charger giving an extra boost to the engine, but there is a price to be paid in added fuel consumption. Donations are like giving a stalled motorcar a push down a hill: if there is no fuel, when it gets to the bottom of the hill it stops rolling.

In this chapter we have looked at how savings, credit and grants can be used to promote self-reliant participatory development. We have also looked at how credit and grants can inhibit genuine development. Development assistance might well be defined as the art of giving poor people access to external resources in a way and at a rate that doesn't destroy the very process that it is trying to promote.

We have also looked at the problems that can arise when external agencies attempt to introduce new technologies to the rural poor, and the need to ensure that the people have the opportunity to shape such technologies to their own social and cultural environment. Development agencies must give as much attention to these human dimensions of development activities as they do to the technical dimensions.

This chapter ends Part II – Action. In it we have looked at the important role to be played by change agents working with the poor and how change agents can be trained and supported for this work. We have presented the need for a radical new approach to preparing and planning rural development programmes. We have established the importance of encouraging the emergence and development of small group efforts within rural society and the problems such groups may confront in their interactions with external forces. This has led to the identification of the need for small groups to combine their efforts within larger associations of the poor. Finally, we have investigated the role of savings and credit in the development process, and the need for a participatory process of technological development.

The next and final part of this examination of self-reliant participatory development is called 'Reflection'. The first chapter attempts to review the general objectives and the basic principles of this approach while the final chapter takes a cautionary look at the potential problems and obstacles to successfully promoting people's development.

Part III
Reflection

10. Objectives and Principles of Self-Reliant Participatory Development

> The input-oriented approach to development is like pouring water into a leaking pot. Without first protecting poor people from different kinds of exploitation, everything poured in runs out.
>
> *Participant*, FFHC/AD Regional Change Agent Training Programme (quoted in *Ideas and Action*, No. 140, FAO, 1981/82)

Self-reliant participatory development is a methodology for assisting the rural poor which is very much based on a particular development philosophy. An excellent summary of this philosophy has been formulated by four South Asian social scientists, Haque, Mehta, Rahman and Wignaraja (1977):

1. The ultimate goal of development is the growth and development of the individual within the context of his or her own collective fellowship, e.g. the family, the group, the community and nation. The measure of development is its effect on the individual and the collective fellowship.
2. Development should lead to the de-alienation of the individual. He or she should feel at home with the process of development in which he or she becomes the subject as well as the object.
3. Development should strengthen the feeling of a collective personality in which men and women find within this fellowship their richest expressions as individuals.
4. Participation is the true form of democracy and the only way in which the individual can become truly integrated with the collective fellowship.
5. Self-reliance is the expression of the individual's faith in his or her own abilities and the foundation on which genuine development can proceed.

The following definition of self-reliant participatory development has been adapted from the work of a group of experienced development workers who met with Ian Askew (1984) at the University of Exeter. It effectively joins the five concepts of the philosophy into an operational unity:

> Self-reliant participatory development is an educational and empowering process in which people, in partnership with each other and with those able to assist them, identify problems and needs, mobilise resources, and assume responsibility themselves to plan, manage, control and assess the individual and collective actions that they themselves decide upon.

This definition contains the following propositions about the nature of self-reliant participatory development:

- It is *educational* because a multidirectional exchange of knowledge takes place in the interactions between individuals, groups, change agents and external institutions. These interactions should be characterised by self-awareness and mutual respect.

- It is *empowering* because experience in how to influence, implement and control activities which improve their living conditions is gained by the people through their active interaction with the change agents and through their own attempts at individual and collective action.
- It is a *process* because people must begin from what they know and from where they are; from this modest start they can gradually increase their knowledge and control over their lives through personal experience. This requires time, but results in changes and transformations that are long-lasting.
- It must be a *partnership* between individuals working together and between the group and the change agents working with it because individuals alone cannot effectively change their socio-economic environment. Eventually this partnership must be extended to include other institutions, and especially the government, so that the people can be assured of access to resources and a stable environment for further development.
- *Problems* and *needs* must be identified by the intended beneficiaries and not be assumed to exist by the external change agents. Only when problems and needs are recognised by individuals and groups will participation in developmental activities be feasible.
- *Resources* must be mobilised to fuel the engine of development. Beginning with the mobilisation of their own meagre resources as the basis of self-reliance, individuals and groups must gradually acquire rightful access to external resources and services on mutually acceptable terms.
- Individuals and groups must assume responsibility for *planning, managing and assessing* their actions if they are to *control* them. This will also ensure maximum self-reliance and continuity of activities when outside support is withdrawn.
- *Collective action* is necessary to achieve empowerment and to address problems requiring resources beyond the means of the individual. Collective undertakings require an organisational structure which is broadly based and ensures continuity of action independent of individual leadership.

The Objectives

On the basis of the philosophy of development and the definition of self-reliant participatory development as expressed above, we can establish the specific objectives of the process:

1. The creation of self-awareness and a conscious understanding of their own situation by the poor, individually and collectively. Such awareness and understanding should lead to an on-going analysis–action–reflection capability directed towards improving their own situation.
2. The creation of self-reliant groups or associations having a strong sense of self-identification and group responsibility and capable through their own

organisation and leadership of setting priorities, planning, implementing and assessing their own projects and activities by mobilising their own, as well as external, resources for the ultimate benefit of the individual members.

3. The establishment of viable, self-sustaining income-generating activities owned and operated by individuals, families or small groups possessing the managerial and technical skills needed to maintain profitability, independence and ecological soundness.

4. The establishment of viable, fair and just political systems and processes which promote human and individual rights, an equitable distribution of resources as well as of the benefits from the use of these resources.

5. The establishment and maintenance of community-supported social service activities in the areas of health, education, water and sanitation in co-operation, where possible, with local government authorities.

Basic Principles

The above sections have discussed various aspects of what is meant by self-reliant participatory development and where it hopefully will lead. In the following paragraphs the basic principles of the self-reliant participatory approach are set down. These are based on the experiences of various groups and organisations working with the genuinely poor and disadvantaged under highly varying conditions in Asia, Africa and Latin America.

1. Interdependence and social transformation

Except for very isolated and primitive communities, no community or group can develop completely independent of national and international political and economic structures. Indeed, these very same political and economic structures can destroy attempts by the poor and disadvantaged to develop themselves. However, no national development policy intended to alleviate the suffering of the poor and disadvantaged can succeed unless the poor and disadvantaged are actively participating in their own development.

Self-reliant participatory development programmes attempt to initiate a process in which the poor acquire greater control over their life situations and solve their fundamental problems. Such programmes operate within existing social, economic and political structures, but aim to enable the poor to transform these structures so that they better serve their interests and enable them to improve their lives.

2. Recognising communities are not homogeneous

Few communities are homogeneous. There will always exist formal and informal power structures within each community which reflect social, economic and political relationships among the members of the community as well as with the outside world. There will be individuals and groups, within the community as well as outside, with considerable power over others. Attempts to transform these power relationships to the advantage of the poor will be met with attempts to obstruct such changes. But, unless changes occur, the poor will remain excluded from development.

3.   Self-reliance
A self-sustaining development process benefiting the poor must be based on their own mobilisation of their resources. In addition the poor must gain access to other available resources to which they are entitled. The amounts of capital necessary in the initial stages of the process are very small. The process must, from the very beginning, be based on individual and group savings which are reinvested in development activities. Once poor groups have demonstrated an inclination and ability to utilise their own group funds for their own benefit, then these can be judiciously supplemented with credits and matching grants. Ultimately, the poor must gain access to existing institutional credit sources.

Injections of large amounts of funding as gifts or even as credit will destroy the self-reliant participatory development process. This process is incompatible with a philosophy of 'giving things to' people or 'doing things for' people which creates greater dependency. Economic development must be based on savings, supplemented by credit, being invested in productive activities which generate new savings and investment. Social development activities must have firm economic and political bases if they are to be sustainable.

4.   Development as a process
Self-reliant participatory development is a process involving many stages and changes unfolding over time. It is complex and difficult to implement, and it does not have a predetermined direction. It attempts to overcome the enormous weight of tradition and the psychological dependence that characterise the lives of the poor. It attempts to change the mentality of being dominated and to develop a conviction among the poor that they have the ability to influence their own future development.

Self-reliant participatory development is a slow-moving process and requires considerable patience, and for the participants it is never-ending. There will be many setbacks and even total failures, but the successes will be genuine and long-lasting.

5.   External change agents
Because of their seriously disadvantaged situation and their inherent lack of cohesion, the poor are seldom able to initiate a self-reliant development process without outside stimulation. An external agent must therefore be the catalyst. The aptitudes and attitudes of such change agents are crucial for the success of such an intervention.

Change agents must be exposed to an intensive participatory training process which is inseparable from development action. The training involves interaction with the poor to investigate the socio-economic realities and contradictions within the community and how these are linked with higher macro-level structures and relationships.

Change agents cannot function effectively if their supporting agency is undemocratic and highly hierarchical. Participatory development cannot be successfully stimulated by agencies which are not themselves internally participatory.

6. Participatory action research

Attempts to initiate a truly self-reliant participatory development process benefiting the poor must be based on a thorough investigation and analysis of the socio-economic relationships existing in each community. Not only is this research intended to deepen the understanding of the change agents but, more importantly, to nurture the skills of the poor in investigation and analysis. The change agents, through dialogue with the poor, seek to arouse the interest of the poor in investigating the root causes of their poverty and potential solutions to their problems. This type of research involves a relatively long period of intimate study, discussion and reflection in which the poor and the change agents interact on an equal footing.

Participatory research is action-oriented. Information is gathered and analysed not primarily for its academic interest, but in order to identify root causes and contributing factors specifically for the purpose of guiding future action. The information stays with the poor as do the skills of data collection, analysis and programme formulation. No development activities should be attempted until participatory action research has been carried out and the socio-economic factors affecting a problem are well understood by the people and the change agents.

7. Conscientisation

Participatory action research is the first step in a process of consciousness-awakening or conscientisation of the people through their own analysis of and reflection on the causes of their poverty and on the socio-economic structures and processes which affect their lives. No development activity can be successful until this process is well underway. Even after activities are started, the people must continue the cycle of analysis–action–reflection. Each new action must be based on reflections about previous actions and an analysis of the new situation. Gradually, their self-awareness and self-confidence increase.

8. Small-scale interest groups

The process of conscientisation and subsequent implementation of development activities must initially be organised around small homogeneous groups of men and/or women sharing common interests. Membership must be voluntary. These groups must structure themselves and be internally autonomous. They must assume complete responsibility for analysing their own needs, setting priorities, mobilising resources, planning, implementing and eventually evaluating their own development activities. The role of the change agent in this process is to facilitate discussion of the problems to be addressed in forming mutual support groups.

All too often groups are formally recognised before their common interests and future courses of action are identified. Change agents should not 'form' groups nor should their work be judged on the number of groups with which they are working. They should encourage people to act on their own behalf and to perceive the added strength of joint action. Groups must evolve through their own efforts if they are to achieve self-reliance and sustainability.

9.   Development activities

Groups of poor people must initially concentrate their efforts on improving their economic situation through increasing the gains from their productive activities or by initiating new productive activities either individually or collectively. The genuinely poor will normally give this their first priority. However, in some cases, the poor may need first to fight and overcome exploitation and social oppression through asserting their human and legal rights. Unless their economic situation is improved all other development activities will be less than successful. Sustainable economic development must be based on savings and reinvestment.

However, once mobilised, groups normally will direct their collective efforts towards solving other non-economic problems. The choice of these activities will depend on local conditions and culture and should be selected by the people on the basis of their own priorities. Past experience has shown that they may give priority to increasing their participation in political decision-making; to conserving and improving their environment; to making improvements in their health, welfare and social security; and to reducing wasteful social expenditures.

It cannot be predicted in advance to which development activities the poor will choose to give priority. Self-reliant participatory projects are therefore not compatible with rigid project plans which predetermine objectives, activities, services and outputs. Such rigid planning will inhibit rather than liberate the creative energies of the poor.

Most development activities will involve the acquisition of new skills and knowledge on the part of the poor as well as the selection and introduction of new technologies and processes. New skills and knowledge must be developed through non-formal educational experiences in which the poor actively participate as 'subjects' instead of remaining passive 'objects'. Participatory technological development involves the poor directly in the processes of selection, experimentation, adaption, implementation and evaluation of new technologies.

10.   Independent autonomous associations

Isolated small groups, like individuals, cannot by themselves maintain a long-lasting, self-reliant development process. They must eventually ally themselves with like-minded neighbouring groups in order to achieve sustained development. These groups and associations may be composed solely of women, or men; or they may be mixed. They will normally be producer groups such as farmers, fishermen or labourers, or they may be multi-purpose welfare and human-rights groups. These local associations may eventually join or evolve into free and independent regional or national associations promoting the interests of their members.

It is essential to begin small – with only a few groups – and do a thorough job. If the initial efforts are carried out correctly, the process will spread by itself. Other poor people, on seeing the success of the original groups, will form their own groups and request assistance – which often can be provided by the original groups. Eventually, associations of groups will need to be formed, but the initiative and driving force must come from the groups themselves rather than from the external change agents.

11. The golden rule

Finally, there is a golden rule which should always be foremost in the thinking of external change agents in order to ensure that new forms of dependency do not evolve:

Don't do anything for people that they can do for themselves.

It is not intended that these principles be held to in every situation encountered, nor that the methodology be slavishly followed. The stating of the principles is intended to serve as a series of reference points for the analysis of each situation and the eventual choice of methodology. However, it would be unwise to deviate from any one principle or to radically change the choice of methods without taking considerable time and effort to analyse the possible consequences that such changes may have on the probability of catalysing a long-lasting and truly self-reliant development process which brings genuine benefits to the poor and disadvantaged.

11. Two Steps Forward, One Step Back . . .

Two Steps Forward

This book is an attempt to present in a systematic manner an interpretation of self-reliant participatory development as it has been defined and developed through research and field experience over the past 15 years. It is a process which is highly sensitive to the specific people involved in a given situation at a given point of time. It cannot therefore be defined in terms of a step-by-step methodology. It is a process which unfolds in response to the interactions of change agents with the poor and with their environment.

A true development process is based on a continuous series of analysis–action–reflection exercises carried out by the poor. Beginning with awareness and analysis, poor people must gain access to and mobilise their own human and material resources as well as link into sources of external credit and technical assistance in order to initiate actions. When these actions have taken place, the results must be reflected upon; these reflections should lead to a new analysis and new actions; and the development process will hopefully take another two steps forward.

One Step Back . . .

I have often been accused by friends in the development business of being overly optimistic about the effectiveness and potential of the self-reliant participatory development methodology. There are of course serious dangers in becoming a 'true believer'. But this does not necessarily mean that one is blind to the problems, risks and obstacles involved in this type of approach. Experience everywhere has shown that economic, political and social development is a long and difficult process in which many are hurt and many fall by the wayside. These difficulties may in themselves be one reason for putting one's faith in the necessity for people to develop themselves.

But let us look briefly at some of the problems that affect attempts to promote a self-reliant participatory methodology. First of all, do poor peasants, the rural proletariat, really respond as positively as the methodology assumes? Well, yes and no. Certainly the totally destitute, the 'poorest of the poor', the starving, and the displaced are not going to have the mental and physical resources to respond. But their predicament calls for relief and charity work. We are talking about development work, and there is a difference.

How many development agencies in practice talk about working with the poorest of the poor or the most destitute 20% of the population? In reality, in most Third World rural areas, 80% or more of the population are either landless labourers or poor or middle peasants whose quality of life is appalling by modern standards. These are the people who ultimately must develop themselves. Granted that many will not respond initially and those who do will often be the more intelligent, the more resourceful, those with a slight edge in human and physical resources. But we must start with a few, and who better to start with? Surely in every poor rural area there are sufficient 'grains of sand' to start a crystallisation process? Most of the others will follow, some will not – but, in any case, what other methodology will bring this minority into the development process?

During my work as a coordinator of change agent training programmes, I have sometimes encountered trainees who say, 'It's all very well what you say, but *our* rural people are genuinely backward! They are superstitious, mistrustful, refuse to co-operate with us or with each other, are resistant to change, and will not listen to good advice.' These trainees are almost always the better educated, those who come with middle-class values. This highlights a real danger in the methodology, especially when attempted by international NGOs, UN and bilateral agencies, or even local NGOs with leaders who are well-educated and urbanised. They tend to recruit the wrong people to be trained as change agents.

Assuming the right change agents are recruited – and I have been enormously impressed with many I have worked with – does the methodology set such enormously high expectations of them that they must be 'a band of self-sacrificial saints'? Yes, if we expect them to produce visible results within the short life-span of the typical development project. Yes, if we expect them to forsake home and family. No, if we can accept that the development of commitment is also a process; that no job can require or needs people to work 24 hours, seven days a week; and that change agents need support, encouragement and security. Change agents who are recruited from their home districts, in which they will work, and with strong roots within the rural population can, and do, commit themselves to the demands of this very difficult career. They are there; the problems arise when agencies cannot take the time nor give enough attention to find them; and do not have the commitment to support and encourage them in what must be a long-term engagement.

Is there a contradiction between self-reliance and the use of external change agents? Once again, I think the answer lies in the fact that development must be a process, and is of course highly dependent on the skill and sensitivity of the change agent. There will be many failures. Even those change agents with the potential to develop such skills and sensitivity will fail in the beginning to find the right balance between 'stirring the pot vigorously and gradually pulling out the stirring spoon'. It would be an injustice to many to say that it can't be done. However, experience strongly indicates that the pot must be stirred.

Which leads us directly into the perhaps frightening prospect that conscientisation, which lies at the core of the methodology, must logically lead to political action. I have attempted to address some aspects of this in Chapter 8. But I think there is an unconscious fear within the development community about this question which may identify the underlying fallacy in most development efforts during the past three decades. Most development agencies, both local and international, have refused, again unconsciously in most cases, to recognise that there is an unavoidable relationship between human, economic, political and social develpment (see Chapter 2).

Most aid agencies direct their activities to social development problems. Human development activities, when they are attempted, are also usually tied to the same problems. That minority of agencies who do try to 'dirty their hands' in economic development activities consistently keep on the side of skill and technology transfer in an attempt to increase productivity and production. Very few get involved in the explosive questions of marketing and control of resources. And when did you last meet an agency which openly was promoting political development? Does this invalidate the methodology because most agencies lack the courage to use it?

And yet there must be political development. Perhaps (a very critical perhaps) the end of the Cold War will create pressures and openings permitting greater involvement in questions of political development. Perhaps we shall see a lessening in the rivalries of ideology which have certainly complicated the issue beyond rationality. Is the self-reliant participatory methodology in any way politically ideological? Although parts of it could be, and are, used by political zealots of various persuasions, it cannot be completely and faithfully used by them because they have a predetermined outcome in mind. My experience is that the rural poor are not ideologically inclined unless they are forced to be.

Where does this leave the change agent caught between the people and the repressors who are not going to leave the stage without a push? And where does it leave the people who may be subjected to even more violent repression? Perhaps caution should have a more central role in the methodology? As discussed in Chapter 8, the change agent must at all costs avoid getting 'caught out in front' of the people; and the people should not push until they are fairly sure that they have the weight to push through. Assuming momentum will not be lost, the revolutions of 1989 in Eastern Europe show what can be done given suitable opportunities and circumstances.

But people and change agents will suffer, and some will die. They already have in Latin America, Asia and South Africa. Development is such a slow and uncertain process that I think it is too early to say that they have suffered and died in vain. Ultimately, it is not development grants, and certainly not development experts, that will push the process through to a positive conclusion, but the people themselves.

I think the greatest contradiction in the methodology is the fact that it relies on development agencies to initiate and sustain it. Almost every development agency today shouts its adherence to 'self-reliance', 'participation', 'awareness building', 'facilitation', 'change agents'. This includes the enormously rich and powerful international agencies, the UN agencies, the bilaterals, Third World and First World NGOs, and especially those with public education in their mandates.

Yet, unfortunately, it is still rare that these concepts are genuinely and with full commitment put into practice. Self-reliance is tempered with a rush to give 'soft' credit and even hand-outs. Participation is participation in what we want to do as set out in our predefined programme descriptions and budgets. Awareness-building means listening to our prepackaged messages; and facilitation is in reality mobilisation. Change agents are employees given work plans and targets. Where is the willingness to let the people progress at their own speed and in their own directions? Are we afraid that the people will take the control of the process out of our hands? Are we afraid of our funders? Or do we think we know better? Should we accept that because the concepts are misused, the methodology is wrong? We shall just have to try harder.

Finally, there is the question of how a few change agents working in a remote and isolated corner of a huge and diverse nation can influence important questions of national policy; and how can the processes which they hopefully will contribute to starting be replicated throughout the land? Well, they can't, and certainly not tomorrow; but if only a fraction of the billions of dollars spent annually on overseas development programmes could be diverted to training and supporting local change agents in every district then the seeds of replication would be sown. And in terms of sustainability, it would be more cost-effective.

As to the question of national policies, these will as always be affected by pressure groups; and presently rural people in the Third World are obviously not an effective pressure group for the most part. But if the people organise – the farmers, the fishermen, the women, the cattlekeepers – first in small groups, then in local associations, and ultimately in regional and national federations, then perhaps policies will begin to reflect the needs and aspirations of the rural population. Perhaps the co-operatives will be freed from government control. Perhaps the monopolistic, inefficient and corrupt marketing boards will be dismantled. Perhaps the laws guaranteeing women's rights will finally be observed. Perhaps the elected local representatives of the people will appoint the chief, the school inspector, the extension officers. Surely this is our goal. How else will it happen if the majority of the people don't take control of their own lives? Should we not help to put the people first?

All of this is not to say that the self-reliant participatory approach to development is sufficient in itself to develop a nation. There will still need to be large-scale programmes for social services (hospitals, vector eradication, colleges, water supply systems) and economic infrastructure (trunk roads, railroads, electrification). There will still need to be national policies affecting investment incentives, import control, export promotion. In emergencies there will need to be relief and rehabilitation programmes. But in terms of development promotion among the masses of the rural poor, I know of no other methodology as effective in releasing the productive and organisational energies of so many people in so many different directions and with so much hope of sustainability.

Stepping Out

The ultimate test of self-reliant participatory development is whether or not the people become self-reliant in the sense that they are able to maintain and advance their socio-economic development *without outside assistance*. This means that at some point in time they have to be left to themselves to get on with it. For the change agent, knowing when to stay a bit longer and when to move on to new areas is as important as all the work leading up to this decision.

It is important to distinguish between groups and projects, i.e. development work in a defined area of activity. One can imagine a situation in which change agents have assisted small groups of milk producers to organise their own co-operative which is, after a few years, able to manage on its own. It would be correct for the change agents to end their regular work with the milk producer groups, but instead of leaving the area, i.e. closing down the project, they could direct their attention to other producer groups.

One can imagine an 'ideal' project which begins in one small area and expands outward encompassing new villages and new producers, while at the same time expanding inward: taking up promotional work with groups and sectors of the poor population who were not absorbed in the first producer groups and associations. This project would not end until all the groups in all the villages within the district or province were organised for participatory development, and were functioning self-reliantly. This type of project would represent a genuine commitment to all the poor of a given area, and might extend over a period of 25 or more years.

Normally, projects are ended and staff withdrawn because someone, somewhere decided at some time that this is a three-year project, or this is a five-year project; this takes no real heed of the needs of the poor. If participatory groups are left on their own before having had time to consolidate their work and build links to similar groups, they will often not be able to sustain what has so far been achieved. On the other hand, it is possible to stay too long, smothering the group in a new form of paternalism.

This dilemma has been elegantly described by the Chilean economist Manfred Max-Neef (1982) who believes that there is an optimal duration for every commitment. Exactly how long that is, is a sensitive question. There are no fixed rules. First of all, a decision will depend – among other things – on the type of commitment under consideration. A project to build a bridge or to construct a dam is, by its very nature, quite different from a programme conceived to improve, through participatory action, the quality of life of a given group of people.

In the latter case, there is a first phase of discovery. Ideally, that should be followed by a phase of true integration between the change agents and the local people for whose benefit the programme has been initiated. This is supposed to be the period of creativity, including the creation of increasing awareness and transformation that should lead into the final phase of maturity, consolidation and greater self-reliance. Max-Neef maintains that this last phase must, however, necessarily be reached after the programme promoters have departed. It must be the work and achievement of the people themselves; and this can only come about if the middle phase is, first, sufficiently enriching and stimulating for the people and, secondly, not extended beyond the limit of its critical duration.

He points out that such a limit cannot be determined in advance or be conclusively identified while underway. Although there are no rules, there are symptoms. Assuming a successful integration during the middle phase, after a certain length of time a crisis will inevitably surface. It may take the shape of growing disagreements, confrontations and disputes between the change agents and the people (which may be a healthy sign), or of increasing submission and dependency of the people with respect to the project (which is definitely an unhealthy and undesirable sign). Whatever the alternative may be in the case of any given intervention, one fact should remain beyond dispute: that this is the moment when it is imperative for the 'umbilical cord' to be severed. Beyond that point there is nothing positive that an outside agent could or should do. From there on, the chosen future and the chosen paths belong exclusively to the people.

Max-Neef believes that in most projects these subtle, yet important, psychological signs are, unfortunately, not taken into account. Durations are rigidly fixed in advance, and desirable aims, goals and outcomes are predetermined by technocrats without any consultation with the people concerned. The 'experts' of such projects, instead of acting as they should, that is, as catalysts for the development of hidden potential, act as they should not, that is, as 'doers' of things that are often not desired. Accordingly, the final outcome in such cases is always the same: it is neither what the technocrats proposed or predicted, nor what the people would have wished. It is simply failure and, eventually, collapse.

In general, it appears that international agencies tend to close down project areas too soon while local agencies working with participatory development stay too long. As Max-Neef pointed out, there are no fixed rules. However, as a rule of thumb, groups should be left alone as soon as they show a capacity to manage their own collective funds and have established workable credit relations with formal credit institutions and contacts with external sources of technical assistance. Areas can be expected to make it on their own with the establishment and stabilisation of independent, federated producers' associations covering the entire area. None of these developments can, however, be forced. They must be given time to emerge from a foundation of inner strength.

The change agents need not stay with us continuously any longer. They may leave, provided they visit us occasionally, and are available for consultation when we need them. They may perhaps work in nearby villages so that we can consult them when we have a problem we cannot solve ourselves. We do not yet have enough knowledge about how to run our organisation in all matters. But we do not want the facilitators permanently because people in other areas also need them.

Member, Malabor Kasama farmers' organisation
(quoted by Rahman, 1983b)

Appendix – Questions for Discussion

The following sets of questions relate to each chapter. Although they can be thought through by the individual reader, it would be far more productive if they are used as the basis for small group discussions. They are by no means all-inclusive, but are merely intended as catalysts for further reflection and analysis.

Chapter 1 – Understanding Poverty

Basic needs and poverty
Which basic needs are most imporant? Why? Can people survive without a community? What is the difference between charity, relief and development assistance? Does your agency claim to work with the 'poorest of the poor'? Do you feel this is accurate?

Identifying and measuring poverty
Collect and analyse national production and income figures, physical quality of life measurements, and basic needs statistics for your country. Are these statistics broken down by regions, districts, etc.? What do these statistics mean in relation to the people with whom you are working? How do their actual conditions relate to these statistics?

Rural poverty unperceived
To what extent do your government and the aid agencies working in your country actually comprehend the extent and degree of rural poverty in your working area? Are the rural people in any way included in your national economic statistics and in the development plans deriving from these statistics?

What are the causes of poverty?
Which category of the causes of poverty (lack of modernisation tendencies, physical limitations, bureaucratic stifling, dependency of Third World countries and exploitation by local elites) do you feel is the most significant? Why? Can you add any more 'reasons' for poverty to those listed? Do you disagree with any of the points made in this section? To which explanations do

you personally give the most importance? Why?

Analysing poverty
Have you made an analysis of the causes of poverty in your working area? Who are the poor people in your area? What do they say about the causes of their situation? What do the rich and well-to-do say? What do government officials say? How much time do you think should be spent investigating causes?

Chapter 2 – What Is Development?

Modernisation – development through growth
Obtain and analyse annual national growth statistics (gross national product and national income) for your country over the past 25 years. Has there been any significant growth in the national economy? If so, who has benefited from this growth? In what ways has your country been 'modernised' during these years?

Dependency theory of underdevelopment
In what ways is the economy of your country dependent on international trade and relations? What are the major exports and imports? What import-substitution industries have been developed? How are they protected or promoted by your government? What products which are presently being imported could be economically manufactured domestically?

Interdependence and development
Obtain and analyse the export and import statistics for your country for the past 10 years. Other than exports, in which other ways does your country earn foreign exchange? What energy sources are utilised in your country? How much of this is imported? How much foreign aid has been extended to your country during the past 10 years? What has this aid been used for? What is the national debt to foreign governments and other overseas lenders? What is the annual interest payment on this debt? Which transnational corporations have established facilities in your country? How are they regulated by the government?

Another development
What is meant by a 'normative approach'? What is meant by 'structural transformation'? What are the different ways in which structural transformations can occur? What structural transformations have taken place in your country during the last 40 years? What have been the positive and the negative aspects of these transformations?

The basic needs approach to development
What needs are basic/less basic? Are basic needs universal and objective? Do human needs apply to all human beings and can they be quantified and

measured? Are they subjective and historically relative? Must they be seen in the context of specific social systems? How does one set priorities among different needs? Who decides? Are there differences between 'material needs' and 'human needs'? Are the First World's perceptions of the 'basic needs' of the Third World realistic?

Ecodevelopment
What are the major ecological problems within your country today? What has caused these problems? What problems can be anticipated in the future? How could these be avoided? What was the traditional attitude in your society regarding the relationship between man and the environment? Have these attitudes changed in modern times? Which attitudes do you feel should be retained and/or revived?

Development from below – people first
How do the development theories described in the text relate to the poor in your country? Do you see any indications that your government or development agencies are placing more emphasis on the needs and priorities of poor rural people in their development plans? Develop your own definitions of personal, political, economic and social development. Do development plans and strategies in your country reflect these definitions?

Chapter 3 – Self-Reliant Participatory Development

What is a community
Do people in your community live tightly together in villages or are they spread out through the countryside? Why? What sense of community is there? Does everyone co-operate for the good of the community? How and why? What socio-economic classes are found in your community? What special interest groups are there? How powerful are they? In what ways? What forms of exploitation, if any, occur? What other forms of conflict are there? Would you say that the communities that you work with are harmonious or not?

Social and cultural change
Discuss examples of how traditional social relations and customs inhibit change and the implementation of new development activities by the poor. Discuss how they can be used to promote new development activities. Discuss with a group of poor people how their social relations and cultural traditions have changed during their lifetimes? Which of these changes do they consider to have been beneficial and which detrimental? Why? What were some of the preconditions for the Tarun Mandal being able to change age-old marriage customs? What role did the detailed analysis of expenditure patterns play in the process? Can you think of other social traditions in the context of your own situation which might be susceptible to change through socio-economic analysis carried out by the group members?

Development as social transformation
Discuss some typical development activities such as a marketing co-operative, an irrigation channel or a bakery in terms of social transformation rather than in merely technical or economic terms. In what ways could these projects entail human, economic, political, ecological and/or institutional transformations? What social and cultural considerations should development workers keep in mind while helping groups to plan their own development activities?

What is self-reliance?
What are the differences between self-reliance and self-sufficiency? Study a rural community. In what ways are individual families self-sufficient? What about the community as a whole? How is it self-reliant? What factors are keeping it from becoming so?

Human development
Discuss how development workers can help people increase their self-confidence and self-respect. Discuss how you would help people to acquire the human skills necessary for self-reliance. Set up a list of practical skills and knowledge that you think would be useful to the poor. How would you go about helping them to acquire these skills and knowledge?

Conscientisation
When does one know that a group is conscientised? What does one do with a group that 'refuses' to become conscientised? What are the dangers of having preconceived ideas – things that you expect to find in a community? How can a development worker avoid pushing the people into accepting an analysis of a situation that may or may not actually exist?

What do we mean by participation?
What does people's participation mean to you? Do you think participation is a means to an end or an end in itself? Is it possible to see participation as *both* a means and an end in terms of people's development? What are some of the key factors which will determine the success of a participatory approach to development? Do you think a participatory approach can succeed in all situations? If not, why not? Do you think any other approach can succeed without participation? Why or why not?

Participatory action research
Do poor rural men and women have the time and interest to become involved with participatory action research? Can you guarantee that PAR will lead to analysis–action–reflection? Is it not inevitable that development workers will 'extract' information without sharing it with the poor? How can development workers stimulate PAR without directing it?

Participation of women in development
What was the traditional view about the role and position of women in your

society? Have viewpoints changed during modern times? If so, have these changes been for the good or bad from the women's viewpoint? What roles do the dominant religions in your society give to women? What are the legal rights of women in your society? Can women own land? Can they obtain credit in their own name? Are women participating equally in educational opportunities?

If you are working with a development agency, are poor women benefiting from the projects? Are women participating as much as or more than the men? Is this genuine participation? What percentage of the programme field staff are women? What percentage are project managers? What percentage are country directors? How many women have a genuine leadership role in the agency?

Participatory development and the time factor
For how many years should a development programme exist before it is terminated? How do we know this? How can we tell whether or not we are progressing too slowly?

Chapter 4 – Agents of Change

What role can development agencies play?
Do you feel that any of the roles suggested in the text are *not* part of the role of a development agency? Why? Can you suggest any additional roles? Which of these roles would you give highest priority? Lowest? Why?

Why external change agents?
Do you agree that external change agents are necessary to catalyse a self-reliant participatory development process in rural communities? Do you know of any such processes which began spontaneously? If so, what were the contributing factors?

What is a change agent?
What other designations have you heard for change agents? Does it make any difference which words you actually use to designate your fieldworkers? What term do you prefer? Why? What about the terms used for other positions in your organisation?

Is there a need for horizontal linkages between change agents working at the same level but in different organisations? Countries? Is there a need for vertical linkages between change agents at different levels? Is there a need for a unifying philosophy or ideology of change to bind them together in the common pursuit of enhancing rather than hindering the cause of development with social justice?

Change agents at the grassroots level
Discuss the problems involved in being truly accepted by the poor? What are the advantages and disadvantages of being from the 'outside' compared to being an 'internal' change agent, i.e. emerging from the people? How can we avoid being fooled into thinking we are accepted when we really are not? How

much time should be taken to become accepted? How does the length of time taken affect the total participatory development process?

The role of change agents
Do you agree with the roles as stated in the text? What would you change? How active should change agents be in helping groups establish external linkages? Is it the role of the change agent to identify/choose leaders?

Change agents and their work
Do you agree that change agents should work together in small teams? Why? If so, how would you put together such a team? How important is it for the change agents to live among the people? How can this be done? What are the problems involved? Is it really possible for middle class change agents to live among the poor, or must they live with the more well-to-do? How would you regulate working hours and free days? What about the family life of change agents?

Characteristics of change agents
Do you agree with the list of characteristics given in the text? With what do you disagree? Why? What about motorised transport? Is it important to use the same means of transport as the people?

Common weaknesses and inadequacies of change agents
Do you agree with the weaknesses and inadequacies suggested in the text? Have you seen or experienced similar weaknesses in development projects? How can these weaknesses be corrected?

Qualifications for change agents?
Do you agree with the list of qualifications given in the text? What are the advantages and disadvantages of various age groups? What about higher education? It has been said, only half-jokingly, that the ideal change agent is a 35-year-old, unmarried female born and raised in a village, but with a university degree. Do you agree? Why?

Recruitment of female fieldworkers
Do you think that women's role in development is being given adequate attention in your own development programme? What percentage of your programme staff are women? Is this adequate? What should be done to improve the role of women in your agency?

Recruitment and selection of change agents
Discuss how you would set up the process for the selection of male and female change agents? Where would you carry out the selection process? How much time would you use? What specific investigations or case studies would you select?

How would you go about advertising for change agents? Prepare your own advertisement text? Where would you post or insert your advertisement? How would you ensure that it reaches potential candidates in the rural areas? What languages would you use? How would you try to ensure enough women apply?

The staying power of change agents

Why do many change agents drop out of rural development programmes? What can be done to stop this leakage? What can be done to attract talented and dedicated young people to this type of work?

Chapter 5 – Training and Support of Change Agents

Traditional training programmes

Analyse the appropriateness of training programmes that you have experienced or are familiar with in relationship to the points raised in the text as well as to the discussion on the role of change agents. How would you design an appropriate training programme?

Objectives of participatory training

Does the list of objectives of participatory training cover the training needs of change agents based on your understanding of their role in participatory development? What additions or changes would you make?

Methodology of participatory training

What do you see as the advantages and disadvantages of a methodology based almost completely on fieldwork and group discussions? Have you ever participated in this type of training before? How does it compare to traditional training methods?

Structure of the training programme

Would you be capable of responding to the responsibility placed upon you as a participant in this type of training programme? As a training co-ordinator, would you be willing to give as much responsibility to the traineees? Decision-making by discussion consumes great amounts of time; is it worth it? Why?

Training content – topics for investigation

What other issues and topics do you feel should be discussed in a participatory training programme for change agents? Why?

Participation of trainees in programme management

How much responsibility for the self-management of a training programme can be given to a group of young trainees? Discuss the problems facing the co-ordinator with regards to participatory training and the natural authority according to him or her as co-ordinator? How should these problems be tackled?

Personal case studies

How 'personal' do you think personal case studies should be? Isn't this an invasion of privacy? Discuss the linkages between lifestyle, beliefs, etc., and participatory work with the poor.

Fieldwork in rural situations
How should trainees introduce themselves to the people of their field area? Who are they? Why are they there? How can the trainees gain the confidence of the various groups within the area, especially the poor, without raising expectations of gain either for the individual or for the group or community?

Reflection, criticism and self-criticism
Which is more important, open criticism or the maintenance of harmony within the group? What is the relationship between criticism, and solidarity and unity? Do you practice self-criticism with others with whom you are working? If not, why not?

Women and development training
Why do men in most societies tend to dominate discussions? Is this intentional or by default? How can you avoid the tendency for men to take a dominating role in discussions and management questions, and a passive or invisible role in the 'housekeeping' functions of a participatory, residential training course?

The role of training co-ordinator
Discuss the types of teachers and trainers that you have experienced. Which were the most effective in helping you to learn? Why? Using a participatory approach, how is discipline to be maintained? What should a co-ordinator do if the training programme is obviously going in the wrong direction?

Summing up participatory training
Do you think participation in this type of participatory training programme will make a change agent out of every trainee? Why? Review the section on the role of change agents. Which of the attitudes, aptitudes and skills associated with the work of change agents could possibly be improved through this type of training? What can be done about the others?

Follow-up and support of change agents
What is your agency doing today to provide support and development opportunities for its staff members? Is this adequate? What more could be done? Are there sufficient opportunities for group discussion? Is the atmosphere conducive to constructive criticism and self-criticism? Are there opportunities for sharing experiences with staff from other organisations or from other programmes being carried out by your agency? What specialised training should be offered to change agents? What career opportunities should be associated with the work of a change agent?

Organisation and leadership
Discuss the organisational structure and decision-making procedures in your

present work situation. In what ways do they contribute to the promotion of participatory development? What factors make participatory development difficult? What steps could be taken to reduce these factors and make your work more effective?

Organisational style and image
In what ways do style and image affect attempts to generate a self-reliant participatory development process? Is it possible for a foreign agency to avoid creating new forms of dependency and feelings of inferiority? How can this be done? Can a change agent be professional and still respect the people with whom he or she is working? How does 'professionalism' divorce a change agent from the people?

Chapter 6 – Getting Started

Which factors have played a role in the past in the selection of project areas by your agency and/or other local and foreign agencies in your country? Which factors should be given more weight? Which should be given less consideration? Is this possible and desirable?

Preparatory studies
What are the advantages of doing careful preparatory studies? What can be the negative effects of such studies? How can these negative effects be reduced or eliminated? Can the time and expense of the participatory action research approach be justified? What about funding and the traditional approach to project planning and proposals? Ten areas of investigation were suggested in the text, what additional areas or questions do you think should be investigated? Is it realistic for poor, uneducated rural men and women to participate in scientific, baseline-data surveys?

Planning and proposals
What are the advantages and disadvantages of detailed project plans prepared prior to approval of the project? Why is it necessary to set up project plans? Is it possible to present a programme proposal based on general guidelines and broad time and space frameworks, and expect to have it approved? If not, why not? What is the difference between a project and a programme? Is it possible to get approval/funding for a programme based on the principles of self-reliant participatory development?

Budgeting and funding
Do you agree with the statement 'Salaries will tend to take up the lion's share of a good programme budget'? How can this be justified? How can it be possible that 'Except for revolving loan funds, outlays for inputs and equipment should usually represent less than 10% of the total budget'? What should be the cost per family of a good self-reliant participatory project? Is such a calculation

possible or even desirable? What factors will determine such a calculation?

Programme size and expansion
Why is flexibility important, especially during the early phases of a programme? What is the relationship between programme size and people's participation? What are the disadvantages associated with the availability of large amounts of project funds? What are the dangers and disadvantages of 'starting small'? What would you consider to be too small? How can one distinguish between healthy growth of a programme and growth which is opportunistic or over-ambitious? What factors are important for determining an optimum rate of growth? Can a self-reliant participatory development process ever become too large in terms of target area?

Programme monitoring
What role can participatory action research play in programme monitoring? How can criticism and self-criticism contribute to better project monitoring? Can this be done in the context of a review workshop? How often should monitoring activities occur? Under what circumstances should external evaluation be carried out? What are the advantages and disadvantages of external evaluation?

Chapter 7 – Working with Groups

Why should change agents work with groups rather than with progressive individuals? Can the self-reliant participatory methodology benefit progressive individuals? If so, how?

The dialogical method
The dialogical method obviously requires considerable time; how can this time be justified? What does one do if the conclusions of an analysis carried out by a group are obviously wrong? There are many things, especially technical knowledge, that poor people just do not know very much about. How can such knowledge be transferred through the dialogical approach to understanding?

What is an interest group?
Should a group have one special interest or can it have a range of interests not equally shared by all of the members? What are the advantages and disadvantages of collective ownership/production/investment? How can it be ensured that group membership benefits the individual members?

Formation of interest groups
In terms of your own experience of being a member of an interest group or of having worked with such groups, discuss the considerations presented in the text, e.g. motivation, voluntary membership, common interests, composition, group size and autonomy. What were the important factors in determining the

success or failure of the groups with which you have been associated? What considerations should the landless and other marginal poor give weight to in making decisions regarding the composition of their groups? What difficulties can arise when groups are composed of both the landless and small or marginal farmers? Will it not be natural that most emerging groups will consist of the stronger, more dynamic and richer members of a community? How can you ensure that the poorest and most vulnerable become part of the development process?

Group leadership and decision-making

Discuss the advantages and disadvantages of elected group leaders serving over longer periods of time. Compare these with a frequent rotation of leadership roles among all members. Discuss the advantages and disadvantages of majority voting. Compare these with decision-making by consensus. How should these questions be decided?

Group meetings

What are the advantages and disadvantages of informality in group meetings? What would be some of the signs indicating that a group is progressing? What would be the danger signs of possible group failure or even dissolution? What should the change agent do if the group continuously turns to him or her for leadership?

Women's groups

Sit together with a group composed of roughly equal numbers of male and female development workers. Discuss the advantages and disadvantages of working with separate women's groups vs. mixed groups. What differences in opinion are there between the men and the women in your group? In your culture, what traditions inhibit women from participating on an equal basis with the men? Do these apply to all socio-economic groups, or are there differences? How can you ensure that poor rural women participate in the development process?

Group activities

Discuss the question of when to intervene and when to let the group make its own mistakes in regards to planning group activities. What should be done when an activity fails or doesn't reach its goals? Why is sustainability critical? How can individual member activities harmonise with and be assisted by the group?

Can we really expect that groups will be able to carry out group activities on the basis of their own resources? How can self-reliance be balanced with the perceived need for external assistance?

Income-generating activities

Do you agree that income-generating activities will normally be the first priority of the poor? Why or why not? Why are social infrastructure activities difficult for small groups? Identify a list of possible investment opportunities in your community? Why did you choose these? Choose one modest investment from your list and do a viability analysis of it? If it is profitable, prepare an implementation plan? How much capital would it need? Where would this capital come from?

Common causes of group failure
Discuss possible ways to avoid the various causes of group failure described in the text. Can you think of any other common causes of group failure?

Chapter 8 – External Relationships

Relations with local elites and the power structure
Who are the local elites in your community? Who are the power-brokers? How did they acquire these positions? How do they benefit at the expense of the rest of the community? Have they ever been challenged by the poor? By outsiders? What happened and why?

Change agents and local elites
Under what circumstances and in what ways should an agency intervene in a serious conflict between poor people's groups and the local power structure? When should the agency not intervene? Why? How can an agency use its position to legitimise people's organisations? In what ways can local elites or power-brokers damage the work of an agency? How can this damage be minimised?

Relations with government officials
Which government officials do the villagers come into contact with? What are the attitudes of these officials to poor people? Do you agree with the statements in the text indicating that poor people often have a negative attitude towards government officials? If so, what do you think are the reasons for these generally negative attitudes?

Do you agree with the characteristics of typical government service at the field level as stated in the text? Is it true that many non-governmental agencies and their fieldworkers could also be described in these terms?

Do you know of any examples of genuinely good relations between poor villagers and individual government officials? If so, what do you think are the basic reasons for these positive relationships having developed? What do you think can be done to promote constructive relations with other less positive officials?

Why are many government officials suspicious of participatory group activities and meetings? How can these suspicions be dispelled and replaced by feelings of understanding and goodwill?

Official interest organisations

What official interest organisations – co-operatives, women's clubs, youth clubs, savings and credit societies, etc. – are found in your district? Who controls them? What decisions can they make without getting permission from higher authorities? What decisions can they not make on their own? Why? Who benefits from them? Why?

Change agents and government officials

What consequences might result in cases where change agents have not maintained good relations with local officials? What are the dangers of maintaining too intimate contact with officials? How should a change agent respond to strongly negative attitudes towards officials expressed by group members?

Interest organisations and associations

Discuss the formal and informal barriers to the emergence of genuinely independent regional or national interest associations in your country. How can these barriers be overcome, if at all. Can local organisations survive over time without the support of broader associations? Do you know of any successful interest organisations either in the Third World or elsewhere? Why have these been successful?

People's organisations and autonomy

Why is autonomy so critically important for a people's organisation? What is the legal position of independent private organisations in your country? How much local autonomy is there in official people's organisations, such as co-operatives? Discuss the advantages and disadvantages of federal and unitary systems of organisation.

Dilemmas of participatory development

How would you try to resolve the four dilemmas facing small groups, associations and change agents? Can you think of other dilemmas that might arise? What about in the relationships of groups and change agents to local elites and government officials?

Chapter 9 – Savings, Credit and Inputs: Essential Components

Factors of production

Which factors are easily available in your community? Which are not? Why? Make a list of all the possible sources of energy that you can think of. What are the advantages and disadvantages of each? How common is entrepreneurship in your community? What can be done to encourage entrepreneurship?

The positive spiral of economic development

Why is it called a spiral rather than a circle? What do you think would be a reasonable balance between consumption, savings and repayment of credit and interest? Why? What would happen if production did not produce a surplus? Can the spiral be started with just land and labour? Grants seem so easy – what are the disadvantages?

Savings and group funds
Is it reasonable (and/or possible) to first promote savings on the part of the nearly destitute poor, before helping them to obtain credit from banking institutions or providing easy credit from the project? Is it possible for international aid agencies to defend such a policy to their donors?

What are the factors inhibiting poor rural people from beginning collective saving and setting up their own revolving loan funds? Discuss how you might set up a revolving group loan fund. Why is it important for groups of poor producers to have full autonomy over and responsibility for their own funds? How would a group pay off a member who for some reason was leaving the group? How would a group calculate member dividends? Is it possible for a group to pay interest on member deposits? How would these be calculated?

External credit
Discuss your personal experiences, if any, with obtaining loans from sources of institutional credit in your country. What problems would groups or associations of poor producers face in trying to obtain institutional loans? What can be done to help them solve these problems? When would you judge a group sufficiently ready to be able to take on the obligations of an institutional loan? What are the dangers involved in taking such a loan too soon?

Donations and matching grants
Discuss the advantages and disadvantages of pure grants, matching grants and credit. When should matching grants be given? Should donations without any matching input ever be given? Why?

Introducing new technologies
How can the introduction of new technologies lead to new dependency relationships? How can this be avoided? How can we ensure that a new technology really is appropriate? Which is more important: the new technology or the process of introduction? Why? Prepare case studies illustrating examples of the introduction of inappropriate, and of appropriate, technologies.

Participatory technological development
The participatory technological development process is going to take much longer than obtaining an appropriate technology from 'off the shelf'; is it worthwhile or not to take this additional time? Why? How can a change agent avoid the probability that the poor will initially almost always choose the technology proposed by the change agent? What should a change agent do if he or she feels that the people have chosen the wrong technology?

Chapter 10 – Objectives and Principles of Self-Reliant Participatory Development

Do you agree with the philosophy of self-reliant participatory development, as expressed in the text? Do you agree with the definition of self-reliant participatory development? What would you change?

What are the objectives of a self-reliant participatory development process?
Do you agree with the five specific objectives? What would you change? Would you add or subtract anything? Why? How does all of this relate to the goals and objectives of your own agency?

The basic principles of self-reliant participatory development
Discuss each of the basic principles individually and then analyse them as a whole. Which principles do you think would be the most difficult to maintain? Why? How does this methodology compare with others that you are aware of or have used? Which do you think are more likely to promote sustainable development?

Chapter 11 – Two Steps Forward, One Step Back – Being Realistic

One step back . . .
Do you believe that rural people will respond to this approach or not? Why? Do you believe that it is possible to find change agents willing and able to do this type of development work or not? Why? Is it possible for change agents not to be co-opted by the government or by development agencies which may divert their efforts from promoting the people's own development? How serious a problem will repression be in your country? Do you think development agencies or the government are really interested in this type of development?

Do you think the rural poor in your country or elsewhere will be able to develop themselves only on the basis of self-reliant participatory development? What other types of development are needed? How are these to be carried out?

Stepping out
Are the poor a good judge of when they should be left on their own? In what matters do you feel that the poor might still feel uncertain of their own abilities? Could this perhaps be because the change agents have done these things for the people instead of making the people do them for themselves? Do you think the viewpoints of the poor might be different if the agency and its change agents are also responsible for distributing material benefits, e.g. loans, materials, etc.? What happens to change agents when a set of groups or a producer association says that they don't need the change agents any longer?

References

Askew, I. (1983), *The Institutionalisation of Participatory Projects: A strategy for self-reliance*, Institute of Population Studies, University of Exeter.

Askew, I. (1984), *Community Participation in Family Planning: A consultation between researchers, practitioners and support agencies*, Institute of Population Studies, University of Exeter.

Bengtsson, B. (ed.) (1979), *Rural Development Research: The role of power relations*, SAREC Report R4, SAREC: Stockholm.

Bhasin, K. (1976), *Participatory Training for Development*, FFHC/AD, FAO: Bangkok.

Bhasin, K. (1977), 'Participation of women in development', in Bhasin, K. and Vimala, R. (eds.) (1980), *Readings on Poverty, Politics and Development*, FFHC/AD, FAO: New Delhi.

Bhasin, K. (1979), *Breaking Barriers: A South Asian experience of training for participatory development*, FAO: Bangkok.

Bhasin, K. (1980a), *The Role and Training of Development Activists*, FFHC/AD, FAO: New Delhi.

Bhasin, K. (1980b), 'Criticism and self-criticism', in Bhasin, K. and Vimala, R. (eds.) (1980), *Readings on Poverty, Politics and Development*, FFHC/AD, FAO: New Delhi.

Bhasin, K. (1982), *Formulating Projects with People: Report of a training programme*, FFHC/AD, FAO: New Delhi.

Bhasin, K. and Vimala, R. (eds.) (1980), *Readings on Poverty, Politics and Development*, FFHC/AD, FAO: Rome.

Blomstrom, M. and Hettne, B. (1984), *Development Theory in Transition*, Zed Books: London.

Bunch, R. (1982), *Two Ears of Corn: A guide to people-centered agricultural improvement*, World Neighbors: Oklahoma City.

Chambers, R. (1983), *Rural Development: Putting the last first*, Longman: London.

Cohen, J. M. and Uphoff, N. T. (1977), *Rural Development Participation: Concepts and measures for project design, implementation and evaluation*, Monograph Series No. 2, Rural Development Committee, Cornell University: Ithaca, NY.

Cohen, S. (ed.) (1980), 'Debaters Comments on *Inquiry into Participation: A research approach* by Pearse and Stiefel', Popular Participation Programme, UNRISD: Geneva.

Comstock, D. E. and Fox, R. (1982), 'Participatory research as critical theory: The North Bonneville, USA experience', paper presented at the 10th World Congress of Sociology, Mexico City, August 1982.

de Silva, G. V. S., Mehta, N., Rahman, Md. A. and Wignaraja, P. (1979), 'Bhoomi Sena: A struggle for people's power', *Development Dialogue*, 1979: 2, Dag Hammarskjöld Foundation: Uppsala.

de Silva, G. V. S., Ahmed, R. U., Dasgupta, S., Espiritu, R. and Tilakaratna, S. (1983), *Cadre Creation and Action Research in Self-Reliant Rural Development*, Rural Employment Policies Branch, ILO: Geneva.

Development Alternatives Inc. (1975), *Strategies for Small Farmer Development: An empirical study of rural development projects*, a report prepared for the Agency for International Development under Contract AID/CM/ta-C-73-41, Westview Press: Boulder.

Fals-Borda, O. (1981), 'The challenge of action research', in Wignaraja, P. (ed.) (1981), *Participation of the Rural Poor in Development*.

Fals-Borda, O. (1983), *Some Premises for the Development of Participatory Action Research in the Third World*, in SID (1983), GRIS Policy Dialogues.

Fals-Borda, O. (1988), *Knowledge and People's Power: Lessons with peasants in Nicaragua, Mexico and Colombia*, Indian Social Institute: New Delhi.

FAO (1978), *Small Farmers Development Manual*, Vol. I and II, FAO: Bangkok.

FAO (1981), *The Peasants' Charter: The declaration of principles and programme of action of the World Conference on Agrarian Reform and Rural Development*, FAO: Rome.

Fayossewo, A. A. (1978), *Motivating Rural Women in the Ivory Coast: An experiment/mid-term report*, FFHC/AD, FAO: Rome.

Freire, P. (1972), *Pedagogy of the Oppressed*, Penguin Books: Harmondsworth.

Frost, D. (1983), *Intermediate Technology Development Group*, IT Publications: London.

Fuglesang, A. (1982), *About Understanding: Ideas and observations on cross-cultural communication*, Dag Hammarskjöld Foundation: Uppsala.

Ghai, D. P., Khan, A. R., Lee, E. L. H. and Alfthan, T. (1977), *The Basic Needs Approach to Development: Some issues regarding concepts and methodology*, ILO: Geneva.

Gianotten, V. and deWit. T. (1983), 'Rural development: education and social research', *Ideas and Action*, No. 153, 1983/5, FFHC/AD, FAO: Rome.

Haque, W., Mehta, N., Rahman, Md. A. and Wignaraja, P. (1977), 'Towards a theory of rural development', *Development Dialogue*, 1977: 2, Dag Hammarskjöld Foundation: Uppsala.

Hettne, B. (1982), 'Development Theory and the Third World', SAREC Report No. 2 (1982), SAREC: Stockholm.

Hollnsteiner, M. R. (1978), *Development from the Bottom Up: Mobilizing the rural poor for self-development*, Quezon City, Philippines.

Hong, E. (1984), 'Rural women in development', in Bawtree (ed.) 1984/4–5.

Hossain, M. (1982), *Conscientizing Rural Disadvantaged Peasants in Bangladesh: Intervention through group action – a case study of PROSHIKA*, WEPR Programme, ILO: Geneva.

Huizer, G. (1971), 'Betting on the weak: from counterpoint towards revolution', in Werthein, W. F., *Buiten de Grenzen*, Meppel.

Huizer, G. (1984), 'Harmony vs. conflict', in Wignaraja, P. (ed.) (1984), *Reversing Anti-rural Development*.

Ideas and Action, FFHC/AD, FAO: Rome
   No. 116, 1977/3–4, 'Participatory training for development: FFHC/AD's regional change agents programme.

No. 140, 1981:2, 'Training change agents in Asia'.

No. 152, 1983:3–4, 'Culture and rural development'.

No. 155, 1984:1, 'An appointment in Rome: some questions and answers about the second international FFHC/AD consultation'.

No. 157, 1984:3, 'Nijera Kori: we will do it ourselves'.

No. 158, 1984:4–5, 'Special issue on rural women'.

Lassen, C. A., (1980), *Reaching the Assetless Poor: Projects and strategies for their self-reliant development*, Special Series on Landlessness and near-Landlessness, No. 6, Rural Development Committee, Cornell University: Ithaca, NY.

Léger, R. (1984), 'The challenge to donors: learning from past experience', in Wignaraja, P. (ed.) (1984), *Reversing Anti-rural Development*.

ILO (1989), 'Promoting people's participation and self-reliance', Proceedings of the regional workshop of trainers in participatory development, Bulawayo, Zimbabwe, ILO: Geneva.

MacDonald, J. J. (1981), 'The theory and practice of integrated rural development', in *Manchester Monographs 19*, University of Manchester: Manchester.

Madeley, J. (1984), 'Giving credit where it's due: banking on the landless in Bangladesh', in Bawtree (ed.), 1984.

Max-Neef, M. A. (1982) (reissued 1992), *From the Outside Looking In: Experiences in 'barefoot economics'*, Zed Books: London.

Mukhopadhyay, M. (1984), *Silver Shackles: Women and development in India*, Oxfam: Oxford.

Nerfin, M. (ed.) (1977), *Another Development: Approaches and strategies*, Dag Hammarskjöld Foundation: Uppsala.

NORAD (1989), *Sør-Nord Utvikling*, No. 5, NORAD: Oslo.

Oakley, P. and Winder, D. (1981), 'The concept and practice of rural social development: current trends in Latin America and India', *Manchester Papers on Development* No. 1, May 1981, University of Manchester: Manchester.

Oakley, P. and Marsden, D. (1984), *Approaches to Participation in Rural Development*, ILO: Geneva.

Oxfam (1987), *A Manual of Credit and Savings for the Poor of Developing Countries*, Oxfam: Oxford.

Partridge, B. (1983), 'Towards development and change: a community in central Mondoro sets a model for self-reliance', American Friends Service Committee, Harare, Zimbabwe.

Pearse, A. and Stiefel, M. (1979), *Inquiry into Participation: A research approach*, Popular Participation Programme, UNRISD/79/C/14, UNRISD: Geneva.

PIDA (1984), 'People's movements and experiments: report of a meeting of South Asian scholars, Kerala, 10–12 March 1984', The United Nations University Asian Perspectives Project (South Asia), PIDA, Colombo.

Pradervand, P. (1990), *Listening to Africa: Developing Africa from the grass roots*, Praeger Publishers: New York.

Rahman, Md. A. (1981), *Some Dimensions of People's Participation in the Bhoomi Sena Movement*, Popular Participation Programme, UNRISD: Geneva.

Rahman, Md. A. (1983a), *Theory and Practice of Participatory Action Research*, WEP 10/WP.29, ILO: Geneva.

Rahman, Md. A. (1983b), *Sarilakas: A pilot project for stimulating grassroots participation in the Philippines*, Technical Co-operation Evaluation Report, ILO: Geneva.

Rahman, Md. A. (1984a), *Grassroots Participation and Self-reliance: Experiences in south and southeast Asia*, Oxford and IBH Publishing Co.: New Delhi.

Rahman, Md. A. (1984b), *Participatory Organizations of the Rural Poor: Introduction to an ILO programme*, ILO: Geneva.

Rahman, Md. A. (1985a), 'Participation of the rural poor in development: Bangladesh field notes' (mimeograph), ILO: Geneva.

Rahman, Md. A. (1985b) 'Catalytic action to promote participatory rural development: a review of methodology and experiences', (unpublished manuscript), ILO: Geneva.

Sachs, I. (1974), 'Ecodevelopment', in *Ceres*, Nov.–Dec. 1974, FAO: Rome.

Savale, D. and Bhasin, K. (1984), *Training Tribal Activists: A report*, FFHC/AD, FAO: New Delhi.

Schumacher, E. F., *Small is Beautiful*.

Seawell, J. P. (1984), 'Towards development and change: a community in central Mondoro sets a model for self-reliance', paper presented at the IACD colloquium, Which Models for Community Development, Marcinelle, Belgium, 10–15 Dec. 1984.

Sethi, H. (1983), 'Development issues in South Asia: the state, voluntary agencies and the rural poor', Second International FFHC/AD Consultation, Rome, 13–16 Sept. 1983, FAO, Rome.

Shanmugaratnam, N. (1984), *International Center for Law and Development: Evaluation report*, SAREC Report No. 1, SAREC: Stockholm.

SID, *GRIS Notes*, Society for International Development, Rome, 1981, No. 1; 1982, No. 2; 1983, No. 3; 1984, No. 4.

Streeten, P. (1979), 'A basic-needs approach to economic development', in Jameson and Wilbur (eds) (1979), *Directions in Economic Development*, University of Notre Dame Press: Terre Haute.

Swantz, M. (1982), 'Women's creative role in development', paper presented at the 10th World Congress of Sociology, Mexico City, August 1982.

Tan, J. G. (1985), 'Some notes on participatory technology development', in *IFDA Dossier 45*, January/February 1985, IFDA: Nyon, Switzerland.

Tilakaratna, S. (1984), 'Grassroots self-reliance in Sri Lanka: organisations of betel and coir producers', in Rahman, Md. A. (ed.) *Grassroots Participation and Self-reliance: Experiences in south and southeast Asia*, Oxford and IBH Publishing: New Delhi.

Tilakaratna, S. (1987), *The Animator in Participatory Rural Development (Concept and Practice)*, ILO: Geneva.

Tilakaratna, S. (1989), *Retrieval of Roots for Self-Reliant Development: Some experiences from Thailand*, ILO: Geneva.

Traitler, R. (1976), 'People's participation in development', in *Betting on the Weak: Some experiences in people's participation in development*, Commission on the Churches' Participation in Development, World Council of Churches: Geneva.

Verhelst, T. G. (1990), *No Life Without Roots: Culture and development*, Zed Books: London.

Wignaraja, P. (ed.), *Development: Seeds of change*, Society for International Development: Rome, (1981) 1, 'Participation of the rural poor in development', and (1984a) 2, 'Reversing anti-rural development'.

Wignaraja, P. (1984b), 'Towards a theory and practice of rural development' in Wignaraja (ed.) (1984a).

Index

A.R. Desai, 43
ACORD rural development programme, xiii
action versus reflection, 178
aid agencies, 50, 110, 113, 123, 124, 125, 126, 158, 196
aid technicians, 153
alcohol: bootleg, 117; drinking of, 41, 49, 66, 150 (rise of, 184)
American Friends Service Committee, 77
Amin, Samir, 197
Anek, Evie, 156
Askew, Ian, 205
audio-visual techniques, 95
authoritarianism, 108
autonomous associations, 210-11
autonomy, 34, 171, 176, 209
Awor, Catherine, 148

bakery, establishment of, 154
Bangladesh, 53, 85, 109, 139, 146, 150, 166, 190
banks, 9, 10, 54, 189, 190, 191; experience of, 187
base communities, xvii
baseline data surveys, 119-20
basic needs, 116; definition of, 3-6; of communities, 3
Basic Needs Approach, 5
Baumgartner, Thomas, 170
behavioural change, time needed for, 69
Bengtsson, B., 34
Bhasin, Kamla, 66, 67, 81, 88, 89, 90, 98, 99, 100, 102, 103, 104, 107, 123, 132, 134, 165, 169
Bhoomi Sena movement (India), 46, 75, 131, 142
Blomstrom, Magnus, 27
Bolivia, 117
bonded labour, 47
book-keeping, 138, 140, 148, 156, 161, 162, 187

Brandt Commission Report, 26, 30
Brazil, xvii
Brett, Teddy, 34
brick-making group, establishment of, 152
budgets of projects, 124, 125, 126, 157
Bunch, Roland, 69, 117, 127, 128, 129, 180
bureaucracy, 6, 11, 19, 125, 169; as stifling development, 8-9
Burkina Faso, 184
bye-laws in groups, establishment of, 141-2

Can Deg Ming Men's Group, 162
Can Ocuka Women's Group, 147-8
Canadian International Development Agency (CIDA), xvii, 121
capital, provision of, 23, 25, 184
Chambers, Robert, 5, 11
change agents, 107, 127, 133, 141, 142, 144, 145, 159, 161, 164, 169, 179, 180, 184, 191, 208-9, 214, 215, 217; and dialogical process, 134; and government officials, 173; and new technology, 200; and relations with elites, 167; career development of, 107; characteristics of, 81-2; contradictory with self-reliance, 213; definition of, 76-83; drop-out of, 107; formal qualifications of, 83-6; golden rule of, 211; life style of, 82; openness of, 134; over-enthusiasm of, 168; recruitment of, 213; role of, 78-81, 132, 151-2, 153; staying power of, 86-7; training of, xii, 88-114; weaknesses of, 83
change agents programmes, xi, xiii, 88, 213
chiefs, village, 41
Chile, 28, 176
chillies, growing of, xi, xv
Chowdhury, Z., 85
circles, for discussions, 93, 145

class structure of rural society, 41, 43
clothing of project staff, 112
Club of Rome, 32
co-operatives, 129, 135, 136, 138, 141, 180, 215, 216; official, 172, 173
Cocoyoc Declaration, 27, 30
Cohen, J.M., 56
Coir Women's Producer Association (Sri Lanka), xi
cola nuts, chewing of, 184
collective purchasing, 174, 177
colonialism, 9; legacies of, 18-20
combining with other groups, 174-8
commitment, as key word, 82
common interest, defining groups, 137-8, 192
communications, lapses of, 129
communism, 165
Community Development Movement, 43
community, definition of, 40-5, 94
comprador development bourgeoisie, 112
Comstock, D.E., 61, 63
conflict resolution, 170
conscientisation, 41, 53-5, 58, 60, 69, 73, 78, 79, 121, 125, 130, 132, 144, 159, 162, 164, 178, 179, 184, 192, 206, 209, 214
Consumers' Association of Penang, 65
corruption, 142, 161, 173, 215
credit, 23, 66, 141, 150, 152, 159, 161, 163, 164, 180-202; external, 189-93; programmes, 191
credit institutions, 10, 189, 190; lacking in poor areas, 192
credit unions, 159, 165, 172
criticism within groups, 145
cultural change, 45-9
cultural traditions, 45, 63; local, integrated in develoment, 48

Dag Hammarskjöld Foundation, 30
data: collection of, 119, 209
De Silva, G.V.S., 159
de Wit, T., 61, 197
debt, 11, 17, 28, 30, 46, 131, 184
decision-making, 142-4, 151, 169, 175; by consensus, 143-4, 145; collective, 163; decentralised, 109
deforestation, 8, 22
democracy, 69, 93, 96, 103, 205
dependence: at village level, 41; minimisation of, 149; on wealthy, 130
dependency, 6, 9-10, 11, 136, 159, 179, 181, 183, 201, 217
dependency theory of underdevelopment, 28-9

development: as process, 208; as social transformation, 48-9; community, 42; definition of, xvii, 28-39; economic, 36 (constraints on, 16); from below, 35; human, 35; people-based, 124; political, 37; programmes for women, 66; rural, 122 (and group formation, 130); social, 37 (constraints on, 16; definition of, 38-9); theories of, 27-32; versus charity, 213
development agencies, role of, 73-6
Development Alternatives Inc., 56
development workers, 19, 38
Dhambi, Annah, 127
dialogical method, 131-4
discussions: group, xiii, 105, 132, 151, 157, 158; in circle shape, 93, 145; on technology, 199
disease, 14, 17; as cause of poverty, 20; as cause of underdevelopment, 12
donations, 193-5, 202
drinking of alcohol, 41, 49, 66, 150
drugs, selling of, 165
drunkenness, at meetings, 142
dualistic nature of underdeveloped economies, 27

ecologically sound development, 31, 32
economic development, 36, 58, 181-2
education, 5, 54, 116, 162, 167, 175, 205, 207; and poverty, 20
El Sayed, Mustafa, 170
élites, 142, 165-8; relations with, 167
Emmanuel, Ongiertho J., 138
empowering, 58, 59, 83, 205, 206
energy supplies, lack of, 23
entrepreneurship, 181
Ethiopia, 4
evaluation procedures for projects, 125
experts: role of, 10; white, 116
extension workers, 158, 164, 171
external relationships, 164-80

facilitation of action, 73
failure of projects, causes of, 159-60
Fals-Borda, Orlando, 57, 63
farmers' associations, 46
Fayossewo, Antoine A., 136
FFHC/AD Consultation, 115
FFHC/AD programme, 136
field staff, 170; conditioning of, 108; turnover of, 87
fieldwork, 91, 92, 94; follow-up of, 92; in rural situations, 97-8
fishing, 7, 23, 78, 139, 147, 162, 168, 177, 186

Food and Agricultural Organisation (FAO), 31, 106, 115, 171, 190; Rural Organisations Action Programme, 172; Small Farmers' Development Manual, 141
foreign exchange, 196
Fox, R., 61, 63
Francis, Can, 189
Freire, Paolo, 8, 9, 51, 54, 55
Frost, Dennis, 196, 197
Fuglesang, Andreas, 34, 45, 47, 52, 107, 109
funding, 178; destructive potential of, 208; easy availability of, 113, 114, 126, 128; external, 75
funds: allocation of, 118; group, 137, 149, 157; pooling of, 152

Germany, 183
Ghai, D.P., 56
give-away inputs, 181; rotting of, 180
Gonoshasthaya Kendra workshop, 53
government officials, 169-73; over-intimate relations with, 171
Grameen Bank, 190
grants: conditions of, 169; dumping of, 164; matching, 193-5; non-viability of, 23
green revolution, 28
group activities, 148-58; financing of, 158; planning of, 156-8; principles for, 149
group formation, 125, 130, 135-48
group funds, 137, 149, 157, 182-8; rotational, 186-9
group meetings, 144-5
group savings, 158, 161, 163
groups: arrangements for members to leave, 142; autonomy of, 141; co-optation into, 164; composition of, 138-40; meetings of, 144; membership of, 161; regulations of, 141; size of, 140-1, 161, 163, 175; small, 174, 175, 190, 209
growth, 27, 30, 32
Guatemala, 4

happiness, as factor of welfare, 5
Haque, W., 198, 205
harmony model of rural community life, 40, 43, 45, 165
health, xvi, 5, 28, 37, 65, 116, 160, 167, 207
health clinics, 10, 13, 22, 111, 123, 167
Hettne, Björn, 27, 29, 33, 34
hierarchy, 109, 169, 175
Holland, 125
Hollnsteiner, Mary Racelis, 106, 124

Hong, Evelyn, 65
hospitals, 13, 215
Hossain, Mosharraf, 85, 109, 139
housing, 14; as indicator of poverty, 12
Huizer, Gerrit, 43, 44, 61
human development, 35, 51-2
hurricane Fifi, 194
hybrid seeds, 7, 153

ideology versus pragmatism, 178
ignorance, as cause of underdevelopment, 12
illiteracy, 4, 140, 148; and poverty, 20
income-generating activities, 152-3, 163, 207, 210; feasibility study of, 156
India, 44, 86
inflation, 29, 183, 192
inputs into projects, 180-202; rotting of, 193
integrated development programmes, 48
integrated rural development projects (IRDPs), 121
interdependence, 51, 207; global, 29-30
interest groups, definition of, 134-5
interest rates, 9, 131, 155, 185, 186, 188, 192
Intermediate Technology Development Group, 196, 197
International Planned Parenthood Federation (IPPF), xvi
International Foundation for Development Alternatives (IFDA), 31
International Fund for Agricultural Development (IFAD), 190
International Labour Office (ILO), 59, 106
investment, 27, 36, 118, 140, 174, 180, 194, 201, 215; group, 153; identification of opportunities, 153-6; individual, 153
irrigation, 6, 157

Jamaica, 28
Japan, 183
jargon of development, 24, 26, 50
Jatex, Odaga, 178
Jocan Penindo Women's Group, 155-6

Kabir, Khushi, 130
Kalu, 131
Kenya, 117
knowledge, and development, 63
Kwo-Lonyo Women's Group, 137

Léger, Ronald, xvii, 121, 122
labour, as input, 182

Lakshmi, goddess, 62
land: as input, 182; destruction of, 17, 18; distribution of, 135; reform of, 40; scarcity of, 17
landless people, 7, 159, 191; interests of, 139
language: choice of, 112; of training programmes, 93, 95; sexism in, 101
Lassen, C.A., 186
latrines, building of, 14, 83
leadership, 80, 102, 107-14, 142-4, 160, 163, 175; changing of, 143, 161; development of, 74; election of, 143; sharing of, 96
lecture, as passive event, 133
literacy, 119, 187; adult, 116; programmes, 120
loan funds, 149, 174
loans of money, 139, 152, 155, 156, 157, 161, 162, 184, 188 *see also* moneylenders
localism versus coalition-building, 179
Lok-tek Group, 187-9
low income, and poverty, 20

MacDonald, J.J., 169
Magandanga, Bless, 146
Malabor Kasama organisation, 218
malnutrition, 4, 8, 13; as cause of poverty, 20
management skills, 36, 181
Mang Pedring, 7
Manley, Michael, 28
Mao Tse-tung, 64
Marsden, D., 58, 78, 83, 145, 146, 148, 149
Marshall Plan, 26
Masefield, Geoffrey, 69
Matsvaire, Evaristo, 180
Max-Neef, Manfred, 216, 217
meetings: domination of, 145; of groups, 161, 163
membership of groups, 175, 178; voluntary, 136, 163, 209
methodologies of work, 124
middlemen, profits of, 165
militant observers, change agents as, 81
Miller, Duncan, 73
Mirla, Lute, 112
mobilisation, 125, 130, 215
modernisation, 6, 11, 27-8, 196
money economy, problem of, 180
moneylenders, 10, 41, 46, 62, 159, 165, 166, 170, 187
Moser, Heinz, 151
Mukhopadhyay, Maitrayee, 150
mulberries, growing of, xi, xv

Nepal, 141, 170, 171
Nestlé company, 9
New International Economic Order (NIEO), 29, 31
Nga Konyi Mixed Group, 185-6
Nijera Kori groups, 109, 110, 146, 147, 150, 166
Nizam, murder of, 165
Nok Cibo Acaye Group, 139-40
non-governmental organisations (NGOs), xv, xvii, 74, 77, 86, 114, 121, 122, 159, 213, 215
Norway, 3, 4
note-taking, on training programmes, 93, 98
Nyakagai Fishing and Farming Group, 137
Nyerere, Julius, 28, 124
Nyundo Women's Club, 127

Oakley, P., 44, 58, 78, 83, 145, 146, 148, 149
OEF International company, 156
Okori, Jesta Akello, 162
organisation, 107-14, 130, 215
Organisation of Rural Associations for Progress (ORAP), xvii
organisational style, 110-11
organisations, co-optation of, 171
over-centralisation, as cause of poverty, 25
over-grazing, 8, 22
Oxfam, 192

Palshikar, Vasant, 130
Paroketo Fishermen's Associations, 177-8
participation: meaning of, 56-60, 94; non-constructive, 160-2; of women, 67; people's, 176
participatory action research, 60-4, 118, 119, 120, 122, 209
participatory development, 75; and time factor, 68-70; dilemmas of, 178-9
Participatory Institute for Development Alternatives (PIDA), xiii, xvii, 42, 88, 131
participatory technological development, 198-202, 210
participatory training: 88-104; methodology of, 90-1; objectives of, 89-90
Partridge, B., 127
Pearse, A., 59
peasants, 42, 46; initiatives of, 123; resistance to development, 44
Peasants' Charter, 33, 56, 67, 131, 176
peripheral/central paradigm, 28

Perlman, Janice, 174
personal case studies, as part of training, 97
Philippines, 17
Physical Quality of Life Index (PQLI), 4
Pinochet, General, 57
planning, 29, 121-8, 156, 169; blueprint approach to, 121
planning-implementation dichotomy, 122
plundering, as social policy, 23
pluralism, definition of, 11
political action, 214
political instability, as cause of poverty, 25
political parties, 176
poor people: and self-reliance, 212; as defaulters, 189; attitudes towards, 85; choosing own priorities, 160; composition of, 41; confrontations with power-holders, 167; conservatism of, 52; discrimination in favour of, 43; discussion with, 117; divisions among, 41, 44; exploitation of, 10-11; motivation of, 136; non-ideological inclination of, 214; participation of, 123; understanding problems of, 118
population growth, 8, 27; and poverty, 20
pottery-making, 155
poverty: absolute, 3; analysis of, xvii, 11-25; causes of, 118, 119, 130; causes of, 6-11, 24-5; factors of, 21; meaning of, 3-25; relative, 4; research on, 61; symptoms of, 22
powdered milk, sale of, 9
power structure of communities, 165, 166, 207
Pradervand, Pierre, 184
pregnancy, 84
preparation of projects, 116-18,
PRODERO project (Honduras), 194, 195
productivity, 153, 196
programme areas, criteria for selecting, 115
programmes: criticism of, 129; feedback from, 129; monitoring of, 128-9; size of, 126-8; small, 128
project compounds, desirability of, 111
projects: as constructs, 115; as means of strengthening self-organisation, 121; closing of, 217; lifespan of, 121; participation in formulation of, 123; planning of, 210; six-month, 118-19; suggestions for new, 115; time scale of, 216
Proshika organisation, 85, 86, 109
pyrethrum production, 117

Quennell, Peter, 171

Rahman, Mohammed Anisur, 48, 49, 57, 58, 61, 63, 75, 104, 112, 127, 139, 146, 201, 205
report-writing, 169
resources: control of, 214; effective use of, 149; inventory of, 154; local, 180; mobilisation of, 206, 207, 208, 209
revolution, 58, 59
risk minimisation strategies, 7
role plays, in training, 96
Roy, Aruna, 66, 68
Rural Action Project (India), 49

Sachs, Ignacy, 32
salaries, 108, 112, 126, 128
sanitation, 5, 8, 14, 119, 160, 207
Sankara, Thomas, 184
Santunino, Cwinya-ai, 186
Saouma, Edouard, 33
SARILAKAS organisation (Philippines), xvii, 48
Savale Bhasin, 41
savings, 27, 36, 172
savings groups, rotational, 184, 185
savings, 180-202; collective, psychological importance of, 185; lack of, 23
school, 10, 110, 133, 167, 194, 215; attendance at, 4
Schumacher, E.F., 196
Scurrah, Martin, 160
Seawell, James P., 77
self-awareness, 135
self-confidence, acquisition of, 53
self-criticism, 98-100
Self Employed Women's Association (SEWA) (India), 150
self-reliance, xvi, 31, 113, 180, 208; meaning of, 50-5, 94; reduced by aid, 114
self-reliant participatory development, xii, 40-70, 73, 122, 126, 127, 135, 151, 159, 165, 174, 180, 181, 201; as ideology, 212; objectives of, 205
Sethi, Harsh, 40, 86, 112, 113, 131
sexism in language, 101
sexual harassment, 150
shyness, overcoming of, 97
signboards, advertising projects, 111
Singer, Burton, 37
Six S's organisation (Sahel), xvii
skills: human, 52, 90, 96, 105, 151, 210; investigation of, 154; lack of, 24; leadership, 80; management, 181
Small Farmers' Development Programme

(Nepal), 190
smoking, 66; rise of, 184
social anthropologists, 116
social change, 45-9
solar energy, 195, 198
solidarity, 99, 151
Solomon, D.D., 170
speaking, encouragement of, 97
Sri Lanka, xi, xii, xvii, 4, 42, 88, 118, 154, 168, 191
staff development, consequences of, 106-7
stepping out of projects, 216-18
Stiefel, M., 59
structural transformation, 31
Swantz, Marja-Liisa, 120
Swaraswati, goddess, 62

Tan, Jake Galvez, 199
Tanzania, 28, 120, 124
team work, 85, 98
technical assistance, as input, 182
technologies, new, introduction of, 195-202
technology, 34, 180; 'hippy', 197; appropriate, 197, 198, 199; elitist, 198; experiments in, 200; inappropriate, 193; indigenous, safeguarding of, 199; lack of, 6-7; next-step, 149; testing of, 200; transfer of, 196
time-scale of interventions, 122, 123, 148
top-down policy formation, xvi, 109
tourism, 40; rural development, 6
training, xiii, 35, 73, 127, 158, 177; content of, 94-6; follow-up of, 104-5; materials for, 95; of change agents, 85, 88-114; organisational, 74; participatory, 88; role of coordinators, 101-3; technical, 74
training programmes: evaluation of, 91; management of, 96-7; structure of, 91-4; traditional, 89
training workshops, 105
transnational corporations, 11, 29
transport, 5, 154; lack of, 23
travel allowances, 170
trickle-down development, 44

Ubanjagiu, Sebi Ali, 140
Uganda, xii, 3, 17, 18, 23, 38, 137, 147-8, 152, 154, 155, 162, 177-8, 184, 185-6, 187-9
Umtali, D.L., 76
underdevelopment, generation of, 28
unions, rural, 172
United Nations (UN), 26, 77, 191, 213, 215

UN Conference on the Environment, 32
UNICEF, xvi, 31, 106
UN Development Decade, 26
UN Research Institute for Social Development (UNRISD), 59
UN Water Decade, 26
UN Women's Decade, 26, 65
Uphoff, N.T., 56
used clothing, sale of, 152

vehicles of project staff, 82, 111, 117, 118, 128
Verhelst, T.G., 46
viability analysis, 156
vicious circles of poverty, 13-17, 22, 182
visitors to projects, 113, 145; white, 113

wages, 10, 65, 179
water, supply of, 8, 10, 14, 49, 116, 123, 207, 215
welfare programmes, as instruments of manipulation, 8 wells, 10, 14, 15
Wignajara, P., 40, 130, 174, 205
Winder, D., 44
women, 41, 53, 54, 78, 98, 104, 116, 117, 120, 135, 136, 138, 147, 150-1, 164, 184, 215; and development training, 100-1; and speaking at meetings, 146; and work, 146; as change agents, 87; development programmes for, 66; groups, 145-8; needs of, 146; participation in development, 64-8; prejudices against, 100; recruitment of, 84-5; role of, 34, 94
World Bank, 4
World Conference on Agrarian Reform and Rural Development, 67, 131, 146
World Neighbors agency, 126

Zaire, 139
Zimbabwe, 77, 127, 150

MANFRED A. MAX-NEEF
From the Outside Looking In
Experiences in 'Barefoot Economics'

This book has become a classic since it was first produced by the Dag Hammarskjöld Foundation. Translated into five languages, it has had an extraordinary influence on grassroots development projects.

Manfred Max-Neef relates two of his own experiences in 'barefoot economics', interspersing these moving and insightful accounts with reflections on development projects and experts, pioneering criticism of orthodox development economics, and a new vision of development in which 'the poor must learn to circumvent the national [economic] system'.

'An unusual volume with an unusual message ... It should be studied carefully by social scientists and policy makers alike.' - Nicholas W. Balabkins, *The Eastern Economic Journal*

'Written with passion, this book also inspires passion in the reader, above all because it views the problems of poverty and marginalisation from a new and more human angle.' - *Development Education Exchange Papers*

'Max-Neef recognises fully that the problems facing us today are profound.' - Edward Goldsmith, *Resurgence*

' A minor masterpiece ... The three "Theoretical Inerludes" are remarkable for their insight and originality.' - John Papworth, *The Fourth World*

'A clear break from the conventional approach to economics.' - *West Africa*

'A well-written book that provides a challenging and welcome break from the repetitive debates about the economics of development.' - *Education with Production*

Manfred Max-Neef is a Chilean economist, the founder and director of the Development Alternatives Centre. He is a member of the council of the Club of Rome and a recipient of the Right Livelihood Award.

Hb 1 85649 187 0 £29.95 $$49.95
Pb 1 85649 188 9 £10.95 $17.50

Also by MANFRED A. MAX-NEEF
Human Scale Development
Conception, Application and Further Reflections

This book presents a fresh approach to meeting human needs, both material and non-material, through the self-reliant efforts of grassroots communities. The people thus become subjects rather than objects of the development process, which must be conducted on a truly human scale. There is no possibility, the book argues, for the active participation of people - essential to sustained development - in gigantic systems where decisions flow from top to bottom.

An imaginative and provocative contribution to the continuing debate on how to build more just and sustainable societies in both North and South.

ISBN 0 945257 35 X £12.95

MD ANISUR RAHMAN
People's Self-development
Perspectives on Participatory Action Research

This book presents Anisur Rahman's reflections on development through collective local initiatives by people themselves - what he has called people's self-development - and how to promote such development. His thinking grew out of his long involvement in popular initiatives, as well as experience of field 'animation' work in Asia and Africa. His very influential ideas have centred on what the notion of self-reliance should actually mean; a formulation of Participatory Action Research (PAR) in terms of the self-emancipation of the popular classes; the importance of knowledge relations in perpetuating domination and an examination of the rationality of collectively generated popular knowledge.

Anisur Rahman's essential contribution has been a creativist view of development which questions the premises of both liberal and socialist schools, and instead outlines an alternative development paradigm and vision of society.

'A timely and most useful work which pulls together 20 years of intellectual support and practical involvement in grassroots, people-led development. Anis Rahman has made a major contribution to alternative development approaches. His writings have served as a challenge and an inspiration to thousands of development workers. This book will be an invaluable source of ideas and references for those seeking to develop more relevant methods of project intervention.' - Peter Oakley, author of *Projects with the People*

'When "development" from above has failed, when planners have failed, Anis Rahman continues to light the way of people's self-development. This is the moment to listen to him.' - Marc Nerfin, President, International Foundation for Development Alternatives

Anisur Rahman - a Harvard-educated economist - ran the ILO's Programme on Participatory Organisations of the Rural Poor (PORP) for many years.

Hb 1 856499 0799 3 £32.95 $55.00
Pb 1 85649 080 7 £12.95 $19.95